W9-ARE-222

A Century of Service: The Story of the DAR

Ann Arnold Hunter

National Society Daughters of the American Revolution
Washington, D.C.

Presented by John Foster Chapter Daughters of the American Revolution

WINGATE UNIVERSITY LIBRARY

Cover: Detail of *Memorial Continental Hall* by P. Buckley Moss
courtesy of the Moss Portfolio, Washington, D.C.
The original painting hangs at DAR National Headquarters, the Centennial
gift of the Virginia Daughters of the American Revolution

© 1991 by the National Society Daughters of the American Revolution

Library of Congress Catalog No. 91-070981

Printed in the United States of America

Published by the National Society Daughters of the American Revolution
1776 D Street, N.W.
Washington, D.C. 20006

Produced by AAH Graphics, Seven Fountains, VA 22652

Foreword

When an organization such as ours has reached its 100th anniversary it certainly seems to be an appropriate time to tell its inspiring story.

What remarkable foresight and vision the Founders possessed when they brought into being this Society.

Over these 100 years more than 730,000 women have found a sense of purpose and service through the Society's three objectives, Historical, Educational and Patriotic.

With the most devoted dedication and perseverance every goal the early members had in mind was achieved.

They dreamed of a home. Today our block of DAR buildings is a reality and is the largest group of buildings in the world owned by women.

They wanted a place to house the artifacts of the Revolutionary era. Today our accredited museum holds over 30,000 items.

Since membership in the Society is based upon lineage, they longed for a library. Today the DAR Library contains more than 95,000 books and pamphlets on genealogy.

Today's organization is a multi-faceted one in which members can work in many fields of endeavor.

The Daughters of the American Revolution work, and they work hard, many long hours to preserve the past, to carry out their obligations to the present, and to build a firm foundation to safeguard the future.

It is hoped you will find this story of the Society's first one hundred years interesting, inspiring and challenging.

A cordial welcome awaits all who visit our DAR Headquarters.

Marie Hirst Yochim
Mrs. Eldred Martin Yochim, President General 1989-1992
National Society Daughters of the American Revolution

Contents

The Founding of the National Society

National Headquarters

Service to the Nation

The author is indebted to Mrs. Eldred Martin Yochim, President General, for giving her the privilege of writing this Centennial volume.

It is a delight to work in the pleasant surroundings of the National Headquarters of the National Society Daughters of the American Revolution. Every office went out of its way to offer help, and where needed, advice. Sincere appreciation to all.

Deep gratitude is extended to the editorial committee consisting of Mrs. Yochim, Mrs. Charles R. Haugh, Vice President General from Virginia, and Miss Jean Jacobs, Executive Secretary to the President General and member, NSDAR. They read the manuscript carefully and tried to keep the author on track.

My husband, Stephen R. Hunter has tolerated my frequent absences and general authorial air of scholarly bemusement with humor and understanding. Thank you, Steve.

Ann Arnold Hunter
February, 1991

When the light of truth is turned upon the page
of history, no matter how many idols it shatters,
what it reveals we must believe.

Mary S. Lockwood, Founder and first Historian General,
American Monthly Magazine, Vol. I, #2, page 122

Part I

The Founding of the National Society

The men and women who achieved American
Independence needed no reminders of what they had
accomplished. The victory itself was the monument to the
spirit. No other was required. Documents, relics and
soldiers' tales were handed down in the traditional way,
through families.

The nation was to endure a devastating war between its
very states, a painful reconstruction, and a proud
centennial before it finally awoke to the ephemeral nature
of the national memory. And then suddenly, it was time
to remember and preserve.

The Strathmore Arms

Time to Remember and Preserve

On October 11, 1890, eighteen ladies and four gentlemen met in Washington at the Strathmore Arms, 810 12th Street, the boarding house and home of Mrs. Mary S. Lockwood, for the purpose of organizing the Daughters of the American Revolution. One hundred years later, the prominent and respected National Society Daughters of the American Revolution bears testimony to their success.

The romantic story of how it all came about deserves to be preserved.

With the exception of the exclusive Society of the Cincinnati, formed in 1783 by officers of the Continental Army, the Revolution spawned no patriotic society until a group called the Sons of Revolutionary Sires was organized in California on October 22, 1875. Next came the Sons of the Revolution in New York in 1883. When the Sons of the American Revolution organized at Fraunces Tavern in New York City on April 30, 1889, it incorporated a number of early State Societies of Sons, including the California group. Some of the SAR societies permitted women; some did not. At its general meeting in Lexington, Kentucky on April 30, 1890, the Sons of the American Revolution made its fateful decision to exclude women and history seized the opportunity to embark upon a major undertaking.

Even in those early days, the news media did their work. The wireless efficiently spread the news of the April discrimination of the Sons of the American Revolution to an interested America. And the newspapers . . . where would we be without newspapers?

At a Washington, D.C. banquet of the Sons on July 11, 1890, Senator John Sherman expressed his regret that women were ineligible.

His remarks that they "kept the country alive" during the War of the Revolution were reported in the *Washington Post* on July 12.

The scorching editorial

Mary Smith Lockwood was ready. She fired off her pen with the scorching editorial "Women Worthy of Honor"(*see Appendix 1*). which appeared in the *Post* on July 13th! Paraphrasing a story published in the New York *Observer* in 1876, "Hannah Arnett's Faith," written by Henrietta Holdich, and adding her own pointed comments, Mrs. Lockwood demonstrated convincingly that women had, indeed, contributed much, and a great deal heretofore not recognized, to the War for Independence. "Were there no mothers of the Revolution?" asked Mrs. Lockwood. "Where will the 'Sons and Daughters of the Revolution' place Hannah Arnett."

William O. McDowell of New Jersey, himself a great-grandson of Hannah Arnett, and New Jersey Number 1, National Number 2013, and Vice President General at large of the Sons of the American Revolution, had believed for some time that the women of America should form their own patriotic society, modeled after that of the Sons.

Following the Sons' disastrous decision in Lexington to keep women out of the SAR, McDowell began preparing a call to the women to organize.

Mrs. Lockwood's letter to the *Post* provided just the opening he needed.

Immediately, William O. McDowell wrote his *own* letter to the *Post*, published on July 21, stating " . . . in the hands of the women of America patriotic undertakings have never failed. Why not, therefore, invite the formation of the National Society of the 'Daughters of the American Revolution' . . . " Mr. McDowell concluded by inviting "every woman in America who has the blood of the heroes of the revolution in her veins" to send her name and address to him for purposes of organization.

Six women: Miss Eugenia Washington, Miss Mary Desha, Mrs. Hannah McLaren

William O. McDowell

Wolff, Mrs. Louise K. Brown, and Mrs. Mary Morris Hallowell, all of Washington, and Mrs. Roger A. Pryor of New York, replied to Mr. McDowell. Miss Desha wrote "I am good for any amount of work."

It was to Mary Desha that William McDowell addressed his next letter, enclosing the names and addresses of those who had replied and suggesting immediate organization followed by a mass meeting on October 11, "the anniversary of the discovery of America."

The deadest place in the United States

On July 29th the first meeting of women interested in organizing was held at the home of Mrs. Louise K. Brown with Miss Washington, Miss Desha, Mrs. Wolff, Mrs. Brown and Mrs. Ellen Hardin Walworth present. It was decided that action should be deferred until autumn because so many ladies were out of town for the summer. "Washington is the deadest place in the United States in summer," wrote Mary Desha. Among the absentees was Mrs. Mary S. Lockwood, who as a Lady Manager of the Columbian Exposition in Chicago, was occupied making plans and attending meetings for that event.

Although Mr. McDowell was notified that organization was to be delayed, he was anything but convinced. Writing Miss Desha on July 30, he insisted that they proceed at once. He sent her a packet containing application blanks of the Sons of the American Revolution, an S.A.R.-based constitution, a plan of organization and a check for $5.00 attached to his own application for membership! "I believe the Society should be one of women, men absolutely excluded and yet it seems to me I should appreciate it very much if the ladies, when fully organized, made one exception."

Imagination must discover the activity of the following week.

On August 8 Miss Washington received Mrs. E.H. Walworth's card. Scribbled on the front in Mary Desha's distinctive writing was the message, "To form the Association of Daughters of the American Revolution. Mrs. E.H. Walworth. The Langham. 8 o'clock Saturday evening Aug. 9th." The inscription on the back, in the same hand, said, "My dear Miss Washington, Mr. McDowell still insists that we shall organize. If you possibly can please meet us tomorrow evening at the Langham. Your friend, M. Desha."

A dark and stormy night

The sultry afternoon of August 9th advanced to evening producing a furious Washington summer thunderstorm. An eyewitness stated that rain filled the streets with water from curb to curb, the thunder was continuous and the lightning incessant, keeping all but the most determined at home.

Three ladies attended Mrs. Walworth's meeting: the hostess, Miss Washington and Miss Desha. Mrs. Walworth, a lawyer, had studied McDowell's constitution with an educated as well as an interested eye. The meeting was productive. It resulted in a thoroughly reconstructed and adopted constitution for an organization *national* in scope. A tentative board of management was proposed. The decision was made to invite Caroline Scott Harrison, wife of United States President Benjamin Harrison, to serve as President of the new society. Miss Desha was to be chairman, Mrs. Walworth, secretary and Miss Washington, registrar. Others named August 9th included Mrs. Mary Orr Earle, Mrs. Hannah McLaren Wolff, Mrs. Flora Adams Darling, Mrs. Louise K. Brown, Miss Sophonisba P. Breckenridge and Miss Virginia Grigsby.

Mr. McDowell's application was not acted upon and his check was not cashed because the society was to be exclusively for women. Appreciating the irony that the first prospective applicant for the "Daughters" was a "Son," the ladies decided to keep Mr. McDowell's application and check on file.

The nine ladies named to the board, and Mr. McDowell, probably constitute the list of those invited to Mrs. Walworth's meeting August 9th. A pamphlet published by the Board of Management, November 1908, attempting to rectify

The Langham, residence of Mrs. Ellen Hardin Walworth

what some members considered to be errors in the story of the founding of the society as known at that time, stated, "Had everyone invited been present there would have been ten founders instead of three [sic] . . . "

Then followed a period of great activity. Correspondence went out to representative women all over the country. A letter to Mrs. Harrison requesting that she accept as President was sent on August 10th. Mary Desha wrote William O. McDowell on August 17th that " . . . we organized and elected officers. By the first of September most people will be home and we will try to have a meeting of all the members . . . "

On August 18th, a notice appeared in the *Washington Post* stating the purposes of the society and the eligibility clause, and requesting women of Revolutionary descent to send their names to the Registrar, Miss Washington, at her residence at 813 13th Street.

By early September, 300 application blanks had been ordered and copies of the Constitution, adopted August 9th, had been distributed to members of the Board for suggestions. Mr. McDowell was planning to spend a day with Miss Desha over preliminary work and was thinking about a DAR badge.

A meeting for organization

While all this work was going on, plans were being made for the mass meeting to be held October 11. Mrs. Earle was appointed to engage rooms for that purpose at the Arlington Hotel.

It would be an error to suppose that the creative winds unleashed in Washington in the summer of 1890 could be sustained without causing some damage: inevitably, there would be misunderstandings. Women of strong personality, laboring to found an enduring society, competed for control.

Flora Adams Darling, an acquaintance of Eugenia Washington, was staying at the Strathmore Arms. Certainly, Mrs. Lockwood and Mrs. Darling knew each other. Mrs. Darling was excited about the planned new society and had been in correspondence with Mr. McDowell. Judging by the evidence, she was a capable woman, confident, pre-emptive and inclined to act independently.

On October 7, 1890 Mrs. Darling apparently seized the initiative and sent letters to the list in her possession stating that Mr. McDowell would be with her at the Strathmore Arms on the 11th of October to organize the Society of the Daughters of the American Revolution.

The first minutes (*see Appendix 2*) of the National Society began:

Minutes, October 11, 1890

A meeting for the organization of the National Society of the Daughters of the American Revolution was called by Mrs. Flora Adams Darling, and held at the Strathmore Arms, 810 12th Street, Washington, D.C., at half past two o'clock in the afternoon of Saturday, October 11, 1890.

The Board of Management's 1908 pamphlet states, "October 11 had been selected as the day on which to celebrate . . . organization of the society, because it was the date of Columbus' discovery of America, and because that discovery was made possible by the generosity of Queen Isabella."

Eighteen women attended the organizing meeting of the National Society of the Daughters of the American Revolution. Their names, in the order they signed the formal draft of organization, were Miss Eugenia Washington, Mrs. Flora Adams Darling, Mrs. Ellen Hardin Walworth, Mrs. Mary Morris Hallowell, Miss Susan Riviere Hetzel, Mrs. Margaret Hetzel, Mrs. Mary V.E. Cabell, Mrs. Mary S. Lockwood, Mrs. Alice Morrow Clark, Miss Pauline McDowell, Mrs. Ada P. Kimberley, Mrs. Aurelia Hadley Mohl, Miss Floride Cunningham, Mrs. Caroline L. Ransom, Mrs. Emily Lee Sherwood, Mrs. Harriet Lincoln Coolidge, Mrs. Jennie D. Garrison and Miss Mary Desha.

Also present were four of the six gentlemen who formed the first Advisory Board to the National Society: Prof. G. Brown Goode, Prof. W.C. Winlock, Mr. Wm. O. McDowell and Mr. Wilson L. Gill. The other two members of the Advisory Board were General H.V. Boynton and General Marcus J. Wright.

At the meeting, the following officers were elected: President General, Mrs. Benjamin Harrison; Vice President in Charge of Organization, Mrs. Flora Adams Darling; seven Vice Presidents General: Mrs. David Porter, Mrs. Mary V.E. Cabell, Mrs. Henry V. Boynton, Mrs. General Greely, Mrs. F.P. St. Clair, Mrs. G. Brown Goode, and Mrs. William C. Winlock; Secretary General, Mrs. Ellen Hardin Walworth; Secretary General, Mrs. William O. Earle; Treasurer General, Mrs. Marshall MacDonald; Registrar General, Miss Eugenia Washington;

Registrar General, Mrs. A. Howard Clark; Historian General, Mrs. Mary S. Lockwood; Surgeon General, Miss Clara Barton, and Chaplain General, Mrs. Teunis S. Hamlin. The executive committee consisted of Miss Mary Desha, Mrs. William D. Cabell, Mrs. E.H. Walworth, Mrs. Marshall MacDonald, Mrs. Mary S. Lockwood, Miss Eugenia Washington and Mrs. Margaret Hetzel.

A tentative constitution subject to revision was adopted, the date of the annual meeting discussed and the meeting *recessed* until October 18. The first resolution of the new society pledged support toward completing the monument to the memory of Mary Washington, mother of George Washington. It was also resolved that the eleventh of October would be the permanent anniversary day of the society.

The October 18, 1890 meeting, called in the minutes the "second session of the meeting for organization of the National Society of the Daughters of the American Revolution," acknowledged the acceptance of Mrs. Benjamin Harrison as President General. The colors, blue and white, were decided upon and the society resolved that its next effort, after assisting in the completion of the Mary Washington monument, would be toward providing a "place for the collection of historical relics . . . ," ultimately the "erection of a fire-proof building." This meeting was adjourned to November 11, 1890.

The "third and last session of the meeting for organization" *was* held November 11 and produced adoption of the revised constitution, a seal and a motto.

It took three meetings to carefully perfect organization of the National Society Daughters of the American Revolution.

A Century of Service begins

DAR service to the nation began on the date of organization, October 11, 1890. When the new society pledged to support the Mary Washington Monument effort, the chapters and members of the Daughters of the American Revolution responded generously, providing almost three-fourths of the cost of the project.

The organizing year, October 11, 1890 – October 11, 1891, was filled with activity. Once the Board of Management was elected, Regents had to be appointed all over the country to begin the work of organizing.

It was decided from the beginning that the society was to be national in scope; members would join the national organization, and where twelve members wished it, they could form local chapters.

The first DAR chapter was formed at Chicago on March 20, 1891 with Mrs. Frank Osborn as Regent; the second was Atlanta Chapter on April 15 closely followed by New York City Chapter on April 19, 1891. A further revision to the Constitution and a meeting on October 11, 1891 clarified some administrative details. The rolls of charter membership closed on October 11, 1891. The last national number assigned during the charter year was 818, representing 816 actual members. Two numbers, 89 and 129, were not used.

All Four Founders of the National Society, Miss Eugenia Washington, Miss Mary Desha, Mrs. Ellen Hardin Walworth, and Mrs. Mary S. Lockwood, were single, self-supporting women. Two were widows; two had never married. Two, Eugenia Washington and Mary Desha, were "government girls." Mary S. Lockwood was a published author and kept a boarding house. Ellen H. Walworth also wrote, and gave lectures in parliamentary law. Their dreams for the National Society were lofty. Intelligent, energetic and able, from distinguished families, they each one, nevertheless, lacked the social and financial support that only a husband could provide in a pre-woman-suffrage society. Well connected, they were able to interest prominent women in their ambitious undertaking. In choosing a leader, they knew from the beginning that they should aim high—as high as possible. Their selection of Mrs. Benjamin Harrison as Honorary President General propelled them into the limelight and secured the nation's interested attention.

Mrs. Harrison accepted her office with the understanding that she would have no actual responsibility. Concurrently, Mrs. William D. Cabell was elected Vice President Presiding. With that title, and later as President Presiding, she led the National Society from its inception October 11, 1890 until October 5, 1893, when she resigned the position.

When the National Society of the Daughters of the American Revolution triumphantly held its First Continental Congress on February 22–23, 1892, it could boast 1,306 proudly patriotic members, headed by the prominent Mrs. Harrison, all firmly committed to their objectives, fueled by that fervor that rightly descends on those who break new ground to high purpose.

On the Fiftieth Anniversary of the founding of the Society, the Washington Star's Clifford K. Berryman expressed hearty congratulations.

100 Years

Thirty-four dedicated women have served the National Society as President General. On February 18, 1901, Mrs. Daniel Manning's address included a message that has been echoed by other "P.G.'s" through the years: "None more than I can tell the closeness of the tie that binds us one and all, and I extend my heartfelt thanks for the good will and confidence with which you have always supported your President General. . . . Have pride in your past, determination in the present, and courageous confidence in the future."

Mrs. Benjamin Harrison
1890–92

Mrs. Adlai E. Stevenson
1893–95 1896–98

Mrs. John W. Foster
1895–96

Mrs. Daniel Manning
1898–01

Mrs. Charles W. Fairbanks
1901–05

Mrs. Donald McLean
1905–09

Mrs. Matthew T. Scott
1909–13

Mrs. William C. Story
1913–17

Mrs. George T. Guernsey
1917–20

# of Presidents General

Mrs. George M. Minor
1920–23

Mrs. Anthony W. Cook
1923–26

Mrs. Grace L.H. Brosseau
1926–29

Mrs. Lowell F. Hobart
1929–32

Mrs. Russell W. Magna
1932–35

Mrs. William A. Becker
1935–38

Mrs. Henry M. Robert, Jr.
1938–41

Mrs. William H. Pouch
1941–44

Mrs. Julius Y. Talmadge
1944–47

Mrs. Roscoe C. O'Byrne
1947–50

Mrs. James B. Patton
1950–53

Miss Gertrude S. Carraway
1953–56

Mrs. Frederic A. Groves
1956–59

Mrs. Ashmead White
1959–62

Mrs. Robert V.H. Duncan
1962–65

Mrs. William H. Sullivan, Jr.
1965–68

Mrs. Erwin F. Seimes
1968–71

Mrs. Donald Spicer
1971–74

Mrs. Henry S. Jones
1974–75

Mrs. Wakelee R. Smith
1975–77

Mrs. George U. Baylies
1977–80

Mrs. Richard D. Shelby
1980–83

Mrs. Walter H. King
1983–86

Mrs. Raymond F. Fleck
1986–89

Mrs. Eldred M. Yochim
1989–92

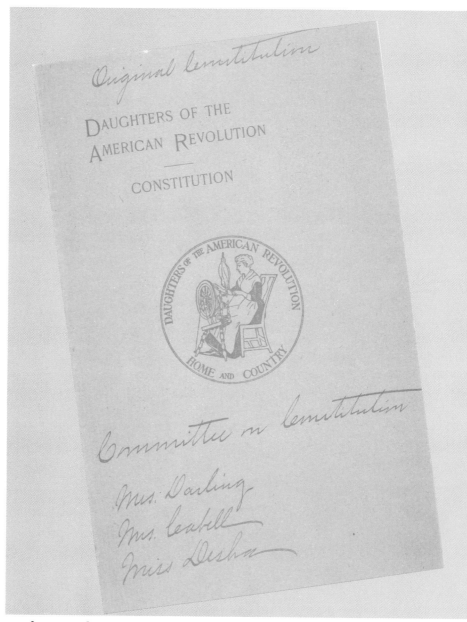

The original 1890 Daughters of the American Revolution Constitution.
Notes on the cover were written by Mary Desha.

What Is the DAR?

*Its laws of membership are equally democratic, for it
requires no test except proven Revolutionary descent and
unblemished good character; it is not a social organization,
although it embraces in its honored membership women of
highest social position and finest attainments; it is an order
patriotic, historical and genealogical, and holds itself
closely to these objects.*

Ellen Hardin Walworth, Founder,
American Monthly Magazine, February 1893

The National Society Daughters of the American
Revolution is, as the name implies, a national organization for women not less than 18 years of age who are in harmony with the objects of the society and who can prove eligibility. There are no restrictions as to race or creed.

Objects

Bylaws of the National Society of the Daughters of the American Revolution

Article II

The objects of this Society shall be:

(1) To perpetuate the memory and spirit of the men and women who achieved American Independence; by the acquisition and protection of historical spots and the erection of monuments; by the encouragement of historical research in relation to the American Revolution and the publication of its results; by the preservation of documents and relics, and of the records of its results; by the preservation of documents and relics, and of the records of the individual services of Revolutionary

soldiers and patriots; and by the promotion of celebrations of all patriotic anniversaries.

(2) To carry out the injunction of Washington in his farewell address to the American people, "to promote, as an object of primary importance, institutions for the general diffusion of knowledge," thus developing an enlightened public opinion, and affording to young and old such advantages as shall develop in them the largest capacity for performing the duties of American Citizens.

(3) To cherish, maintain and extend the institutions of American freedom, to foster true patriotism and love of country, and to aid in securing for mankind all the blessings of liberty.

Eligibility

Article III

Section 1. Any woman is eligible for membership in the National Society of the Daughters of the American Revolution who is not less than eighteen years of age, and who is descended from a man or woman who, with unfailing loyalty to the cause of American Independence, served as a sailor, or a soldier or civil officer in one of the several Colonies or States, or in the United Colonies or States or as a recognized patriot, or rendered material aid thereto; provided the applicant is personally acceptable to the society.

The entire endeavor of the DAR is toward fulfilling its three objectives: historic, educational and patriotic. It is interesting to note that the objectives of the DAR today are identical to those decided upon on October 11, 1890. In 100 years of active service, the National Society has never swerved or strayed from its high purpose.

Advancing the work

To advance these interests, committees are appointed by the President General. National committee chairmen propose and direct projects through their counterparts on division, state and chapter levels who in turn report back their accomplishments to the national chairman. The annual report of each national chairman is published in the *Proceedings of the Continental Congress,* In addition, states and chapters initiate projects of local interest. All this activity is reported, recorded and becomes a part of the permanent written record of the work of the National Society.

Originally, a constitution ruled the organization. Today the society is governed by bylaws which cover all such organizational topics as membership, officers, meetings, executive committee, chapters and states. The Bylaws set forth the objects, eligibility, seal and Insignia of the Society, as well as certifying *Robert's Rules of Order Newly Revised* as parliamentary authority and providing disciplinary measures for any member conducting herself in a way calculated to disturb the harmony of the National Society. The Bylaws of the National Society also make provision for their own amendment.

National officers are elected for a three-year term. Once in each administration a *National Bylaws and DAR Handbook* is published. This contains the Act of Incorporation, the latest revision of the National Bylaws and a complete outline of the work of the DAR. The role of the national officers, the scope of the committees, and information for states and chapters are given. There is even a "thumbnail sketch" summary of the administration of each President General from the beginning, which provides a brief history of the society. The *DAR Handbook*, available to the general public, is so comprehensive that it answers all ordinary questions.

Act of Incorporation

The National Society Daughters of the American Revolution was incorporated under the laws of Congress for the District of Columbia on June 8, 1891. The signers of the act of incorporation were Mrs. Caroline Scott Harrison, Mrs. Henrietta Greely, Mrs. Sara E. Goode, Mrs. Mary E. McDonald, Mrs. Mary V.E. Cabell, Mrs. Helen M. Boynton, Miss Eugenia Washington, and Miss Mary Desha. The objects were the same on that date as the objects adopted in the constitution of October 11, 1890; the same objectives that guide the National Society Daughters of the American Revolution today.

The incorporation gave the society the legal identity it needed and provided temporary satisfaction to the incorporators.

They knew, however, that the society they envisioned, with a character national in scope, must be sanctioned, not by local law, but through endorsement by the primary legislators of the land. Congressional recognition, legal affirmation of the noble motives governing their organization, was necessary if it was to assume the dominant role planned for it.

During Mrs. Adlai E. Stevenson's term of office, and while her husband was Vice President of the United States, the desired Act of the Fifty-Fourth Congress of the United States of America was passed on December 2, 1895.

The first section of the Act created a body corporate and politic, in the District of Columbia, by the name of the National Society of the Daughters of the American Revolution, for patriotic, historical and educational purposes, and then, using the same language found in the most recent edition of the Bylaws of the National Society of the Daughters of the American Revolution, described those purposes in detail.

Stating that the headquarters would be at Washington, D.C., Section 2 authorized the society to hold real and personal estate, limiting the value to $500,000, and permitted the adoption of a constitution, and seal.

Most significantly, Section 3 ordered the society to report annually to the Secretary of the Smithsonian Institution, and permitted the National Society to deposit materials in the Smithsonian Institution or in the National Museum.

Approved February 20, 1896 and signed by President Grover Cleveland, Speaker of the House of Representatives, Thomas B. Reed and Vice-President of the United States and President of the Senate, A.E. Stevenson, this action had the desired effect of reinforcing the national importance of the society.

Amendments by the 63rd, 69th, 82nd and 94th Congresses increased the amount of permissible real and personal estate holdings and protected the society by granting exclusivity of the name "National Society of the Daughters of the American Revolution" and of adopted emblems, seals and badges of the organization.

*1890 and 1972
Seals of the
National Society.*

Colors, seal, Insignia, motto

The minutes of the organizing meeting of the National Society Daughters of the American Revolution on October 11, 1890 state that "the ribbon of our badge and rosette be red with white edges" (but action was deferred). The minutes of the October 18th meeting state that a "discussion ensued . . . between the advocates of Red and White, and those of Blue and White . . . . it was Resolved, that the colors be blue and white." The colors chosen memorialized the dark blue and white of George Washington's staff. Later, the blue was modified to its present shade.

On October 18th, the committee on Insignia and Seal reported that the design for the seal should be "the figure of Abigail Adams in the costume of 1776 seated at a spinning wheel." The idea found favor but the suggestion that a cradle be added with the motto "The hand that rocks the cradle rules the world," caused enough critical dialogue that a decision was postponed and the committee was asked to give the matter further thought. The November 11, 1890 report of the committee that "the Seal of the Society should be two and three eighths of an inch in diameter, charged with the figure of a dame sitting at her spinning wheel: The legend to be: 'Daughters of the American Revolution,'" resulted in favorable action. The committee also presented two choices for a motto, *Libertas et Patria* and *Amor Patriae*. *Amor Patriae* was accepted as the motto of the NSDAR for one month. At the request of Mrs. Flora Adams Darling, it was changed on December 11, 1890 to *Home and Country* which was expanded to *God, Home and Country* in 1972.

Equally as important as the seal and motto, the National Society needed a distinctive badge.

In a most attractive way, the spinning wheel symbolizes the virtuous woman of *Proverbs 31:10:* faithful, loyal to home, and productive. In a letter to Mrs. Mary V.E. Cabell, Vice President Presiding, dated November 14, 1890, Mrs. Flora Adams Darling commented, "I regarded the spinning wheel as an accepted fact. . . . I like it much better than a teapot." This comment suggests that a teapot was at least discussed as an emblem for the Daughters! Fortunately, the wheel prevailed.

A Resolution passed October 11, 1890 called for the appointment of a Committee on Insignia and Seal. The young and gifted Miss Sophonisba P. Breckinridge, soon to be the first female lawyer in Kentucky and first chairman of the Seal and Insignia Committee, left on a trip abroad before bringing the wheel design to fruition. Her successor, Mrs. G. Brown Goode, was able in short order to produce an emblem that pleased the members, thanks to the inspiration of her husband, Dr. Goode, Chairman of the Advisory Board and assistant secretary of the Smithsonian Institution.

Dr. Goode studied the spinning wheel standing in his dining room; the very wheel made between 1775 and 1825 that belonged to his grandmother, Rebecca Hayes Goode of Amelia County, Virginia. Quickly, Dr. Goode made some sketches. Where his mother's wheel had fourteen spokes, Dr. Goode pictured thirteen, to correspond to the original thirteen states. One drawing showed stars projecting from the wheel like handles. In another, the distaff pointed to the right instead of to the left, and its tip, aimed lower down, suggested a cannon. However, one of the sketches presented the badge in its present form, "the gold wheel over a distaff filled with silver flax, the wheel with thirteen spokes, having opposite the end of each a star intended for the reception of a jewel." Dr. Goode's design included the rim with letters of gold on blue enamel, "Daughters of the American Revolution."

Mr. Paul Brockett, an associate of Dr. Goode's at the Smithsonian, prepared a finished sketch which was presented to the committee and accepted by the Board of Management and approved on May 26, 1891.

During the development of a badge, a number of jewelers were contacted. The final choice of J.E. Caldwell and Co. was based largely upon their offer to manufacture the dies at no cost provided that each member of the Board of Management agreed to be responsible for selling ten badges. It was Caldwell who suggested that the flax in the design be fashioned of platinum rather than of silver, to avoid tarnishing. The first badge left Caldwell on July 1, 1891. On August 3, 1891, Dr. Goode applied for a patent in the name of the National Society, which was granted September 22, 1891; Design No. 21053, Serial No. 401,584.

Who Organized the DAR?

This vast army of women is lineally descended from the founders of America who fought for individual liberty and freedom.

Mrs. Julius Young Talmadge, President General, 1944 – 1947

The Daughters of the American Revolution, an idea whose time had come, grew astonishingly. Eighteen women attended the organizational meeting on October 11, 1890, eleven of whom paid their dues and joined on that day. The society grew rapidly;

A vast army of women descended

membership reached 816 a year later when Charter Membership closed, and had increased to over 23,000 by 1898.

It is hard for us today to comprehend just how devoted those early Daughters were. Mountainous correspondence was carried on primarily through hand-written notes. A "call" was a visit, not a telephone conversation. There was plenty of work for the printer: invitation cards, announcements, application forms, and all the paraphernalia that go with establishing a society that was from the very beginning intended to be great.

Special recognition

Fitting recognition of living benefactors is far better than the erection of monuments to their memory after they have passed away unnoticed.
First Report to Smithsonian Institution, 1899

A number of women were instrumental in the successful organiza-

from the founders of America.

tion of the National Society. The Sixth Continental Congress singled out four for special recognition. A resolution passed on February 27, 1897 declared that Eugenia Washington, Mary Desha, Ellen H. Walworth and Mary Smith Lockwood were the Founders of the DAR.

The resolution as originally proposed honored the three women who met August 9, 1890 to plan the National Society: Eugenia Washington, Mary Desha and Ellen Hardin Walworth. The resolution was amended to include Mary Smith Lockwood, whose letter to the *Washington Post* began the whole movement. The amended resolution was adopted:

> WHEREAS, Miss Eugenia Washington, Miss Mary Desha and Mrs. Ellen Hardin Walworth did, on August 9, 1890, prepare the constitution and appoint the leading officers of the National Society, which were confirmed at the first public meeting, on October 11, 1890, and did in the interval prepare, publish and circulate application papers and other appliances for organization, and thus initiated and established the Society, which therefore entered upon its successful career; and

> WHEREAS, Mrs. Mary S. Lockwood inspired a general interest in this subject, this founding, by her pen, in the article published July 13, 1890, that she be recognized as a Founder and four medals be awarded to these Founders of the Society.

> RESOLVED, That these Four Founders of the National Society of the Daughters of the American Revolution, viz: Eugenia Washington, Mary Desha, Ellen Hardin Walworth, and Mary S. Lockwood shall be, and hereby are, officially recognized as Founders.

> RESOLVED, That a committee be appointed by the Continental Congress to prepare four medals to be commemorative of the work done by the said Four Founders, the same to be designed by a skilled artist, and that said medals be formally presented to the said Founders—Eugenia Washington, Mary Desha, Ellen Hardin Walworth, and Mary S. Lockwood—to be retained by them during their lifetime, and at their demise to be returned to the Society, there to be deposited among the valuable historical mementos of our Society; and be it

> RESOLVED, That all expenses attending the procurement and presentation of said medals be paid from any moneys in the treasury not otherwise appropriated.

A committee was appointed to procure the medals. Four identical jeweled medals were commissioned from Gorham & Co. at a cost of

The Founders' Medals honored Mrs. Lockwood for "Service" and Miss Desha, Miss Washington, and Mrs. Walworth as "Founders."

$250 each. However, a rift that had been present since the resolution was first passed grew serious enough to require attention.

Eugenia Washington and Ellen Hardin Walworth were adamantly opposed to Mary Smith Lockwood's recognition as a Founder. They maintained that the founding of the National Society took place on August 9, 1890, and that they, along with Mary Desha, being the only ones present on that occasion, were the only possible Founders of the Society. They were prepared to refuse to accept a medal that failed to recognize this essential distinction.

The compromise solution honored Mary S. Lockwood for "Service" and the others as "Founders." All four solid gold medals are equally valuable, identical in size, and similar in appearance. On each medal the seal of the National Society is surrounded on two sides and the bottom by the figure of an American eagle; on the medals presented to Miss Washington, Miss Desha and Mrs. Walworth, the position above the seal is occupied by an enameled United States shield, and flying above that, a banner emblazoned with the word *Founder*. Mrs. Lockwood's medal substitutes a fourth eagle for the shield, engraved on her banner is the word *Service* and a quill pen rests upon the banner.

The reverse side of each of the four medals is engraved with the recipient's name and national number and the words "National Society, Founded Aug. 9, 1890, Medal ordered by Sixth Continental Congress 1897."

The Seventh Continental Congress decided that the medals were to be absolute gifts to the Four Founders, with no need that they ever be returned to the National Society. Nevertheless, each medal did come home to the National Society following the death of its owner and all are now on display and may be viewed in the Assembly Room of the Administration Building at DAR Headquarters.

The Founders received their medals during the Seventh Continental Congress, February 28, 1898. The medals were presented and the Founders made their responses. Then there was "a change of scene; in an instant the lights were out, dense darkness obtained, and the vast audience sat in voiceless expectancy. Suddenly the large Insignia hanging above the stage glowed with brilliant light, and the national colors sprang forth from the darkness . . . "

A newspaper dated March 5, 1898 stated that Mrs. Walworth "shook hands with a thousand daughters" in the receiving line following the presentation.

On April 17, 1929 the National Society dedicated a memorial to the Four Founders. Located on the C Street side of the DAR complex of buildings in Washington, D.C., the Founders' Memorial Monument pays tribute to the wisdom, inspiration and mighty deeds of the four exceptional women. Gertrude Vanderbilt Whitney, a DAR member and artist of international fame, was selected to sculpt the graceful marble figure. Poised in an attitude of protection and sympathy, her outstretched arms call for unity; the whole embodying the ideals animating

The Founders' Memorial Monument, dedicated April 17, 1929.

the National Society. On the panels flanking the statue are replicas of the medals these four women received for their services; their names, dates of birth and death engraved there in perpetual remembrance.

Accepting the memorial for the National Society, Mrs. Alfred J. Brosseau, President General 1926 – 1929, said that since two of the Four Founders were born in the north, two in the south, " . . . in the very beginning were strong ties created, binding together the women of both sections of our country into one harmonious whole . . . " She saw in the beckoning gesture of the figure an "appeal to carry on despite all obstacles and discouragements; to see no bitterness or pain in service, but only its joy and beauty, and to work unitedly in the well-loved cause." The ceremony of dedication closed with the singing of "Blest Be the Tie That Binds," followed by the benediction and "Taps."

The Founders

Mrs. Mary Smith Lockwood—*"Were there no mothers of the Revolution? I have heard of a man who had a dam by a mill site, while he had "no mill by a dam site," but I have yet to hear of a man who had a Revolutionary sire without a dam by the home site."*

Writer, suffragist and hostess of the Strathmore Arms hotel in Washington, D.C., Mary Smith Lockwood wrote the words that triggered the organization of the National Society of the Daughters of the American Revolution. Her article, "Women Worthy of Honor," appearing in the 16-page July 13, 1890 issue of the *Washington Post*, struck the first spark that ignited the patriotic passion blazing in the breasts of the women of America.

The Founders' Medal presented to Mrs. Lockwood, with its graceful quill pen resting over the word, *Service*, illustrates the first of her two unofficial titles, *Pen Founder*. In later years

Mary Smith Lockwood

she was affectionately called *Little Mother,* as her continuing service and charming personality won the love and esteem of the entire society.

Small and slender, with a firm carriage and sympathetic manner, Mrs. Mary S. Lockwood served the National Society from July 12, 1890, the day on which she penned her famous letter, until her death on November 9, 1922 at the age of 92. In her, womanly grace was combined with physical loveliness, intellectual wit and executive ability.

Over the years she spoke frequently at Continental Congress. Others might salute the audience formally from the rostrum; Mary Lockwood had the endearing habit of standing at the edge of the platform and addressing the members as "girls."

When she was asked to speak at the 27th Continental Congress in April, 1918, her thoughts were on the war. Setting her prepared remarks aside, "I have changed my mind," she said. She went on to quote Henry Ward Beecher, preparing to deliver a sermon at the beginning of the Civil War. "He laid his sermon on the counter and said, 'I am not a-going to use it. In coming down this morning I passed a group of soldiers marching down the street on their way to war. I have changed my sermon.' And that's where I am tonight." Delivering a rousing extemporaneous patriotic speech, she received tremendous applause. Then 27 Pages, one for each year in the life of the National Society, came up the middle aisle to the platform and presented Mrs. Lockwood with an American Beauty rose. Mary S. Lockwood responded, typically:

> I cannot say any more—I am overpowered. Now there are times when even little Mary gets rattled; and I am—you may know how my heart feels. Like a woman I saw in church the other day, who said, "My boy has gone to the war." "Why," I said, "You don't tell me." But she says, "I am glad of it; I wouldn't respect him if he hadn't gone—but my heart is broken." And I feel a little bit that way now—my heart is kind of giving out, girls. Thank you.

She had the gift of timing. When the Seventh Continental Congress was discussing the bestowing of the Founders' Medals, it was necessary to decide how to alter the identical medals to make them distinct; rearranging the American eagles was one possible solution. In the end, Mrs. Lockwood's medal retained all four of its eagles. But the irrepressible Little Mother had the Congress in stitches when she said, "As to this motion that the eagles be removed, I have always loved the eagle for some reason; but I think I could go through life knowing it is the emblem of my country without having it upon a medal given to me. Any old bird will do." This, of course, brought down the house. Mrs. Lockwood followed up with, "I would prefer a dove, however." It was this ability of Mary S. Lockwood to heal with humor and gentle chiding that won her the lasting affection of the DAR.

Mrs. Lockwood was born in Hanover, Chautauqua County, New York on October 24, 1831. The widow of a Union soldier, Henry C. Lockwood, she was a member of the Woman's Relief Corps, auxiliary to the Grand Army of the Republic.

Her only daughter, Miss Lillian M. Lockwood, who served for many years as business manager of the *American Monthly Magazine*, died on December 3, 1909.

Beyond her service to the National Society as Founder, Mary Smith Lockwood held numerous national offices. As the first Historian General, on October 18, 1890 Mrs. Lockwood, echoing her prescience of July 13, 1890, offered the motion that gave voice to a dream and ultimately resulted in the building of Memorial Continental Hall.

She later served as Vice President General, Chaplain General, State Regent of the District of Columbia and, for six years, from 1894 to 1900, editor of *American Monthly Magazine* (later *Daughters of the American Revolution Magazine*).

Mrs. Lockwood gave more service, for a longer period of time, than any of the other Founders. Long after the others were laid to their final rest, she continued as an active officer. No wonder her influence on the society was so profound. She worked hard. So did they all. More to the point, she lived long. Outliving even Mrs. Walworth by seven years, Mrs. Lockwood was regarded as the living symbol of the Daughters of the American Revolution at a time when the memory of the other Founders and many of the other early members had faded irretrievably from the scene.

However, Mary S. Lockwood had great difficulty proving her eligibility. She owned an ancient trunk. In the trunk were preserved a three-cornered hat, a presentation sword and other Revolutionary gear. Oral tradition preserved the story, but it took almost a year to find documentary proof. Mary S. Lockwood, Pen Founder of the National Society Daughters of the American Revolution, just barely qualified in time to be listed as a charter member! A prestigious low national number was held open for her, but it was not within the first four or five. The demand was great for the distinguished digits, and others pressed their claims.

At the time of her death she held the offices of Honorary Chaplain General and Honorary Vice President General. Her National Number was 27. At her passing, the society she helped found had grown to a membership of almost 140,000.

Miss Eugenia Washington—*"We want a society founded on service."*

Eugenia Washington

National Number 1, Eugenia Washington was one of the six women who replied to William O. McDowell's call to organize, published in the *Washington Post* on July 21, 1890. She was also present at the informal meeting in the home of Mrs. Louise K. Brown in late July, 1890, and one of the three attending a meeting in the home of Mrs. Ellen Hardin Walworth on August 9, 1890. There a constitution was adopted and important groundwork laid for the founding of the society. Although the National Society opted to focus on October 11, 1890, Miss Washington strongly believed and maintained to the end of her life that August 9, 1890 was the founding date of the National Society. Her service was devoted and extensive.

Unmarried, from an illustrious family that was ruined by the War Between the States, Miss Washington supported herself as a government clerk. From the day she believed that organization was possible, she spent every moment outside of her employment for the advancement of the cause.

The Founders' Medal presented to Miss Eugenia Washington on February 28, 1898 is identical to those presented to Miss Mary Desha and Mrs. Ellen Hardin Walworth. With its three American eagles and the ribbon carrying the word "Founder," it illustrates and commemorates the organizational planning of Miss Washington, Miss Desha and Mrs. Walworth.

A descendant of Samuel, brother of George, Washington, Eugenia Washington was born on June 24, 1840 in Jefferson County, near Harpers Ferry, Virginia (now West Virginia) to William Temple and Margaret Calhoun Fletcher Washington. Her early life typified the gentle existence of well-bred southern girls of her era.

Her father, son of George Steptoe Washington, a graduate of William and Mary College, Williamsburg, Virginia, educated his daughter, Eugenia, and her two sisters at home. Domestic pleasures, country recreation and the society of her family occupied her days.

The family moved to Falmouth, near Fredericksburg, Virginia about 1859. There the Washingtons lived "between the contending armies of the civil war."

One episode serves to illuminate the character of Eugenia Washington. During the Battle of Fredericksburg it fell to Eugenia's lot to leave her home and take her paralytic father to safety, but she delayed. Precious hours slipped away as Eugenia nursed the wounded of both sides. Fleeing at last, Eugenia and her father were trapped on the battlefield. There was no shelter. The girl placed her father in a furrow left by a passing cannon and then, lying beside him, protected him with her own body. Prostrate on the field through the entire day, Eugenia waited through the duration of the battle, witnessing unspeakable death and destruction before she was finally able to remove her father.

The end of the war found the family destitute. The mother was dead; her sisters were married. Eugenia, being offered a government position, took her father to Washington, D.C. where she cared for him and provided his sole support for the remaining seven years of his life.

Her war experience could be expected to change her life. She might have grown bitter toward the country that had used her so badly. Instead, she helped found a National Society that transcended the recent struggle and united women of the North and the South in a patriotic effort to preserve their common glorious heritage.

Eugenia Washington saw no need to tolerate sloppy or casual attention to detail. Making her report as joint Registrar General with Mrs. A. Howard Clark at the First Continental Congress, she spoke out for careful records. She was concerned that applications with incomplete information would prove to be of defective historical value.

> The records of the services of these 1,306 patriots thus preserved, form volumes of most interesting as well as valuable history. Yet this history will lose much of its value if the statements contained therein are not to be relied upon. Therefore we recommend to the Regents and delegates present, as well as to all applicants to the Society of the Daughters of the American Revolution, to give an exact as well as full statement of the ancestors' service during the war, as far as possible, the regiment and company in which such service was rendered, and authority for the statement must be given. Any interesting bit of family tradition may be added, but should be mentioned as such. For these records, we should remember, are collected not only for present use, but shall stand through future generations as monuments to our noble sires.

Although she often spoke her mind without hesitation, her complete devotion to the Daughters of the American Revolution won her the love and respect of the members, who affectionately called her "Miss Eugy."

Following the organization of the National Society, Miss Eugenia Washington served as its first Registrar General, and later as Secretary General, Vice President General, and in 1895, Honorary Vice President General.

She suffered from eye trouble. The constant reading and evaluation of handwritten membership applications in her years as Registrar General was performed at great cost to her sight.

In 1895 she was invited to speak on "Our History" for DAR Day at the Atlanta Exposition, Atlanta, Georgia. Her failing eyesight prevented her from either writing or delivering her paper. Miss Janet Richards, a prominent lecturer, and charter member of the DAR, assembled Eugenia's data into a fine paper and later read it for her on DAR Day.

When the Seventh Continental Congress honored Miss Washington as a Founder, she was unable to do more than take her place on the platform. Recently ill, she was too weak to make a speech. Mrs. Ellen H. Walworth said a few informal words of acceptance on her behalf before beginning her own prepared remarks.

Eugenia Washington died on Thanksgiving Day, November 30,

1900 and was buried at Falmouth, Virginia. On June 27, 1979, her grave was marked by the Virginia Daughters of the American Revolution in a ceremony conducted by Mrs. Eldred Martin Yochim, State Regent, 1977 – 1980.

Miss Mary Desha—*I am good for any amount of work.*

So she said, and so it was. Mary Desha used those very words when she responded to William O. McDowell's call to organize the Daughters of the American Revolution, published in the *Washington Post,* July 21, 1890.

She was known as a tireless worker. Laboring every day at her government job until four o'clock, Mary Desha devoted her personal hours to the great organization she founded, nurtured and loved.

At the 20th Continental Congress, Mary S. Lockwood memorializing her said, "She worked hard. If I have any picture in my mind it is of Mary Desha with a bundle of papers in her hand that pertained to the Daughters of the American Revolution."

Mary Desha

Born in 1850 in Lexington, Kentucky to Dr. John Randolph Desha and Mary Bracken Curry, Mary Desha proudly traced her ancestry to Katherine Montgomery, a "dispatch bearer" during the Revolution and wife of Isaac Bledsoe, a colonel in the Continental Army and Joseph Wheeler, Lieutenant in Braddock's Army. She was the granddaughter of Joseph Desha, a private in the Revolution, Major General in the War of 1812, and Governor of Kentucky in 1825.

"Miss Molly," as she was called, was born to position and prosperity. Like Eugenia Washington, her fortunes were reversed by the War between the States. To support herself she taught—she and her mother operated a private school specializing in French, Latin and mathematics. Miss Desha later worked in the public schools. Well-educated for those days, for a short time she attended State College (now the University of Kentucky).

The election of Grover Cleveland, a Democrat, to the presidency in 1884 signaled an improvement in Mary Desha's life.

Through her brother-in-law, W.C.P. Breckinridge, newly-elected to Congress, she tried to secure an appointment as postmistress of Lexington, Kentucky. Failing in that, she took a "position in one of the departments," and in 1885 arrived in Washington, D.C.

In 1888, at the age of 38, she embarked on an amazing adventure. She accepted a teaching position in Alaska. There her main duty would be to instill discipline in a classroom of 40 children: 14 Americans, the rest Russian.

Mary Desha left Louisville in mid-August.

It took six days to cross the continent by train. Sailing on a steamer from Olympia, Washington around August 24, Mary reached Sitka, Alaska in mid-September. Along the way, she saw gold mines, American Indians, Chinese, and such beautiful landscapes she stayed on deck as much as possible. "I have my sea legs on and have no idea of losing any of the scenery by returning to my state room," she wrote to "everyone at home." The trip cost $150 for "ticket, sleeper and meals." She wrote with gusto of the cuisine and gained ten pounds.

Alaska proved to be filled with contrasts and conflicts. Miss Mary Desha was appalled by the rampant immorality. American men took numerous Indian wives. Russian women took any number of husbands. "I don't suppose Sodom and Gomorrah were any worse than this same town of Sitka," commented Mary in a letter to her sister. Still, she made some good friends and found the climate agreeable. Of the moon, shining bright at four p.m. she wrote, "I don't believe heaven will be any more beautiful."

Mary Desha's idea of an insult was to call someone a Yankee. Although she planned to stay in Alaska for a year, the presidential election of November, won by a "Yankee," changed all that. On November 29, 1888 she learned that Republican Benjamin Harrison had been elected.

Devastated, she and all the other Democrats whose positions had been secured through political appointments began making plans for their inevitable return home. By January 1889 she was on her way.

Back in Washington, Mary Desha worked hard in the Pension office and waited for fate to present her with a new cause.

Little more than a year-and-a-half would elapse before Mary Desha would help to found the organization whose first President General would be the wife of that same Republican president whose election had changed her life's direction.

When Mary S. Lockwood's letter appeared in the *Washington Post*, Mary Desha replied to her enthusiastically. Again, when William O. McDowell's response was printed a week later, Mary Desha was the very first to answer his call.

Like Eugenia Washington, Mary Desha attended the July 29, 1890 meeting at Mrs. Louise K. Brown's and Mrs. Walworth's August 9th meeting.

The early members of the DAR, like today's members, felt they had a mission to perform in fulfilling the historical, patriotic and educational goals of the National Society. This mission was referred to as "the work."

From the day she began it, on July 13, 1890, until death literally snatched her away in mid-stride on January 29, 1911, Mary Desha never laid the work aside. She died in an instant, apparently of a stroke, as she walked home from her day's labor, the ubiquitous bundle of papers in her hand.

She is known for her devotion to the Constitution of the National Society, and her insistence that it must always be adhered to. She won that reputation early on. When the First Continental Congress convened, most of the women present had very little experience in parliamentary procedure. On one day alone, Wednesday, February 24, 1892, Mary Desha's words in support of faithful observance of the Constitution are recorded in sixteen separate places. A few examples:

> We can correct the error but we cannot alter the Constitution. . . . We have to vote by ballot, according to the Constitution. . . . the Constitution must be adhered to. . . . The people who are entitled to vote are named in Article V, Section 1 of the Constitution . . . . With all due deference to our President, I wish to say that if we can change one word in this Constitution, we can change it all. . . . It is not a legal point. It is a constitutional point. . . . I want it to go on record that I wish to adhere to the strict letter of the Constitution.

In 1898 she was appointed Assistant Director of the DAR Hospital Corps under Dr. Anita Newcomb McGee. There she helped pass on the applications of more than 4,500 women who aspired to serve as nurses in the Spanish-American War. She also took charge of supplying the twelve aprons that were provided to each nurse sent to the army by direct endorsement of the DAR.

As a working woman, Miss Desha left her office at 4 p.m. During the entire five-months' service of the DAR Hospital Corps, she attended the Corps office every evening from 4 p.m. to midnight. Eulogizing her, Dr. Anita Newcomb McGee said, "When you crown the Founder, who has so lately passed from us, with a wreath of laurel, may one leaf of it represent her efforts in promoting the saving of lives of our soldiers in the Spanish War."

Mary Desha held National Number 4. She was elected Vice President General on October 11, 1890. Later she was the first Recording Secretary General, and also held the offices of Vice President General in Charge of Organization, Surgeon General, Corresponding Secretary General and Honorary Vice President General.

Hers was the only funeral service ever held in Memorial Continental Hall. From there her remains were borne to Lexington, Kentucky. During the funereal period, the flag at Memorial Continental Hall flew at half-staff. At the unveiling of a monument dedicated to her memory by the Katherine Montgomery Chapter and the Kentucky Daughters of the American Revolution on December 16, 1915, the audience sang "Blest Be the Tie That Binds."

Mrs. Ellen Hardin Walworth—*"A respect for the flag teaches a respect for the rights of others—it teaches a regard for the property of others—a lesson much needed."*

She held National Number 5. Ellen Hardin Walworth called the National Society Daughters of the American Revolution one of the important movements of the century.

As Founder, as Secretary General elected at the organizing meeting, as founding editor of *American Monthly Magazine*, as Vice President General and Honorary Vice President General, Ellen Hardin Walworth gave noble service.

A highly educated woman, she was a published author, a parliamentarian, a lawyer; she chose to devote her energies to the National Society.

It was at Ellen Walworth's home in The Langham that three women, the hostess, Eugenia Washington and Mary Desha met on August 9, 1890 and formulated plans that culminated in the organization of the National Society on October 11, 1890.

On December 14, 1891 Mrs. Ellen H. Walworth presented the Resolution that "a committee be appointed to consider ways and means of erecting a fire-proof building and founding a home for the society, which shall also be the Memorial Hall of the Daughters of the American Revolution, and that the said committee be instructed to bring an early report to the Board." This Resolution is recognized as the official beginning of Memorial Continental Hall.

Ellen Hardin Walworth

Writing in August, 1892, in the second number of the handsome publication that ultimately was named *DAR Magazine*, she honored others, primarily Mrs. Mary V.E. Cabell, Vice President Presiding. Her words apply equally to herself:

> The highest esteem should be awarded the few persons who, like Mrs. Cabell, bravely assumed the responsibility of inaugurating this patriotic society among the most retired and conservative women of America. From the beginning its founders were viewed with suspicion; on the one hand as advocates of a foolish and disloyal aristocracy, and on the other as upholders of methods which would bring women into undue prominence. That both these criticisms have by abundant proof been shown to present false views of the society, is largely due to the uncompromising principle, high-minded courtesy and unruffled amiability of Mrs. Cabell and many officers who assisted her. This union and co-operation of American-born women is one of the important movements of the century, and as the birth of a great measure involves the pains incidental to every creation, so trials have come with the new organization, which its presiding officer was well prepared to meet with

courage, and with the greatest confidence in the good cause in which she was enlisted.

Ellen Hardin's roots were in Kentucky, she was born in Illinois and became a New Yorker by marriage. Her ancestors included an Indian fighter, generals, lawyers and a United States Senator. She equated her background with the admirable aim of uniting the women from the divided North and South of the United States in a single patriotic society emphasizing history, education and patriotism.

Like the other Founders, Ellen enjoyed a close relationship with her father, John Hardin. Kentucky born, Hardin, a lawyer and farmer, took his bride to Jacksonville, Illinois. There Ellen was born on October 20, 1832. When she was twelve or thirteen years old he became a member of the United States Congress. He was killed in 1846, leading his regiment in the Mexican War at the battle of Buena Vista.

Ellen's mother remarried in 1851, the Hon. Reuben Hyde Walworth, last Chancellor of New York, and the family moved to Saratoga Springs, New York. In 1852 Ellen Hardin married the Chancellor's youngest son, Mansfield Tracy Walworth. The marriage lasted until his death in 1873. Following his loss, to support her family she accepted pupils for private instruction. Later, she took her law degree at the University of New York, and was admitted to the bar in New York and the District of Columbia. Her justifiable pride in this achievement was evidenced by her choice of attire: she loved to appear in academic dress; some of the formal portraits of distinguished Daughters at early Continental Congresses include Ellen Hardin Walworth in mortar board cap and gown.

Her daughter, Reubena Hyde Walworth, National Number 47, typified the ideal maiden of the era. Reubena was talented; she studied art and graduated from Vassar. Her poems and drawings grace the pages of the *American Monthly Magazine*. She was modern. Enthusiastically she worked side by side with her mother to help organize the Daughters. She was beautiful and the undisputed joy of her mother's heart. She was in love. As the Spanish-American War riveted the attention of the nation and the National Society, Reubena looked forward to her approaching marriage.

With the DAR Hospital Corps working around the clock certifying nurses to send to the front, "Ruby" and her mother volunteered for relief work in New York. Reubena devoted herself to nursing sick American soldiers in the contagious wards of the detention hospital at Montauk Point. Engrossed in the sacrifice of service, she worked long and exhausting hours. There she, too, fell ill with typhoid fever and died on October 18, 1898.

Reubena Hyde Walworth's portrait was hung in Memorial Continental Hall as a Daughter who died in the service of her country.

An imposing monument, not a broken pillar symbolizing an incomplete life, but a tall, plain, white symmetrical shaft, representing life's purity, funded by contributions from DAR chapters all over the country, was erected at her grave at Greenridge Cemetery, Saratoga Springs, New York. Over 4,000 people attended the unveiling on October 18, 1899. The front of the monument, in bronze letters, reads:

REUBENA HYDE WALWORTH

OCTOBER 18, 1898

SHE SERVED HER COUNTRY NOT AS MAN

BUT BETTER STILL

AS ONLY WOMAN CAN.

The DAR Insignia, the legend "Erected by the Daughters of the American Revolution" and the words "Fortress Monroe, Montauk, Spanish-American War, 1898" complete the inscriptions on the monument.

Ellen Hardin Walworth never fully recovered from the loss of her daughter. A son was also lost, to consumption. Fortunately there was one last son with whom she made her home in later years. However, the joy escaped from her pen with Reubena's loss. Valiantly she carried on but it may be truly said that she was never again the same.

She died on June 23, 1915, just a few short weeks before the twenty-fifth anniversary of the society she helped found. The tribute to Ellen Hardin Walworth given at the 25th Continental Congress concluded with the following words:

> She leaves us a heritage that will go from generation to genera-
> tion—the heritage of faithful work, of absolute devotion to duty as she
> saw it, of unfailing readiness to sacrifice when needs arise, and constant

fidelity to the highest ideals of our Society, that must bear fruit in the inspiration that she is to every one of us.

She was buried in the family lot of the Hardins and Walworths at Green Ridge, near Saratoga, New York.

The first President General

. . . The object and aim of the Society is to keep first in the minds of the coming generation the struggles of the founders of this nation—make them familiar with American History . . .

> *Letter from Caroline Scott Harrison, President General 1890 – 1892, to Mrs. Perrin, April 4, 1892*

To demonstrate the merit, unique mission and essential validity of their enterprise, the organizers of the Daughters of the American Revolution sought a titular head of the first order. They knew that the wife of a man of national prominence would attract the widespread notice they needed, and encourage eligible women to flock to organization.

Caroline Scott Harrison

Dauntless, the founders aimed high, setting their sights and their hearts on the wife of the President of the United States of America.

On August 10th, 1890, Miss Mary Desha penned a letter inviting Mrs. Benjamin Harrison to become the president of the new society.

Attracted to the idea of valuable service, but concerned lest her patronage should provoke division, Mrs. Harrison agreed to take the position only if she were elected unanimously. She sent a letter accepting the office of *Honorary President General*, but by the time the society's first letterhead was printed, she was listed as President General. The distinction had been intended to make allowance for the fact that Mrs. Harrison's DAR responsibilities must never interfere with her duties as "first lady of the land."

The presiding officer would be elected from the Vice Presidents General and would relieve Mrs. Harrison of the burden of most of the work. Mrs. Mary V. E. Cabell was elected and served under the titles of Acting President General and Vice President Presiding during Mrs. Harrison's two terms of office.

Caroline Scott Harrison, National Number 7, had a genuine belief in the National Society and its objectives. Although her unique position as wife of the president demanded much of her time and attention, she frequently attended meetings, free to slip away as her schedule required. She was present, with Mrs. Cabell presiding, on October 18, 1890, when her letter of acceptance was read and spread on the minutes.

Executive Mansion
Washington

My dear Mrs. Darling:

Many thanks for your kind note, and Mrs. Harrison desires me to say that she will accept the position as Honorary President General of the Society and thanks you and the other ladies for their cordiality in the matter.

(Signed) Mrs. Dimmick

(Mrs. Dimmick was Mrs. Harrison's niece and served as her social secretary. Many of Caroline Scott Harrison's letters were written and signed by Mrs. Dimmick.)

Mrs. Benjamin Harrison attended the Second Meeting for Organization of the National Society Daughters of the American Revolution, held October 18, 1890, and her service as President General began on that day. She served with gentleness and dignity through all the tumultuous days of the organizing year, and although the heavy correspondence and the unusual magnitude of some of the challenges fell largely on Mrs. Cabell, Mrs. Harrison kept herself abreast of the situation. It is especially significant that during a period that could have been an embarrassment to one in her public position, Mrs. Harrison remained faithful, and continued to lend her prestige to the infant organization.

Socially, her presence added glitter. On February 22, 1891, Mr. and Mrs. William Cabell entertained the Sons and the Daughters of the American Revolution at a grand reception intended to thrust the new society brilliantly into the Washington "season." No effort was spared, from elegantly engraved invitations issued in the joint names of the National Society Daughters of the American Revolution and the District Society Sons of the American Revolution, to flags, bunting, flowers, and a double line of guards dressed in the Continental buff and blue. Decorations reflected the blue and white of the two organizations. Patriotism was the dominant note. Mrs. Harrison received and the Washington "media" were favorably impressed.

Caroline Scott Harrison was a signatory to the Act of Incorporation of the National Society of the Daughters of the American Revolution entered June 8, 1891.

During the organizing year, October 11, 1890 – October 11, 1891, Mrs. William D. Cabell's impressive home at 1407 Massachusetts Avenue, N.W. served as the society's headquarters. There, on October 6, 1891, Mrs. Harrison presided at the first conference of national officers, state and chapter regents, where a full statement of the plans and methods of the society were presented. On July 1, 1891 the office of Vice President in Charge of Organization had been declared vacant. Confusion existed about appointments of regents. The conference was called to clarify the situation. The next day Mrs. Harrison entertained the officers and members at the White House.

The First Continental Congress was held February 22–24, 1892 at the Church of Our Father, Thirteenth and L Streets, N.W., Washington, D.C. Mrs. Harrison opened the congress.

In the first public address ever made by a first lady of the United States she called attention to the rapid growth of the society, to over thirteen hundred members, with thirty-eight chapter regents and nineteen state regents in thirty-one States of the Union. She continued:

> We now feel that this Society is firmly established and in good condition for continued success. It remains with us all to see that it still lives and grows to greater and better ends. We have within ourselves the only element of destruction; our foes are from within, not without. . . . Our hope is in unity and self-sacrifice. Since this Society has been organized, and so much thought and reading directed to the early struggle of this country, it has been made plain that much of its success was due to the character of the women of that era. The unselfish part they acted constantly commends itself to our admiration and example. If there is no abatement in this element of success in our

Mrs William D. Cabell's home at 1407 Massachusetts Avenue, N.W.

ranks I feel sure their daughters can perpetuate a society worth the cause and worthy of themselves.

Mrs. Harrison entertained the delegates to the First Continental Congress at tea at the White House on February 22, 1892. She and President Harrison received the guests until, becoming fatigued, Mrs. Harrison retired and Mrs. Mary V.E. Cabell took her place.

Mrs. Caroline Scott Harrison presided one last time at the March 19, 1892 meeting of the National Board of Management. Her service was extraordinary, given the circumstances. One can only imagine that, had illness not intervened, she would have taken an ever-increasing role in the society which owed her so much.

Caroline Lavinia Scott Harrison, daughter of Mary Neal and Rev. John Witterspoon Scott, was born October 1, 1832 at Oxford, Ohio. Mrs. Harrison's great, great grandfather was John Scott, Commissary-General of the Pennsylvania Line in the War of the Revolution. Her father was a founder, an incorporator and President of the Oxford Female Institute established in 1830. The school later became the Oxford College for women which merged with Miami University in 1928. The main building at Oxford College was rehabilitated and converted into a dormitory by the National Society as a tribute in memory of its first President General, Mrs. Harrison at the time of the merger.

Caroline Scott graduated from Oxford Female Institute on June 22, 1852 and married Benjamin Harrison on October 20, 1853. She was a gifted artist, specializing in painting flowers in water colors and on china. Her calm, gentle and considerate manner endeared her to everyone. Like the Revolutionary era women she admired, the scope of her influence was broadened by her firm character and her unselfish devotion.

During Mrs. Harrison's term of office the constitution, seal, motto, Insignia and colors were adopted. The resolution to contribute support toward completing the monument to Mary Washington was adopted at the Organizing Meeting. The society was incorporated under the laws of the District of Columbia on June 8, 1891. On December 14, 1891 the Board of Management adopted a resolution to consider ways and means of erecting a permanent home for the society. The *American Monthly*, first magazine of the DAR, was authorized on May 26, 1892.

Growing in confidence, and enjoying her position, Caroline Scott Harrison was unanimously reelected President General at the First Continental Congress, but her health was in decline. On April 4th, 1892, she wrote Mrs. John F. Perrin of Lafayette, Indiana, "I . . . have been far from well for the past three weeks. I hope however to be myself before long." It was not to be. Mrs. Harrison presided for the last time at a meeting of the National Board of Management on March 19, 1892. Her death from cancer on October 25, 1892 plunged the National Society and, in fact, the entire nation into grief. During her term of office the National Society Daughters of the American Revolution, grew from 11 members with $33 in the treasury to a noteworthy enterprise, over 1800 strong.

A portrait of Caroline Scott Harrison, painted by Daniel Huntington, was unveiled at the Third Continental Congress, on February 22, 1894. It was placed in the White House, her home during her tenure in office as the first President General of the National Society, a gift to the American people from the Daughters of the American Revolution. As a 50th Anniversary project, during the administration of Mrs. Henry M. Robert, Jr., President General 1938 – 1941, on October 11, 1939 the National Society presented a copy of the full-length portrait to the Harrison Mansion at Indianapolis, Indiana.

The Vice President Presiding

State Pride is a good, a noble thing, but we hold that love of country is better.
    Mary Virginia Ellet Cabell, Vice President Presiding 1890 – 1892, President Presiding 1892 – 1893, meeting of the National Board of Management, August 10, 1891

Mary Virginia Ellet Cabell

If it is possible to single out the one person most responsible for the early success of the National Society, that person was Mrs. William D. Cabell.

Mary Virginia Ellet Cabell, National Number 6, the daughter of Charles Ellet, Jr. and Elvira Augusta Daniel, was born in 1839 at "Point of Honor," the home of her grandfather, Judge Daniel, near Lynchburg, Virginia. She died, aged 91, on July 4, 1930 at the summer home of her daughters, Misses Elvira and Margaret Cabell in Michigan City, Indiana and is buried in the Cabell family plot in Berryville, Virginia.

As a child, she was extremely close to her father, Charles Ellet, Jr. a prominent civil engineer, and often accompanied him in his travels. At age nine she spent several months with him at Niagara Falls when he constructed the first bridge across the Niagara River below the Falls. Many times she crossed the river in the "iron basket" used to convey men and materials during the early stages of construction. Her father told the impressionable young girl that she was the first "woman" to view the Falls from the bridge before its completion.

Charles Ellet, Jr. was a man of many accomplishments. He built the first suspension bridge in the United States, over the Schuylkill River at Philadelphia; invented the steam ram and constructed and commanded the United States Ram fleet in the battle of Memphis in the Civil War. Injured there, he died in 1862, age 52, in the presence of his wife and daughter, and was honored by being given a military funeral from Independence Hall in Philadelphia. Mary Ellet lost her mother the same year and her brother the following year.

Tragedy thrust responsibility on the young woman. On her shoulders fell the care of two younger children and her elderly grandmother.

Following the close of the war, Mary Ellet married William D. Cabell of Norwood, Virginia. At Norwood the young couple struggled to rebuild his ruined estate by conducting a school for boys.

Later, the Cabells, with their six children, moved to Washington, D.C. There Mrs. Cabell opened the Norwood Institute, a school for the education of her own daughters and their acquaintances, at their stately residence on Massachusetts Avenue. She was socially known in Washington through her father's connections. Her prominence increased as her school became an important feature in Washington life and society.

Mrs. Mary V.E. Cabell "yielded to the repeated exhortations of that indefatigable pioneer, Miss Mary Desha," and attended the First Meeting for Organization of the National Society on October 11, 1890. Years afterward, she recalled:

> I was not influenced by the refusal of the Sons of the American Revolution to admit women to their organization. Nor had I ever read the interesting story of Hannah Arnett. . . . In Washington, where I lived, women in the same social circle but from different sections of the country looked coldly on one another. Another spirit, another creed, was needed. Women, who best conserve the old, might best promote the new. This was a task for Daughters of the American Revolution.

Mrs. Cabell was placed in the chair at that first meeting, and presided. Later the same day she, with Mr. William O. McDowell, called on Mrs. Benjamin Harrison to obtain, if possible, her acceptance of the invitation to become president of the society. On Mrs. Cabell's promise to assume the heavier part of the work Mrs. Harrison agreed to accept the office.

As Vice President Presiding, it was Mrs. Cabell's role not only to preside during the anticipated frequent absences of the President General, but also to handle all the day-to-day details of her office. During the first year of the National Society, this inevitably went far beyond routine. Mrs. Cabell had to be able to forge policy, solve problems, and make a new organization, with an untried constitution, work. The challenges were enormous. The rewards, as with virtue, were intangible.

Mrs. Cabell's home was the official home of the society for more than a year. There the Board met monthly, beginning with the Second Meeting for Organization, on October 18, 1890.

On February 22, 1892, following the welcoming address of Mrs. Benjamin Harrison, President General, Mrs. Cabell presided at all sessions of the First Continental Congress. Her report to the Congress stated that interested persons in different sections of the country were asking certain questions:

> What is your object; what do you propose; what good will you do; what is the use of such an organization? What does thou work?

Mrs. Cabell proposed, as an "outward and visible sign of an inward and spiritual grace, the building of a House Beautiful . . . the finest building ever owned by women . . . an enterprise which men and women will arise and call blessed because of its wide and spreading influence and the magnificent possibilities it offers to our sisterhood, the patriotic, home-loving and country-loving women of America."

She lived to see, not only the House Beautiful, Memorial Continental Hall, a reality, but also the Administration Building and Constitution Hall.

After the death of President General, Caroline Scott Harrison, Mrs. Cabell, as Acting President General, presided over the meetings of the Second Continental Congress in February, 1893. At that congress she was nominated for the office of President General but withdrew in favor of Mrs. Adlai E. Stevenson, sharing the feeling originated by the Founders that the National Society "should be presided over by a lady prominent in the United States."

The Second Continental Congress, in gratitude, recognized Mrs. Cabell's unique contribution by electing her President Presiding, which office she held until October 5, 1893, when she stepped down. Never again did the National Society elect either a Vice President Presiding or a President Presiding. Those singular offices belonged to the singular Mrs. Cabell alone.

In 1898, following the presentation of the bejeweled medals to the Four Founders, Mrs. Cabell was elected Honorary Vice President

General. In nominating her, Mrs. George H. Shields stated clearly how instrumental Mrs. Cabell had been in the founding of the National Society:

> There is a woman to whom we owe more than to any other woman in our midst. It is our first Vice President General Presiding. Mrs. Harrison was unable by the cares that pressed upon her, as well as by ill-health, to preside—Mrs. Cabell . . . took all this labor upon herself. Moreover, we were in those days a feeble folk; we had no income; we wrote our own letters; we paid our own postage; we had no office; the official home of the Daughters of the American Revolution was the home of Mrs. Cabell; in her beautiful drawing room our Board met; her dining room was our Banquet Hall; her money and her time were ours.

Mary V.E. Cabell had a descriptive ability that enabled her to express great thoughts with elegant simplicity. Speaking in May, 1893 at a meeting held under the auspices of the World's Congress of Representative Women, Mrs. Cabell said:

> Our inspiration lies in those two talismanic words dear to every American Heart,—the house we teach our daughters to grace; the country we rear our sons to defend.

After her resignation as President Presiding, she never again took an active office in the National Society. In 1901 she was elected Honorary President Presiding, a position recognizing her unique contribution; an honor held by no other before or since.

Several years after the death of Mr. Cabell in 1904 Mrs. Cabell moved to Chicago, Illinois with her daughter. There she remained with only occasional visits to the "House Beautiful" she had dreamed of in 1892. She never joined a chapter, feeling that her peculiar relation to the National Society, like no other's, was more clearly defined by limiting her association to national membership.

Mrs. Cabell was invited, with other early members, to attend the 27th Continental Congress, on April 17, 1918, as an honored guest. Mrs. George Thacher Guernsey, President General 1917–1920, introduced the program saying, "When I began coming to the congresses a number of years ago, the first thought in my mind always was that the first people I wanted to see were the ones who made this organization, and it was most interesting to me to have them pointed out."

Mrs. Cabell was given charge of the program that evening. She was to preside while many of the living early members reminisced about the society's beginnings and brought greetings to the Opening Night assembly. Because the Great War dominated her thoughts, Mrs. Cabell found it hard to enter into the spirit of the occasion.

> For myself, I will ask you, instead of dwelling on the past, to look with me for a moment upon the stupendous present, this "present laden with the past and pregnant with the future," which is surging around us with a deafening roar and threatening to engulf not only our work, friends and countrywomen, but the work of those from whom we take our name, from whom we boast our descent—

She asked the members to think of the words of the Commander-in-Chief, President Woodrow Wilson:

> The eyes of the world are upon you, because you are in a certain sense the soldiers of freedom. Therefore, let it be your pride to show the world not only what good soldiers you are, but what good men you are, keeping yourselves fit and straight all the time and everywhere, pure and clean through and through.

> Set your standard so high that it is a glory to try to live up to it; and then so live up to it as to add by your conduct a new laurel to the crown of America. And may God be with you and keep you.

In response to a request from her cousin to describe the organizing of the National Society and particularly, the role of Mrs. Cabell, herself, she wrote:

> The fact is, my dear Bertha, that at our "organizing meeting" or session, officially so-called—I was so impressed with the potentialities (great) of our undertaking—particularly in the way of obliterating the bitterness still cherished in 1890 as a result of our terrible Civil War by bringing into close relationship for a noble patriotic purpose women from the North and South, that I paid the least possible attention to petty personal considerations. My time was more than occupied by the efforts and duties of the important office devolved upon me.

Mrs. Cabell outlived even Mrs. Mary S. Lockwood. Had she chosen to remain active, she would undoubtedly be better known today. The early members acknowledged that it was she who enabled the National Society to thrive and survive its first tumultuous year. She gave generously of her talents and resources, and when she had accomplished what she set out to do, she gracefully retired. On October 11, 1990, the Centennial anniversary of the National Society, in the administration of Mrs. Eldred Martin Yochim, President General 1989 – 1992, a tablet honoring Mrs. Cabell's contribution was placed near the Founders' Memorial Monument. Mrs. Yochim noted that Mrs. Cabell was:

> . . . a founder and charter member who, with quiet dignity, led the newly organized society through its infancy. Her gentle touch is reflected throughout the early history of the society and we should be deeply indebted to her for her wisdom, courage and dedication.

The inscription on the plaque says:

IN LOVING MEMORY OF MARY VIRGINIA ELLET CABELL

(MRS. WILLIAM DANIEL)

VICE PRESIDENT GENERAL HONORARY VICE PRESIDENT GENERAL

ONLY

VICE PRESIDENT PRESIDING—1890 – 1892

PRESIDENT PRESIDING—1893

HONORARY PRESIDENT PRESIDING

OCTOBER 11, 1990

Mary Virginia Ellet Cabell's portrait hangs in the President General's Reception Room at Constitution Hall, the gift in 1932 of her daughter, Miss Elvira Cabell. Painted several years before her death by Paul Trebilcock, it is a faithful likeness of the quiet and capable President Presiding of the National Society Daughters of the American Revolution.

The organizing members

In addition to the Four Founders and Mrs. Cabell, thirteen other women attended the organizing meeting of the National Society of the Daughters of the American Revolution. Each had her own story.

Mrs. Flora Adams Darling wanted to be known as *the* organizer of the DAR. She spent the summer of 1890 in Culpeper, Virginia. In August and September she corresponded with the Founders and Mr. McDowell about the planned new society. Her surprise tactic of calling the Organizing Meeting (albeit on the pre-planned date) won her immediate enmity, but was overlooked in the interests of harmony.

Mrs. Darling was deaf and, mercifully, felt that her condition prevented her from seeking the highest office. However, she was elected Vice President in Charge of Organization, and her name was listed third on the National Society's first letterhead, behind only Mrs. Harrison and Mrs. Cabell.

By November 11, 1890 she had begun causing serious friction. Traveling about the country in her task of organization she was enthusiastic, dedicated and sincere, but her favoritism and unpredictability at once both attracted and repelled. Erratic communications and haphazard record-keeping frustrated those in Washington trying valiantly to certify records, and issue Commissions and Membership Certificates. Conflicting letters of criticism and accusation flew back and forth. The newspapers in Washington and New York City happily published everything they heard. The deteriorating situation required much of Mrs. Cabell's energy and tact to contain.

The adoption of a revised constitution on May 26, 1891 signaled the beginning of the end. In June Mrs. Darling wrote that she would not recognize the authority of the Board, and forbade the society to use her name. The Board retaliated on July 1, 1891 by declaring her office vacant.

Mrs. Darling resigned from the National Society on August 7, 1891 and demanded that all traces of her membership be deleted from society records. To the extent that it was humanly possible, this was done. Her application paper was removed from the files, presumably to be returned to her or destroyed, and her National Number, 1, was reassigned to Miss Eugenia Washington. The entire unpleasant episode was, quite frankly, hushed up.

Miss Margaret Cabell, daughter of Mrs. Mary V.E. Cabell, attended Continental Congress for the first time in April, 1940. On September 16, 1940, she wrote a letter offering to donate to the new Americana Room, valuable papers relating to the organization of the National Society. She expressed the materials from Charlottesville, Virginia on September 24, 1940. An invitation to attend the Golden Jubilee anniversary dinner and historical evening October 10 – 11, 1940 was never received, for Miss Cabell, her archival concern satisfied, died four or five days after shipping the papers.

In 1980 the Cabell family presented a further collection of original correspondence and memorabilia.

Among the original documents in the Cabell collection is Flora Adams Darling's application paper for membership in the Daughters of the American Revolution, signed by Eugenia Washington, Registrar and Mary L. Shields, Recording Secretary.

Mrs. Mary Morris Hallowell, National Number 20, who lived in France, died April 2, 1913. Like many of the early members, she was a contributor to *American Monthly Magazine.*

Mrs. Margaret Hetzel, National Number 12, served the National Society as its first Honorary Vice President General. She was the first secretary of the Mary Washington Monument Association, spearheading the drive to restore the monument to Mary Washington. As Mary Desha expressed it in *American Monthly Magazine,* "She wrote the first letter, gave the first dollar and lived to see the work completed." Mrs. Hetzel died on December 16, 1899.

Her daughter, **Miss Susan Riviere Hetzel,** National Number 13, was also prominent in the movement to honor the mother of Washington. Susan Riviere Hetzel served the National Society as Registrar General and as Historian General. Following her death on June 4, 1908 she was buried at Arlington National Cemetery.

Alice Morrow Clark (Mrs. A. Howard Clark), National Number 16, was elected joint Registrar with Miss Eugenia Washington on October 11, 1890. A descendant of John and Priscilla Alden, Mrs. Clark became a speaker of note, who traveled from coast to coast lecturing. In June, 1894, at a National Board meeting, she offered a resolution that all Daughters of the American Revolution celebrate the anniversary of the adoption of the flag, June 14, as Flag Day, and commemorate it by displaying the flag in their homes. Speaking at the 27th Continental Congress, Mrs. Clark was thinking of the war and said, "The men of our whole allied world are offering up their lives for the spirit of the little phrase which we selected long ago as our motto, Home and Country! . . . our very motto itself urges us to protect, not only our homes and our country, but those of our friends and allies." She is remembered for a dramatic tour she made in the 1920's speaking against the dangers of bolshevism, socialism and pacifism, "I did raise my boy to be a soldier, so he could go when his country needed him." Mrs. Clark died on February 24, 1927.

Miss Floride Cunningham qualified for membership in 1893 with National Number 4850. She was especially interested in historic preservation. A niece of Ann Pamela Cunningham, originator and first Regent of the Mount Vernon Ladies Association, she knew at firsthand of the successful fight to save Mt. Vernon. Floride Cunningham was another organizer present at the 27th Continental Congress. The Official Reader read her message, the frail Miss Cunningham standing at her side. It said in part, "My faith in you is as strong as is my faith in our God-inspired President, Woodrow Wilson, our glorious army at the front, and those who are following them in their unyielding determination to win our cause."

The young daughter of William O. McDowell, *Miss Pauline McDowell*, National Number 98, had not yet attained the required age of eighteen years at the organizing meeting, but so disappointed was the father at his exclusion from the new society, an exception was made in her case and she was allowed to sign as an organizing member. A member of Nova Caesarea Chapter, she lived until November 17, 1968 and was memorialized at the 78th Continental Congress, April 13, 1969 as Pauline McDowell Atkins. The National Society has always appreciated the encouragement shown by William O. McDowell. As one writer said, "The fact that we never adopted a single paper, or did a single thing in the way he proposed, does not in the least diminish our gratitude for his good will."

Mrs. Ada P. Kimberley, National Number 110, served the National Society long and faithfully. An Honorary State Regent of Wisconsin, she was unable to accept the invitation of the President General, Mrs. George Thacher Guernsey, to participate in the 27th Continental Congress in 1918 but sent a letter: "As I have often said, October 11, 1890 was one of the most delightful and beautiful days in my life." She mentioned that Wisconsin Daughters were working like true Badgers, devoting their time and energies sewing garments for American fighting men and for French and Belgian children. She noted that she was familiarly known as Wisconsin's Little Godmother. Mrs. Kimberley died on September 16, 1930.

Mrs. Aurelia Hadley Mohl was interested in the National Society and attended the Organizing Meeting on October 11, 1890, but never qualified for membership.

Some who were present at the Organizing Meeting joined, but left little or no record. **Mrs. Caroline L. Ransom**, National Number 52, enjoyed almost 20 years of membership. The files show that in March 1908, she resigned her membership, was reinstated in April, 1909 and died in February, 1910. Similarly, **Mrs. Harriet Lincoln Coolidge**, National Number 115, was dropped for nonpayment of her dues on July 1, 1901, but was reinstated three months before her death on May 17, 1902.

Mrs. Emily Lee Sherwood, National Number 60, later married William H. Ragan and co-authored with Mrs. Mary S. Lockwood one of the early histories of the society, *The Story of the Records; D.A.R.*, published in 1906. Mrs. Ragan resigned from the DAR in 1902 but was reinstated a year later, on March 23, 1903. She died on April 19, 1916.

Mrs. Jennie D. Garrison, National Number 64, was known as a strong supporter of Continental Hall. She is listed in the 1909 Directory of Committees as a member of the Continental Hall Committee. Enjoying a long life, she went to her rest on August 24, 1928.

Many women joined the National Society during the organizing year, October 11, 1890 – October 11, 1891, and are honored as charter members. The last National Number issued during the organizing year was 818. The last National Number issued as of October 11, 1990, 100 years later, was 733577.

Through the years, each new member has responded to the invitation of the National Society to participate in its historic, educational and patriotic objectives. Each has contributed a part of herself. The National Society Daughters of the American Revolution is, in a very real sense, the sum of all the three-quarters of a million women who have made this contribution during the last 100 years. With over 200,000 active members today, the National Society Daughters of the American Revolution begins its second century of service proud of the accomplishments of the past, mindful of the challenges of the present, and eager to realize the promise of the future.

How Does the DAR Function?

The Daughters of the American Revolution is a *national* organization. Members belong first, to the National Society, and second, to their chapter. This point has been emphasized from day one of the organization and is largely responsible for the great strength of the National Society, its growth through the years, and the loyalty of its members. It is even possible, though not recommended, to belong to the National Society and, as a member-at-large, bypass chapter membership altogether.

The chief executive officer of the DAR is the President General, elected, with a slate of officers, to serve a three-year term. In the earliest days of the National Society women were elected to the office of President General based on the name-recognition value of their husbands. This device helped immeasurably in securing interest in and publicity for the DAR. However, by 1905 the organization had developed a corps of potential officers, trained in DAR leadership through service in the ranks, and women were able to qualify for national office on their own merits

In addition to the President General, the Executive Officers are First Vice President General, Chaplain General, Recording Secretary General, Corresponding Secretary General, Organizing Secretary General, Treasurer General, Registrar General, Historian General, Librarian General, Curator General and Reporter General. Twenty-one other Vice Presidents General are also elected to three-year terms, seven each year. These, with the State Regents (or in their absence the State Vice Regents), constitute the National Board of Management.

Chapters work in communities

*The chapter feature is a peculiarly happy one. Composed
of accepted members of the society, drawn together
because of mutual congeniality, supplementing the great
common interests of the society, these local associations
develop a social feature of great worth and dignity.*
                        Mary Virginia Ellet Cabell

By the time the first chapter was organized at Chicago on March
20, 1891 with about 30 organizing members, patriotic women were lining
up to join. A year later, at the First Continental Congress, Mrs. Frank
Osborn, Chapter Regent, was able to report that 80 women had been
admitted and the local registrar had just approved the papers of ten
more. They were anticipating the coming World's Columbian Exposition
and hoping for DAR participation. Concerned by rapid social change
because of immigration, Mrs. Osborn said, "We do not wish to forget
that we grew from mixed nationalities. Side by side representatives from
the wide world over fought in our Revolution, and side by side evolved
our glorious Constitution." Although the First Continental Congress
hesitated to commit itself to participation at the Exposition, the Second
Congress felt no such reluctance. When the Exposition opened in 1893,
the National Society and Chicago Chapter were well-represented.

Atlanta Chapter was formed on April 15, 1891, the first chapter to
be formed in the deep south. In 1892 members responded enthusiastically to a resolution passed by the National Board of Management that
Daughters of the American Revolution should display the American flag
upon their residences on the Fourth of July, 1892. As an Atlanta paper
reported, "The Flag to Go Up—Daughters of the American Revolution
to Raise It." The chapter reported that "for several years" (probably
since 1861) Georgians had neglected the Fourth and that the "patriotic
women of Atlanta will display upon their homes our country's flag, which
our sons and daughters should be taught to love."

On April 19, 1891 the third chapter was formed, at New York City
with 37 members. Mrs. Roger A. Pryor was the first Regent, but by the
First Continental Congress had withdrawn because of ill-health. Mrs.
R. Ogden Doremus, who succeeded her, amused the Congress by

relating that the chapter was "like the farmer, who, his wife being dangerously ill, sent for a physician. When the doctor got there the woman was dead, and the physician said to the husband, 'was she resigned?' 'Yes,' the husband replied, 'she had to be.' So we had to be resigned when Mrs. Pryor left us."

Mrs. Pryor was one of the six women who answered William O. McDowell's letter in the *Post* on July 20, 1890, and was appointed Regent for New York at the organizing meeting, October 11, 1890. A victim of Flora Adams Darling's vagaries, she was frustrated and disappointed that her chapter was not the first in the nation.

As the *First Report to the Smithsonian Institution,* published in 1899 by the Government Printing Office, said, "The chapters in every locality have reviewed our country's history and have tried to make it interesting to others."

Units Overseas

Patriotism knows neither latitude nor longitude. It is not climatic.

> *Mrs. William Cumming Story, President General, 1913 – 1917*

By 1897, the National Society had attracted members in Paris, Naples, Samoa, China, South Africa and Honolulu. Primarily Americans living abroad, these women had special reasons to hunger for patriotic activities. If such far-distant members were to become active, they needed to organize into chapters.

Throughout the years, 26 different chapters were organized in various locations around the globe, including Hawaii, the Philippine Islands, China, Australia, France, England, Italy, Germany, Mexico, Cuba, Puerto Rico, Venezuela, Alaska and Canada. Changing circumstances have controlled the continuance or disbandment of each chapter. World War II disrupted several. Attainment of statehood changed the status of chapters in Alaska and Hawaii from Units Overseas to State Societies. At this writing there are active DAR chapters in Australia, Canada, England, France and Mexico.

Great distances and the uncertainties of communication create certain difficulties for chapters striving to work in harmony with the

United States mainland. Still, until the intervention of World War II the overseas chapters functioned more or less successfully, depending upon the leadership available at any given moment, and the impetus derived from occasional visitors from home. Following the many changes wrought by World War II, in 1947 the Units Overseas Committee was formed to coordinate overseas chapter activity, and assist with the special needs of DAR chapters on foreign soil.

Real Daughters

By 1893, it was realized that some women were joining whose fathers had actually served the cause of American freedom in the Revolutionary War. Recognizing, locating, and enrolling these *Real Daughters* in the National Society sparked enthusiasm throughout the chapters. In 1895 it was decided to honor each actual Daughter who joined with the gift of a special gold souvenir spoon. Ornamenting the handle, thirteen stars appear upon a canopy of flax, with the motto, "Home and Country," above the dame at the spinning wheel. Spun flax cascades down the handle and into the heart-shaped bowl, and forms the letters DAR with its floating ends. Engraved on the back are the Real Daughter's initials and National Number on a shield with eagle and olive branch.

The society's interest in Real Daughters went far beyond the initial spoon presentation. These special members were chronicled in the *American Monthly Magazine* and greeted from Continental Congress. Those who knew poverty were given aid and support. Food, clothing, household goods, and where necessary, pensions, were provided by the National Society and individual chapters.

Not all, of course, were needy. Their membership was also sought and honored. Eagerly the first-hand stories contributed by these dual Daughters were collected and shared.

Through the years, 757 Real Daughters were located and enrolled. The next to the last surviving Real Daughter of the American Revolution was Mrs. Caroline P. Randall, of Springfield, Vermont, who was born on September 19, 1849, when her father, Stephen Hassam, was 90 years of age. He, at the age of 15, carried water to the Colonial troops at the Battle of Bunker Hill. She lived to age 92, sharing generously her memories of earlier times, and enjoying the association, and died on July 14, 1942. In her last years, the National Society provided her sole support.

The last Real Daughter, Mrs. Annie Knight Gregory of Williamsport, Pennsylvania, was born on March 23, 1843. Her grandfather, Conrad Knight, enlisted in the Revolutionary forces in 1777. A widower, he took his 11 year old son, Richard, with him as a drummer boy. Richard, Mrs. Gregory's father, also served in the War of 1812. The National Society paid loving tribute on her 100th birthday with more than 2,000 cards, telegrams and gifts. That day, she issued a message that:

Annie Knight Gregory, last Real Daughter

> I have lived from the days of the pony express to the wireless telephone and radio, from the spinning wheel and loom to textile plants and factories. Now in my 100th year the wish, the request, the admonition that I would leave with you and those who come after is, that you inculcate into the minds of our *youth* the lessons of the hardships and sacrifices which have entered into the making of our country and that if we would keep our nation what our fathers made it, the present and the coming generations must work and struggle and save, and keep away from lives of idleness and ease.

Purchasing a war bond she said, "It will be my investment in the future of my great-grandchildren, just as my father and

Mary H. Washington, first Real Daughter

grandfather invested in the America we enjoy and defend today." Her death on December 1, 1943 not only brought grief to the National Society and her many friends, it also ended an era.

A bust of the first Real Daughter in the National Society, Mary Hammond Washington, National Number 81, was placed in Memorial Continental Hall in 1912. Mrs. Washington was the first Chapter Regent in Georgia, at Macon, and held that office until her death on November 2, 1901. She was elected an Honorary State Regent in 1899. She was born in St. Louis, Missouri, May 12, 1816, where her father, Col. Samuel Hammond had been appointed military and civil commander by Jefferson in 1804. The family returned to Georgia in 1825, where she spent the rest of her life. Her son, Hugh Vernon Washington gave the final $1,000 for Memorial Continental Hall.

The bust, placed in honor of *all* Real Daughters, was sculpted by F. Landi of New York. As a gift coming from the entire National Society, it served as a "token of their regard for the Daughters of those men who fought to make us a nation." It may be seen today on the main floor of the DAR Library.

Well-known members

> *I hope in your selections you will be exceedingly careful to distinguish those actions in which our Revolutionary mothers took part.*
>
> Susan B. Anthony, letter to Kentucky DAR, 1897

The National Society was founded by women who were either famous in their own right or able through their connections to influence others. The coup of securing Caroline Scott Harrison, the wife of the President of the United States, for first President General of the DAR assured immediate publicity.

Women's rights were in the air and leaders of the movement were keenly interested in the prospects of the new organization. Frances E. Willard, prominent temperance leader, was a charter member.

Mary Baker Eddy, the founder of Christian Science, joined on March 28, 1892, as a Life Member.

Susan B. Anthony, pre-eminent suffragist, observed the fledgling society with interest and signaled her approval by joining in 1898. Explaining why she was unable to take a more active role in the society's affairs, she wrote, "I have been and must continue to be busy working to secure to the women of this day the paramount rights for which the Revolutionary War was waged." Attending the 11th Continental Congress in 1902, she received a standing ovation. In her last public speech, her 86th birthday celebration on February 15, 1906, she correctly prophesied, "Failure is impossible." At her death later that year, Irondequoit Chapter recalled her "sturdy virtues" and, amplifying Tennyson's "Ode on the Death of the Duke of Wellington," mourned that

Susan B. Anthony

they would miss "the good gray head that all men loved." 39 years later, the National Society passed a resolution urging her admission to the Hall of Fame. Although that attempt failed, she was admitted in 1950.

Julia Dent Grant, wife of Gen. Ulysses S. Grant was a member, as were other presidents' wives: Edith Carow Roosevelt, Florence Kling Harding, Eleanor Roosevelt Roosevelt, and Mamie Doud Eisenhower. Jean Faircloth MacArthur, wife of Gen. Douglas MacArthur, is a member of long standing.

The White House has been represented in more recent years by Rosalynn Smith Carter, Nancy Davis Reagan and Barbara Pierce Bush, as well as "first daughter" Julie Nixon Eisenhower.

Author of the popular children's series, *Five Little Peppers*, Margaret Sidney, joined the National Society in 1893 under her real name, Harriett Stone Lothrop. Continuing her interest in youth, under the auspices of the DAR she founded the National Society Children of the American Revolution in 1895.

Other writers of children's books included Annie Fellows Johnston who wrote the *Little Colonel* series and Laura Howe Richards, author of *Captain January*. Journalists have been represented through the years. Founder, Mary Smith Lockwood, was president of the Women's National Press Club, while current member, Sarah McClendon, well-known newspaper woman covering the White House beat, belongs to the National Press Club.

Ella Wheeler Wilcox, the noted poet who wrote, "Laugh, and the world laughs with you; Weep, and you weep alone," was a member, and wrote the ode, "Woman," for the Eighteenth Continental Congress, in 1909. The two concluding stanzas describe the utopia to be achieved with the attainment of women's equality:

> *Brave forefathers, and heroes who fought*
> *Under the flag of the Revolution,*
> *War, was the price of the freedom you bought,*
> *But peace, is the watchword of Evolution.*
> *The progress of woman, means progress of peace;*
> *She wars on war, and its hosts alarming;*
> *And her great love-battle will never cease*
> *Till the glory is seen of a world disarming.*
>
> *The woman wonder, with heart of flame,*
> *The Coming Man of the race shall find her,*
> *For narrowing purpose, and petty aim,*
> *And fault, and flaw, she will leave behind her,*
> *He grown tender, and she grown wise,*
> *They shall enter the Eden by both created,*
> *The broadened kingdom of Paradise—*
> *And love and mate as the first pair mated.*

Miss Wilcox would have appreciated the spirit of DAR member Jeanette Ridlon Piccard. Presented with a balloon from the Chicago World's Fair in 1933, the next year she became the first woman in the world to pilot the unique conveyance. Her husband went along for the ride. Later in life she became an Episcopal priest.

Representative Alice Robertson of Oklahoma was the first Daughter to serve in the United States Congress. A third-generation missionary to the American Indians, she spoke at the 30th Continental Congress of the great loyalty of the American Indian during World War I. "Brave people, these Indian people . . . .Out of something over 17,000 who were called through the draft, 212 asked exemption,—a little less than one percent. Do you know how many white men asked exemption? Ten

Margaret Chase Smith

percent . . . . Have you no room for the Indian? Do you owe them nothing?"

The world of politics has also contributed congresswomen Clare Booth Luce, Edith Nourse Rogers, and Ruth Bryan Rohde; senators Rose McConnell Long and Margaret Chase Smith; and author and activist Phyllis Schlafly, while the conservationists are represented by Mary Eno Pinchot.

The Infanta Eulalia, of Spain, joined in 1895. She qualified for membership through her great-great-grandfather, Carlos III of Spain, who "rendered material aid to the cause of independence by sending money and ships."

Theatrical performers have included the diminutive Lavinia Warren (Mrs. Tom) Thumb, Edie Adams, Lillian Gish, Harriet Hilliard Nelson, Virginia Mayo, Dina Merrill and Ginger Rogers. The Miss America Pageant has contributed winners Mary Ann Mobley and Tawney Elaine Godin. Music is also represented. Julia Ward Howe, author of "The Battle Hymn of the Republic" and Tryphose Bates Batchellor, singer and lecturer, were members.

Anna Mary Robertson Moses, the beloved "Grandma Moses" was a DAR. So was Anna Hyatt Huntington, sculptor of the magnificent "Sybil Ludington, the female Paul Revere." She presented a small copy of the heroic statue to the DAR. It may be seen outside the New York Room in Memorial Continental Hall. Member Gertrude Vanderbilt Whitney sculpted the deeply symbolic Founders' Memorial Monument located on the grounds of NSDAR National Headquarters.

The medical field is well represented. Clara Barton, founder of the American Red Cross, was elected Surgeon General at the organizing meeting, October 11, 1890. Dr. Anita Newcomb McGee was the first Librarian General of the National Society, and director of the DAR Hospital Corps during the Spanish-American War. A marker in her

Clara Barton   *Dr. Anita Newcomb McGee*

memory, at the right of the Founders' Memorial Monument at DAR Headquarters, was restored and rededicated on October 11, 1990, by the Centennial President General, Mrs. Eldred Martin Yochim. Dr. Kate Waller Barrett, a physician noted for her work with unwed mothers and the Florence Crittendon Mission was prominent in DAR; so was Jane A. Delano, developer of the Red Cross Nursing Service. Member, Miss Mabel T. Boardman, as Secretary of the American Red Cross, brought greetings to the National Society on the occasion of the Dedication of Constitution Hall on April 19, 1929.

A poignant story attached to member, Dr. Mary Edwards Walker, the Civil War physician and surgeon. Because of her "patriotism, bravery, and untiring services in attending the sick and wounded" during the Civil War, she was recommended by President Abraham Lincoln, endorsed by President Andrew Johnson, and subsequently awarded the Medal of Honor, the only woman ever to receive the award. A controversial figure, she was stripped of the medal during her lifetime by the Adverse Action Medal of Honor Board in 1917; their excuse was

Jane A. Delano   *Dr. Mary Edwards Walker*

that the award was not legal because specific acts of valor were not cited. A Joint Resolution "Requiring that the Congressional Medal of Honor previously awarded to Doctor Mary Edwards Walker in 1865 be restored to her" was passed in the U.S. Senate on March 2, 1977 and referred to the Committee on Armed Services. S.J.Res. 33 cited several specific acts: that she "dedicated seven years to voluntary service in the Union Army as the first woman commissioned assistant surgeon, treating Union soldiers at such battles as Bull Run and Gettysburg"; that she, "despite the risk of capture, crossed enemy lines to attend to destitute Southern civilians near Chattanooga who desperately needed professional attention"; and that she "endured four months' imprisonment by the Confederate Army, during which time she continued to attend to ailing prisoners of war." The official restoration took place on June 10, 1977, 58 years after her death.

Large numbers of members have answered the call to duty as members of the nation's uniformed services. Let the names of two stand for all: Rear Admiral Grace Hopper, United States Navy, honored at her retirement in 1984 as the nation's oldest active military officer (she was 79); and demonstrating the ties of the National Society with the 21st century, Dr. Margaret Rhea Seddon, astronaut. A DAR Insignia carried by Dr. Seddon aboard the space shuttle *Discovery* April 12 – 19, 1985 is now an up-to-the-minute part of the Americana Collection of historic documents.

DAR politics

*I feel that I have been in a constant caucus since the 11th
of October 1890.*

  Mary Desha

Some love it; others hate it. The DAR form of representative government has always inspired dynamic member participation at election time. From day one of the organization the selection of national officers has been a matter of the greatest interest and debate.

In the beginning years of the society, every national office was filled by election every year. Much precious time at Continental Congress was spent on nominations. Members vied to deliver seconding orations.

In 1898 the Congress voted that, beginning in 1899 the term of office would be two years. The excitement only increased.

The Fourteenth Continental Congress provides a good example. Mrs. Charles W. Fairbanks had served two highly productive terms as President General and had the exhilarating experience of presiding at her final Continental Congress, in April 1905, in the partially completed Memorial Continental Hall.

A very lively election campaign, with three candidates for President General, animated the congressional proceedings. Although Mrs. Fairbanks repeatedly forbade campaign speeches from the platform, members were unable to resist the urge, from time to time, to try.

Mrs. Fairbanks never shirked at chastising offenders. Typically, members would "rise to a question of privilege" and then misuse the privilege to make a humorous, but inappropriate, comment. "Madame, you are out of order. Take your seat," Mrs. Fairbanks would order, and the delinquent would sit meekly down, no doubt mugging and glancing about at her supporters as she descended.

On the evening of the second day of congress, it was time to nominate candidates for President General. Mrs. Fairbanks stated that she would hear the nominations first, followed by as many seconding speeches as the delegates would listen to.

First to be nominated was Mrs. George M. Sternberg of Washington, D.C., followed by Mrs. Charles Warren Lippett of Rhode Island and finally Mrs. Donald McLean of New York. Mrs. Sternberg, had served as Vice President General and as Chairman of the Ways and Means Committee for Memorial Continental Hall. Mrs. Lippett had given four years as State Regent of Rhode Island. Mrs. McLean had attended every Continental Congress, and served in many important capacities, including State Regent of New York. She had run for the office previously, and lost to Mrs. Fairbanks.

When the seconding speeches began, they tried to be fair, taking turns honoring their candidates, but maintaining a ladylike regard for the rights of everyone. The *Proceedings* of the congress records that Mrs. Sternberg received 26 seconding speeches; 17 spoke for Mrs. Lippett; and 33 earnest Daughters went on record in favor of Mrs. McLean.

As enthusiasm grew, one member said she thought it would be

more orderly to allow State Regents to speak first, followed by Chapter Regents. However, the President General, to great applause, said she would recognize the first to come, "every Daughter being alike on the floor."

The hour grew so late that nominations for other offices had to be postponed until the following day.

707 ballots were cast. When they were counted, Mrs. McLean fell twelve short of a majority. Mrs. Lippett withdrew as a candidate and balloting began again.

The hall was closed to all but voters. Delegations were called by state to receive their ballots. Writing her choice of candidate on the ballot, the voter deposited it in the box and was then permitted to leave. The Virginia delegation, exhausted by the previous day's voting, requested that the reader begin at the other end of the alphabet. They had missed their dinner the night before. This appeal was granted and Wyoming was called to vote. Balloting was completed in about an hour and a half.

Although most of Mrs. Lippett's support went to Mrs. Sternberg, Mrs. McLean was the victor, 362 to 322. Both candidates received enthusiastic applause when the results were announced. Mrs. Sternberg moved that the election of Mrs. McLean be made unanimous, which Mrs. Lippett immediately seconded. Almost everyone voted "aye," but there were a few rebellious "noes" followed by a number of hisses. The President General requested that "hissing should cease in this house. The Daughters of the American Revolution do not hiss their sisters." To great applause, she then asked all those who had voted "no" to join in the "ayes."

This election of 1905 ended harmoniously. Mrs. McLean was the first President General to have worked her way up through the ranks and to have served as a State Regent. She had a strong sense of being prepared for her job through DAR experience. As she put it, "I am the only President General who knows just what it is to sit under the gallery." Calling her fellow candidates to stand with her and share in the warmth of the moment, Mrs. McLean spoke generously. Her concluding words go far toward explaining the enthusiasm generated during today's triennial election campaigns in the National Society: " . . . no woman need feel ashamed to wish to be President General."

Ribbons and pins

*Mrs. Harrison wore an elegant gown of gray striped satin
trimmed with fur and diamonds, and on her gown was the
jeweled badge of the society. Mrs. Cabell was in a gray
brocade, Miss Cabell in green corded lace and silk.*
                                   Washington Evening Star, February 23, 1892

The distinctive badge of the National Society, adopted on May 26,
1891 and patented for the society by George Brown Goode on September
22, 1891, has never been changed. The graceful spinning wheel with its
thirteen spokes, thirteen stars and distaff filled with platinum flax was
immediately popular. Set with diamonds or other stones, it became a
rich and noticeable jewel. Nevertheless, for style and true elegance, the
gold, enamel and platinum design required no embellishment.

The right to manufacture and sell the official Insignia belonged to
J.E. Caldwell & Company. The price of $8.00 purchased a 14-carat gold
Insignia filled with platinum flax. Beginning in 1901, a contract with
Mrs. Ellenore Dutcher Key permitted her to provide an enameled
"recognition pin" bearing a recognizable rendering of a miniature
Insignia in a vehicle of her own design for $1.00. When the cost of
manufacturing the recognition pin rose to $1.29, the 29th Continental
Congress approved a price increase to $1.50. The 34th Continental
Congress authorized the pierced "official recognition pin" for sale by
J.E. Caldwell at $4.75, but continued to promote Mrs. Key's pin as an
official pin for several years. Ultimately, Caldwell secured the exclusive
right to produce and sell all three pins. However, as the National Society
authorized new pins to be worn on the ribbon, various firms won
contracts to manufacture them.

When other manufacturers attempted, from time to time, to
establish a business of providing Insignia pins to the growing society,
they were vigorously pursued for infringement of patent. That patent,
of course, required renewal on a regular basis, as do all patents. Through
the years, this necessitated the passage of several bills by the United
States Congress. If there were, occasionally, a preoccupied or otherwise
uncooperative Congress, the integrity of the Insignia became endan-
gered. On October 1, 1976, during the administration of Mrs. Wakelee

Rawson Smith, President General, 1975–1977, the Charter of the National Society was amended to give the society the exclusive and sole right to use, or to allow or refuse the use of, its emblems, seals and badges.

In the earliest portraits available, dating from 1892, members wore the unaccompanied Insignia, pinned usually at the neck or on the left breast. Nothing further was authorized until after the members began dressing it up. By 1893 it appeared dependent from the blue and white ribbon of the National Society, secured by a bar. By 1898 the ribbons were lengthening, and bars began to proliferate. The Board of Management decided that the bars should bear the names of "ancestors through whom the wearer has secured admission to the National Society." Further, it authorized a committee to investigate the bars being worn. By 1900 it was decided that the ancestral bars should be patented and issued only by permit, and that State Regents should wear the ribbon around the neck, with the Insignia. Further, any officer supplying the badge to a lady not entitled to wear it, would forfeit her own right to use it. A State Regent's badge, combining the DAR Insignia with the State seal, was authorized in 1913.

The 23rd Continental Congress, meeting in 1914, set out to address the growing desire for more pins. The Insignia Committee recommended authorization of a specially designed President General's badge, and a special bar for Chapter Regents and Ex-Chapter Regents, all of which were happily agreed to. A delegate who had noticed a certain casualness toward the Insignia noted that we should "have as much respect for our own emblems as we are asked to have for our country's flag." Ushers of the Congress were seen wearing the Insignia on their shoulders, "etc." The Constitution stated that the Insignia be worn only on the left breast. She moved that this should be enforced and everyone should "ascertain where that Insignia is and place it where it should be." The motion carried.

The beautiful gold and jeweled badge of her office was presented to Mrs. William Cumming Story, President General, at the 24th Continental Congress. Made by Bailey, Banks & Biddle, the pendant of the handsome badge carried the seal of the National Society surrounded by diamonds, with golden rays of light paved with diamonds and sapphires radiating in every direction. The American Eagle on the

President General's badge of office.

bar memorialized the patriotic and national spirit of the National Society while the laurel wreath, paved with diamonds, with the wording "President General" in full relief on a ribbon, symbolized the authority and honor of that office. The bar would be retained by the President General; the pendant, affixed to a new bar, would be passed on to her successor. The four living Honorary Presidents General, Mrs. John W. Foster, Mrs. Daniel Manning, Mrs. Donald McLean and Mrs. Matthew T. Scott were presented with bars identical to Mrs. Story's, with the word "Honorary" placed above those of "President General."

On April 6, 1917 the United States declared war with Germany. On April 21, 1917, at the close of the 26th Continental Congress, the badge of office was presented to Mrs. George Thacher Guernsey, newly elected President General. It was timely and topical that the October, 1918 issue of *Daughters of the American Revolution Magazine* opened with an illustrated feature story entitled "The War Medals of the Allies." With a jolt, the chairman of the Insignia Committee realized that the ray design of the plaque or star of the British Order of the Bath, only slightly altered, formed the brilliant pendant of the President General's Badge. When she wore the jeweled insignia of her office, the President General of the National Society Daughters of the American Revolution was wearing, in all innocence, a modified "Order of the Bath."

The designer of the badge, unconcerned, stated that there was no copyright on the ray design. The National Society, however, moved to rectify a potentially embarrassing situation immediately. The offending insignia was delivered to J.E. Caldwell who submitted new designs.

After the National Board of Management made its choice at its meeting on June 25, 1919, Caldwell manufactured the new and exclusive President General's bar and badge from the jewels and gold of the former one. Caldwell performed this service at no cost. Mrs. Guernsey presented it at the close of the 29th Continental Congress to her newly-elected successor, Mrs. George Maynard Minor, President General 1920 – 1923. It has been handed down since then to each succeeding President General in turn. Shortly after settling the matter of the President General's badge, the National Board of Management took steps to terminate its various jewelry contracts with all other suppliers.

With the exception of the recognition pin and the miniature Insignia, the DAR Insignia is used only for official DAR events. Members enjoy wearing the DAR Insignia and pins. The design of each pin suggests its meaning. There are laurel wreathes, eagles, flags and drums, not to mention ships, maps and the *Spirit of '76*. There are books, envelopes, and quill pens; crosses, gavels and money bags, and more. The first pins designed to be worn on the official ribbon were genealogical in nature. Later, service bars or pins were added, showing offices and chairmanships held. In general, each service pin worn on today's DAR ribbon represents three years of volunteer service. There are also pins to commemorate great events such as the Bicentennial of the United States of America, or the Centennial of the National Society Daughters of the American Revolution. In addition, pins may be worn that show a special monetary contribution to the National Society, or that represent membership in such an organization as a State Officers Club or the Outstanding Junior Club.

Committees

The first committee authorized by the National Society was that for Insignia and Seal, on October 11, 1890. It achieved passage of a motto and seal on November 11, 1890, but the finished form of the Insignia eluded it until the spring of 1891. Additional committees appointed on December 11, 1890 were on Finance, Auditing, Printing, Constitution and Revolutionary Relics. With these six committees, the National Society was able to begin functioning. The President General and Board of Management could add others as they were needed.

From the beginning, the society recognized the efficacy of working through committees. That system has grown, been refined, and remained in practice for a hundred years. It provides a finely-honed two-way network of unsurpassed efficiency for information distribution and reporting. The President General appoints the national chairmen, and eight divisional vice chairmen for each committee. The State Regent appoints corresponding state chairmen and the Chapter Regent, chapter chairmen. In the summer, a packet of material is mailed to each State and Chapter Regent from DAR Headquarters in Washington, D.C. The packet consists of informative messages and guidelines for the year from each national chairman, and is meant to be distributed to the corresponding state and chapter chairmen. Divisional vice chairmen receive copies of their national chairman's letter. Guided by the suggestions in the letters, the state and chapter chairmen develop their programs.

A national chairman may, without undertaking a major mailing, communicate with the more than 3,000 women nationwide who work with her particular committee by writing her eight vice chairmen. They then contact the state chairmen in their division, who pass the information along to the chapter chairmen. The larger and more populous states may field a district chairman between the chapter and the state.

When the work for the year is reported, it is tallied in reverse, from chapter, to state, to division, to national. This system has worked effectively from the early days of the society and has facilitated the compiling of the enviable record of public service of the DAR.

Within the scope of historic, educational and patriotic endeavor, the National Society promotes a wide variety of projects through its committees.

At this writing, the 27 national committees of the National Society are: American Heritage, American History Month, American Indians, Americanism and DAR Manual for Citizenship, Children of the American Revolution, Conservation, Constitution Week, DAR Good Citizens, DAR Magazine, DAR Magazine Advertising, DAR Museum, DAR Scholarship, DAR School, DAR Service for Veteran-Patients, The Flag of the United States of America, Genealogical Records, Honor Roll, Junior American Citizens, Junior Membership, Lineage Research, Membership, Motion Picture, Radio & Television, National Defense, Program, Public Relations, and Seimes Microfilm Center.

In addition there are special national committees, appointed to meet current special needs. At this writing, the 20 special national committees are: Bicentennial of the Constitution of the United States of America, Centennial Jubilee NSDAR, Columbus Quincentennial, DAR Patriot Index, DAR Speakers Staff, Ellis Island Restoration, Ethics, Friends of the Library, Insignia, Long-Range Planning Commission, Literacy Challenge, Museum Docents, NSDAR Museum Correspondent Docents, President General's Project, Program Reviewing, Units Overseas, Volunteer Genealogists, Ways and Means, National Board Dinners, and State Regents Dinners.

Congressional committees are responsible for specific aspects of the annual Continental Congress of the National Society Daughters of the American Revolution, held in Washington, D.C. during the week in which the 19th of April falls.

There are standing committees for Auditing, Building and Grounds, Bylaws, Finance, Personnel, Printing and Resolutions, while today's administrative committees are the Board of Consultants, DAR Handbook, Advisory Board, Protocol and Art Critics.

JUNIOR MEMBERSHIP

Junior Members are DAR members ages 18 through 35. The Junior Membership Committee was instituted in 1937 during Mrs. William A. Becker's term as President General. The national Junior Membership fund-raising project, the Helen Pouch Memorial Fund, provides scholarships, medical and general financial assistance to Kate Duncan Smith and Tamassee DAR Schools. This drawing originally appeared in the January 1940 issue of National Historical Magazine.

Continental Congress

*It is safe to assert that no such community of feeling had
ever been aroused among the women of the country. The
sense of a common heritage in the flag, of a common
concern in the welfare of the land, for which the fathers
fought side by side, made this meeting more memorable
than was realized at the time.*

> The First Continental Congress, as reported in
> the First Report of the Daughters of the
> American Revolution to the Smithsonian
> Institution, 1899

Continental Congress, the great annual meeting of the
Daughters of the American Revolution at Washington, D.C., was envisioned at the organizing meeting of the society
on October 11, 1890. The First Continental Congress, held February
22 – 24, 1892, was enormously successful, bringing together as it did the
multiple aspects of the society. The members had already accomplished
a formidable body of work; they were justifiably proud of their reports.
Parliamentary procedure was new to most of them; valiantly, and
frequently aggressively, they struggled to master the niceties of points
of personal privilege, points of order, and calling for the question.
Business sessions were stimulating; social gatherings, satisfying; pages,
young members dressed in white, assisted. The newspapers did what
newspapers ought to do: they paid attention.

Mrs. Benjamin C. Kennard of Connecticut told her chapter about
the Fourth Continental Congress, which met in February 1895. She
found anecdotal reports far more interesting than those that dwelt on

statistics. Reporting that Mrs. Mary S. Lockwood was elected presiding officer for the first day, Mrs. Kennard said that:

> Notwithstanding Mrs. Lockwood had done excellent work in the use of the gavel, she had evidently had enough of it and positively declined reelection on Wednesday. Mrs. Marguerite Dickens was unanimously chosen for the day and succeeded in keeping good order—considering the exceedingly patriotic character of the Congress. . . . Much merriment was caused when the violent use of the gavel again and again beheaded it and the hammer fell to the floor with a thud. But Mrs. Dickens, nothing daunted, as often picked it up and replacing it upon its handle went on with vigorous pounding until quiet was restored.

Mrs. Kennard was again present in 1898, and attended a gala official reception at the Arlington Hotel. Writing home, she said that it eclipsed all previous years in brilliancy and attendance. The 1,500 guests were impressed by the floral display of palms and azaleas flanking "the badge of the order, a design in red, white and blue immortelles jeweled with fairy electric lights in the same colors." The Marine Band played. In the first parlor, Mrs. Adlai E. Stevenson, President General, Mrs. Rose A. Brackett, Vice President General, and Mrs. William D. Cabell, Honorary Vice President General, received. The second parlor was less formal. There one could converse with Vice Presidents General and State Regents. Finally, in the last parlor, were the candidates for election as President General, "Mrs. Manning in light blue satin, flashing diamonds, and Mrs. McLean in

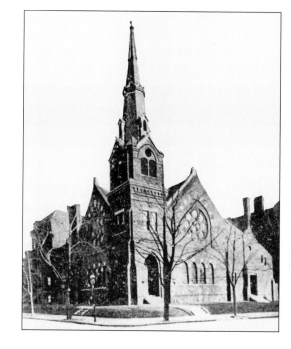

The First through the Sixth Continental Congress met at the Church of Our Father.

black velvet—the sole ornament being the beautiful jeweled crescent, the gift of her chapter." Mrs. Kennard predicted, correctly, that although Mrs. McLean was obviously a woman of great ability, Mrs. Manning would undoubtedly be elected. Mrs. McLean's ambition led her through three election campaigns, in 1898, 1901 and finally 1905, before she finally met with success.

From the day the DAR was founded, meetings have been held in conjunction with significant dates; in that way, the gathering itself becomes a commemoration. The organizing meeting was selected to celebrate Columbus' sighting of the New World. Twelve Continental Congresses, from 1892 through 1903, were held during the week of George Washington's Birthday in February. But February had a reputation. In 1898, Mrs. Kinney, State Regent, hoped that her state, "Connecticut, being the banner state, would go in large numbers, and take Washington by storm, and if Washington was equal to her past record, it would take us by storm." In 1901, Mrs. Kennard told her chapter that changing the date of the congress had been discussed for years, "but this year, as if to be contrary, all was sunshine and brightness." For the first and only time, Washington weather was pleasant for a February congress. Although George Washington was certainly first in the hearts of the Daughters, the observation of an event falling at a milder time of year would contribute to the comfort of the delegates attending the congress. The Battle of Lexington, April 19, occupied the perfect spot on the calendar. Consequently, the 13th Continental Congress

The Seventh through the Thirteenth Continental Congress met at Chase's Opera House.

Matthew Brady photographed the dignitaries in attendance at the First Continental Congress. A key to the photograph was published in American Monthly Magazine in March 1893. Left to right: Row 1 (seated) Mrs. F.O. St. Clair, Mrs. R.W. Smith, Mrs. Marshall MacDonald, Mrs. M.G. Devereux, Mrs. M.V.E. Cabell, Mrs. Caroline Scott Harrison, Miss Eugenia Washington, Mrs. A. Leo Knott, Mrs. T.H. Alexander, Mrs. Margaret

Hetzel. Row 2: Mrs. Sylvia DeWolf Ostrander, Miss Lillian Evans, Miss M.D. Everhart, Miss F.I. Forsey, Mrs. H. Jackson, Mrs. G.H. Shields, Mrs. R.O. Doremus, Mrs. Mary S. Lockwood, Mrs. J.G. Cilley, Mrs. Robinson, Mrs. Donald McLean, Miss Mary Desha. Row 3: Mrs. F.S. Osborn, Mrs. E. Dickson, Mrs. Hugh Hagen, Mrs. Joshua Wilbour, Mrs. F.R. Moran, Mrs. Kendall, Miss M.G. Forsyth.

was held during the week of that battle, April 18–23, 1904, at Chase's Opera House, 15th and Pennsylvania Avenue, N.W. Furthermore, additional honors were scheduled to accrue to the date of April 19. In her opening address, the President General, Mrs. Fairbanks said, "The 19th of April, 1904, will be henceforth a most significant one in your society; for it will be famed for the laying of the cornerstone of your greatest work, your building, erected to commemorate the virtues of a devoted people,—the men and women who made America free." Amazingly, on April 17, 1905, just one year later, the rap of the gavel called to order the 14th Continental Congress meeting for the first time in the new headquarters building of the National Society Daughters of the American Revolution, Memorial Continental Hall.

> Some come to attend all the deliberations and help carry through the projects which have made our Society what it is. Others come purely with the intent and no other thought, to see who are elected to the offices, and they do not attend the meetings, but spend all their time in the lobby making such a noise that those who want to cannot hear. We have another class, who come merely to see what is going on and to take back to their homes knowledge of the work. They are our faithful alternates and members.
>
> *Mrs. George Thacher Guernsey, President General 1917–1920, 29th Continental Congress, 1920*

There comes a time when the order of business has been completed and the Congress remains in session only to await election returns. Then, sometimes, when the schedule has been satisfied, and only the stalwart enthusiasts remain in the Hall, may come something memorable, something unique.

In 1974, while awaiting the report of the Tellers, during the Thursday afternoon session of the 83rd Continental Congress, President General Mrs. Donald Spicer sought to locate the one who had attended the most consecutive Congresses. Mrs. John Morrison Kerr of the District of Columbia, but attending from Hawaii, had been present for 58 years. She said that she attended her first Congress as a Page in 1917, and had attended ever since. Mrs. Helen Adams, of New York, said:

> I insist upon your knowing that I attended the Congress of 1899

with my mother. I was a very small child but I heard Mrs. Donald McLean announce herself, "Mrs. Donald McLean of New York." They didn't have loudspeakers in those days but she didn't need one. She wore a lovely coat and had feathers around her neck.

Mrs. Henry Grady Jacobs, then Chairman of the Board of Kate Duncan Smith DAR School, was asked to tell a story. She chose to tell of her first Congress, in 1922, when she was invited to sit by the State Regent of Alabama.

It had been the custom since the organization of the Society for Kate Duncan Smith (Mrs. J. Morgan) to sing two solos. Each time it was the same two solos and she had refused that time to sing because she said she was getting too old and her voice was cracking. Now, Mrs. Smith really had a beautiful voice so they just kept clapping and begging her to sing and she said, "Well, if you insist, I will sing one." So, her voice did crack and I said to the State Regent, "Oh, I'm so sorry they asked her to sing because she knew better than to get up with that beautiful voice." She took out her lorgnette and looked down at me and she said, "What are you and who are you, little upstart, to criticize Kate Duncan Smith?" So, I haven't criticized anybody since.

Mrs. Spicer asked the Honorary Presidents General for some reminiscences. Mrs. Robert V.H. Duncan, President General 1962–1965, recalled serving during the administration of Miss Gertrude Carraway, President General 1953–1956:

. . . she would look at you and say, "Isn't that splendid!" and always she was talking about DAR and then she would look around and say, "I tell you, it's splendid. Now, isn't that splendid?" and I looked at her one day and I said, "After you have said it four times, who can say it is not splendid?"

The work of the Daughters has been splendid, indeed. For 100 years, this organization, the NSDAR, has successfully strived to uphold its noble objectives. From a strong beginning in 1890, DAR has served and grown—served faithfully and grown stronger. Mrs. George W.S. Musgrave, Honorary Vice President General, speaking at the 83rd Continental Congress, gave the explanation:

The DAR is strong because of fidelity to principle. Whatever the question, the decision is based upon the principle involved and fidelity to it.

Part II

National Headquarters

At first all papers and records of the society were stored in the homes of the registrars and other officers. But the rapid growth of the society made this arrangement impractical. A step toward establishing a permanent national headquarters was taken in July, 1891, when an office was rented at 1505 Pennsylvania Avenue and a clerk, Miss Mary Ball, was installed. By October 5, 1893 that location was outgrown and the society secured rooms in the Kellogg Building, 1416 F Street. In November Miss Nellie Stone was employed to do typewriting and stenography; a typewriting machine was purchased in January. There was some dissatisfaction with the new location but a third move, on August 18, 1894, to the "fireproof" Washington Loan and Trust Building, 902 F Street provided peace of mind, and adequate space for the business offices of the National Society.

The rented office was a temporary solution
to a permanent need.

The North Portico, Memorial Continental Hall

The House Beautiful—Memorial Continental Hall

It was the prophetic Mary S. Lockwood who, on October 18, 1890, gave first voice to the idea which evolved into a dream and finally a magnificent reality:

> RESOLVED that after this association has assisted in the completion of the monument to Mary Washington, the next effort shall be to provide a place for the collection of Historical relics which will accumulate at the World's Fair, and for all other relics which may come to the Society, and for historical portraits, pictures, etc. This may first be in rooms, and later in the erection of a fire-proof building.

At the Conference of State and Chapter Regents held at the residence of Mrs. William D. Cabell on October 6 and 7, 1891, Mrs. Cabell said in part:

> What the Society needs most and first is a home. The women of America want a house where their historic records can be lodged—to grow, it is hoped into the finest collection of Colonial and Revolutionary literature in the world—a spacious hall where debates and addresses can take place—fireproof apartments where the relics and treasures of the Society can be preserved—a commodious place of business where officers and members can meet for the transaction of their affairs.

Mrs. Cabell was in an excellent position to assess the need of the Daughters for a home. For the first year of the society's existence, *her* home was the society's home. Beginning on October 18, 1890, the Second Meeting for Organization, monthly meetings of the entire National Society until May 26, 1891, and twice-monthly meetings of the

Board of Management thereafter were held at her residence. There she hosted the dazzling reception of February 22, 1891 which introduced the National Society to Washington society and in October, 1891, the important Conference of national officers, State and Chapter Regents.

In preparation for the First Continental Congress, the meeting of the Board of Management on December 14, 1891, approved Mrs. Ellen H. Walworth's resolution, proposed October 24, 1891 that:

> . . . a committee be appointed to consider ways and means of erecting a fire-proof building and founding a home for the society, which shall also be the Memorial Hall of the Daughters of the American Revolution, and that the said committee be instructed to bring an early report to the Board.

And further, at the urging of Mrs. Marshall MacDonald, Treasurer General, it was decided that all fees received from life memberships and chapter charters would be set aside as a permanent building fund.

Now the dream was giving way to reality. Mrs. Harrison appointed a committee, as authorized by the Board, and funds began to accumulate. By the First Continental Congress, the permanent fund had reached $650.

Mrs. Mary V.E. Cabell, Vice President Presiding, devoted her report at that first Continental Congress to a persuasive appeal. Telling the assembly that the public was demanding to know what the Daughters were going to accomplish, she said:

> We feel that the question answers itself—is fully answered in our beautiful name. "What must be the objects of the Daughters of the American Revolution?" We reply: None of the old heroes are alive for us to nurse, to support in hospitals, to provide with pensions. The matrons who melted down their treasures of silver and pewter, and tore their linen into bandages, and stinted themselves and their families in order to feed the patriot band have gone to their long rest with their husbands, fathers and sons. The whole majestic generation has passed away. What task then has come down to the *daughters* of the men and women of the Revolution?
>
> . . . The demand of our age is for something more tangible than any sentiment however ennobling . . . and the Society, which for this moment I have the honor to represent, is prepared to meet the call . . . . This . . . outward and visible sign of what we believe to be an inward and spiritual grace, is the building of a house—a House Beautiful—to

Mrs. William D. Cabell's parlor, the society's first home.

be the property in fee-simple of these American women calling themselves by inherited right Daughters of the American Revolution. This house should be builded upon a hill, that all may see and know it. It should be located in or near the beautiful Capital City named for Washington, the immortal. It should be the finest building ever owned by women. . . . Purely American should this structure be; every fluted column, every gorgeous capital should owe its loveliness to the hand of an American artist. A great hall for lectures, addresses and general conventions of the Society . . . Offices and committee-rooms . . . for the business of the Society, ... Safes . . . for the preservation of documents and relics. There should be a library . . . . an art gallery . . . .

Mrs. Cabell went on to explain how the building could be expected to employ a considerable number of women and told of the President General, Mrs. Harrison's enthusiastic support. She concluded by saying that she felt "impelled to advance and advocate" such an enterprise with the magnificent possibilities it offered to the patriotic, home-loving and country-loving women of America.

The fund grew slowly at first—$1,407.37 at the Second Continental Congress; $2,128.40 at the Third Continental Congress; $3,623.34 at the Fourth Continental Congress. By the Fifth Continental Congress, in 1896, $5,772.82 had accumulated and enthusiasm for the project began to spread. The fund reached $11,231.98 in 1897 and the Daughters decided that they were ready to begin.

A committee was appointed to ask the United States Congress to give the National Society a site of ground on which to erect Memorial Continental Hall. A bill passed both houses of the second session of the Fifty-fourth Congress in 1897, granting the permanent use of a plot of public land 200 feet square to the National Society Daughters of the American Revolution. But by error the site selected turned out to be a portion of the Washington Monument grounds and was, by law, not available.

This disappointment had no deleterious effect on the movement to secure a home for the Daughters. If anything, it stimulated that extra surge of adrenalin that rushed the ladies toward dedicated determination.

A circular distributed May 3, 1899 under the auspices of Mrs. Daniel Manning, President General 1898 – 1901, called for $200,000 to be raised, and proclaimed:

> Daughters of the American Revolution! You are equal to this responsibility; you have shown this in your past. This Memorial is assured, and will stand—strong, enduring, magnificent—pointing to the pure white light of heaven, since you have set forth with a purpose born of God, on the consecrated road to its achievement.

Through receptions, concerts, galas, subscriptions and every imaginable fund raising event, the money rolled in. A large amount of cash was raised in small increments. For instance, in 1900, the District of Columbia chapters sponsored a luncheon for twenty-five cents at Willard's Hall, from February 20th to 24th inclusive, from 12 to 2:30 p.m. The District Daughters contributed $333 to Memorial Continental Hall that year.

The State Regent of South Dakota, Mrs. Andrew J. Kellar, asked the veterans residing at the Soldiers' Home of Hot Springs, South Dakota to contribute ten cents each because "they were the men who had fought to *save* the Republic, and we were keeping the memory of those who had *made* the Republic." The veterans generously gave $10.00.

At a bazaar held in Copley Hall, Boston, Boston Tea Party Chapter served the beverage which "cheers but does not inebriate" and displayed the tea chest rescued after the Boston Tea Party. Other Massachusetts chapters provided coat check booths, "gypsie" fortune-tellers, refreshments and needlework for sale, and Revolutionary-era artifacts for display.

Large and small, the donations flowed in. Mrs. Charles W. Fairbanks, President General 1901 – 1905, brought fresh enthusiasm to the cause. On June 4, 1902, the Committee on Memorial Continental Hall, meeting in her home, decided that with $82,190.57 in the bank, the time had come to act.

The Committee on Investigation of a Site had been working all spring, pursuing dozens of leads. They wanted a location near enough to hotels, apartments and boarding houses to be convenient for delegates attending Continental Congress. The streets must be wide enough to permit the parking of carriages. Many attractive lots were suggested by the local realtors. The committee investigated an offering between Connecticut Avenue and 17th on M Street, but it was rejected because the street was too narrow. Octagon House was "out of the question because it is an historical mansion and we cannot tear down such a house, according to our Constitution." Serious consideration was given to "The Corcoran Gardens" on Connecticut Avenue between H and I Streets, at $6.00 per square foot. A sudden death had tied up the title to one lot of Square 172, the tract occupied today by the national headquarters of the American Red Cross.

Several factors influenced the decision to locate on 17th Street between C and D. Price was certainly important. Costs decreased dramatically as the distance from Pennsylvania Avenue increased. Much of the land in question had been purchased speculatively when Memorial Bridge was first discussed. Square 173 was held in small lots by an assortment of owners. It was expected that, sooner or later, the government would buy it; but there had been no movement in the immediate area for a long time. Values had remained low and static.

James McMillan, Chairman of the Senate Subcommittee on the Improvement of the Park System, wrote the President General, Mrs. Fairbanks, assuring her that the area being considered would be an excellent location. " . . . it is proposed to make Seventeenth Street one of the great park approaches, and a thoroughfare of importance."

The geological composition of the tract was questioned. A letter from the Assistant to the Engineer Commissioner, Captain Harding, on

May 31, 1902 states that the greater portion of the surface of Square 173 is "made ground." But his office "has *no* record [that it] was once the site of an old swamp. . . . [but] a basement below street grade would be liable to flooding."

Mr. Edward L. Morse wrote Dr. Anita Newcomb McGee, a member of the Site Subcommittee of the Memorial Continental Hall Committee, that *his* committee had passed a resolution that "the erection of a public hall in the locality of the Corcoran Art Gallery would not meet the public needs of Washington . . . " Perhaps the implied criticism sealed the matter! Certainly the Site Subcommittee did not allow itself to be unduly influenced by the outsiders' opinion.

They did very well for themselves. Expending $50,285.41, they purchased a lot of approximately 35,069.85 square feet at an average $1.42 per square foot. A pamphlet prepared by the committee described it as being "a most beautiful and suitable site for the purpose, on Seventeenth Street, extending from D to C streets, with a frontage of the entire block 210 feet in length, facing the public reservation, known as the White House Lot, and closely adjacent to the new Corcoran Art Gallery."

Honest Davy Burnes

The parcel of land selected for building by the National Society Daughters of the American Revolution was originally owned, like much of downtown Washington, by a Scot reputed to be crusty, difficult and illiterate, "the obstinate Mr. Burnes." Mary Desha, however, called him "honest Davy Burnes."

David Burnes, a farmer, lived in a ramshackle cottage situated exactly where the building of the Organization of American States stands today, on 17th Street one block south of DAR National Headquarters. He won his reputation for stubbornness from George Washington, who, instructing agents to negotiate the purchase of land for the Federal City, told them "to so conduct themselves as to excite no suspicion that they are on behalf of the public." Burnes "the obstinate" refused to sell at $32, or $48 or even $67 an acre. Not until Washington met the landowners face to face was he able to work out an agreement. Land required for public buildings and improvements would yield $125 an acre. The rest would be laid out in building lots; the original owners and the government to share in the proceeds.

The Evening Star of Saturday, June 7, 1902 indicated approval of the choice of site and said that "it is safe to say that the ladies have got more land for their money by going where they did than they could possibly in any other section of the city that is equally as central in location."

Although the National Society tried to conceal its identity, and made its purchases through an agent, as news of the sale spread, prices began to rise. Further land acquisition was desired, but it was decided to allow negotiations to cool off for a while. In a committee report dated April 9, 1903, Dr. Anita Newcomb McGee explained, "Probably the longer we wait before beginning further negotiations, the lower we can get the land." Enough had been acquired to make a beginning.

We go forth in the rain

The ground breaking took place on a dark, rainy Saturday, October 11, 1902. The weather was unable to dampen the spirits of the Daughters, who attended in great numbers. A tent over the platform was crowded with National Officers, State Regents and distinguished guests. Mrs. Mary S. Lockwood and Miss Susan Riviere Hetzel were the only representatives of the 18 original members present. The United States Engineer Band played "Hail Columbia" and General Edwin Warfield, President General, National Society Sons of the American Revolution gave an address.

The second President General of the National Society, Mrs. Adlai E. Stevenson, described the ceremony in her book, *Brief History, National Society Daughters of the American Revolution*, which was published in 1913:

> The President General, Mrs. Fairbanks, broke the ground with a spade made of Montana copper, the gift of the Montana Daughters; the handle was made of wood cut from the pathway of Lewis & Clark as they wended their weary way through the western wilderness, part of which is now Montana . . . .Mrs. Fairbanks delivered an inspiring address and then introduced Mrs. Lockwood, who broke the earth upon which the beautiful home of the Daughters now stands.

Mrs. Fairbanks said, in part:

> We go forth in the rain to our duty but our ancestors did more during the Revolution. . . . We are here because we represent those virtues for which our forefathers struggled, achieved and oftimes lost life and fortune in building up. We are not here in any pride of family or blood. We are here to aid in preserving the eternal principles of liberty, and it behooves us not to think of the society alone, it behooves us to think greatly of the splendid work achieved by our revered ancestors, the men and women of the Revolution, and to do our humble best to emulate that work and aid in preserving intact the splendid heritage of free homes, a free country where prevail the principles of justice and liberty.

A block of white marble inscribed: "From the home of the First President General of the Daughters of the American Revolution," sent later from the White House was kept to be used in the interior of Memorial Continental Hall. That block of marble has interested a number of researchers over the years. The conclusion must be reached that it is indeed in the interior of the building—buried out of sight, its location forgotten.

By February, 1903, after purchase of the site, the fund had rebounded to $59,222. A "Competition for Memorial Continental Hall" resulted in the selection of Edward Pearce Casey, of New York City, as architect. The architect's plans and preliminary sketches for a "monument to the heroic men and women of the Revolution, as well as an administration building for the Society, classic in design," were accepted on January 8, 1904. Contracts for excavation and building foundation were approved and signed the following March 18.

The Sons of the American Revolution, constantly enthusiastic and supportive, presented a flag on February 23, 1903, which was planted on the place where the ground was broken. Dr. Bayne, President of the District of Columbia S.A.R., described it as:

> . . . a storm flag that has been presented by the District of Columbia society—a flag that is intended to wave continuously night and day, through fair weather and stormy weather, until that beautiful building that you have in contemplation is completed.

Public Law No. 118, An Act To exempt from taxation certain property of the Daughters of the American Revolution in Washington,

District of Columbia, was approved by the Senate and the House of Representatives on February 27, 1903:

> That the property situated in square numbered one hundred and seventy-three, in Washington City, District of Columbia, occupied by the Daughters of the American Revolution, be, and the same is hereby, exempt from all taxation so long as the same is so occupied and used, subject to the provisions of section eight of the Act approved March third, eighteen hundred and seventy-seven, providing for exemptions of church and school property, and Acts amendatory thereof.

The Assessor moved swiftly to levy taxes on the vacant parcel. But in the opinion of the Corporation Counsel, it was exempt. District Commissioner MacFarland pointed out that the property, "although unimproved is occupied by a flag pole from which floats the American Stars and Stripes" constituting occupation in the law's intent.

The Assessor continued to grumble that although he was opposed to hauling down the American flag, he did not "believe a flag pole could completely occupy a ten-acre lot." Nevertheless, the *Evening Star* of February 5, 1904 reported that the District Commissioners had that day approved the Corporation Counsel's opinion. Thus, the gift by the Sons of the American Revolution of a United States flag secured the legal rights of the National Society.

Laying the cornerstone

A "memorable day," April 19, 1904, was the 129th anniversary of the Battle of Lexington and the 2nd day of the 13th Continental Congress. Drawing a parallel between the minute man with his musket and the President General with her trowel, the Daughters placed their cornerstone. By all reports it was an impressive service. The Marine Band played. The four former Presidents General, Mrs. Harrison, Mrs. Stevenson, Mrs. Foster and Mrs. Manning were honored. The three living Founders, Mrs. Walworth, Miss Desha and Mrs. Lockwood were present. The Rev. Edward Everett Hale, chaplain of the United States Senate, pronounced the invocation and the Children of the American Revolution saluted the flag.

Mrs. Adlai E. Stevenson, President General 1893 – 1895 and 1896 – 1898, described the event:

The ceremonies attending the laying of the cornerstone were in charge of the Masonic order and were accompanied by Masonic rites. The lighted candles on the four corners of the stone and the intoning of the service were most impressive. The gavel was the one used by George Washington in laying the cornerstone of the national capitol, September 18, 1793, which was afterwards presented to Potomac Lodge, No. 5, and by them loaned for this occasion.

According to the *Proceedings of the 13th Continental Congress*, Mr. Fred D. Owen, Chairman of the Committee on Arrangements, handed articles to be placed in the cornerstone to Grand Treasurer James A. Sample, who placed them in a large copper box to be enclosed in the stone. The list of articles begins with "The Holy Bible, property of a Revolutionary soldier; copy of the Declaration of Independence, imprint of the seal of the United States, the American flag, the insignia of the Daughters of the American Revolution" and then goes on to enumerate an additional 50 items, starting with "portraits of the Founders," and ending with "daily papers, current issue." Mr. Owen then handed the President General, Mrs. Charles W. Fairbanks, a shiny new trowel with red, white and blue ribbons attached. Grand Master James A. Mason said that the "trowel will be used in spreading the cement which shall unite this building into one common mass." The Grand Master, Mrs. Fairbanks, Mrs. Walworth, Miss Desha and Mrs. Lockwood each spread a trowelful of cement on the foundation. A Masonic ceremony followed, after which, "The Grand Master struck the stone three times with the gavel used by Bro. George Washington when he laid the cornerstone of the Capitol on September 18, 1793."

In his address, Mr. Wetmore said that Washington and all of his generals, without exception, were "Masons, including the generous and chivalrous Lafayette, the masterful Baron von Steuben and the intrepid sea captain, John Paul Jones . . . .we feel that patriotism and Masonry, symbolized by the sword and the trowel, were so closely associated with the lives of the persons whose history is to be preserved by the Society of the Daughters of the American Revolution, that we may take an interest in the work you are doing, and in what this edifice shall stand for."

Mrs. Walworth extended greetings. Reminding the audience of the origins of the National Society, she said that "The spirit, the sentiment

Memorial Continental Hall, January 1, 1905.
The 14th Continental Congress met there in April the same year.

which brought this society into existence was in the air; it was a great natural force that swept over the hearts of the people of the country after the Centennial of 1876." She was obviously thinking of her own deceased daughter, Reubena, when she said:

> This day makes an era for American women. Will it be denied that this event marks and typifies a subtle, a mysterious union between Daughters of the American Revolution and the government of this country? Men administer the government; women love it, they guard it, they would willingly die for it; some have so died.

Wind storm rearranges the schedule

Before the ceremonies were completed, the weather changed. The President General said, " . . . because of the inclement weather and the biting winds and blinding blasts of sand," that following the benediction, further ceremonies were postponed to the 8 p.m. session of the congress, that evening.

The first speaker on the program was Mrs. Mary S. Lockwood, Founder and dedicated suffragist, who made her point with the first sentence she uttered. With significant glance and exaggerated inflection, the spirited Mrs. Lockwood began, "Madam President and *fellow-citizens* of this Republic—(I say citizens advisedly):" The audience roared.

Mrs. Lockwood traced the contributions of American women to the Revolutionary struggle and to the Spanish-American war. She compared them to the United States flag and said:

> It is this multitude of stars in our citizenship that has remained a hundred years unnamed and unhonored, that the Daughters of the American Revolution are resurrecting and recording, and hereafter they will be on the honor roll of this country.

Then followed a multitude of eloquent addresses and the reading of congratulatory telegrams from prominent members who were unable to be present, including past Presidents General M. Margaretta Manning and Letitia Green Stevenson. One signed "An old friend and co-worker, Mary Virginia Ellet Cabell" drew particular applause.

The dream comes true

The great edifice rose rapidly; first the steel super-structure, and then block upon block of white Vermont marble. This classic building would assuredly be the finest in the world! Two days short of one year later, on April 17, 1905, during the 14th Continental Congress, with great rejoicing Memorial Continental Hall was dedicated. Never mind that a temporary roof had to be erected over the auditorium. Never mind that there were no porches, no pillars. The furnace was temporary; so were the seats in the auditorium. Four long years would elapse before the hall was truly complete and the offices of the society could occupy it. But there was a building, a house, a home, and it was truly beautiful.

Memorial Continental Hall before the addition of the porticoes, circa 1906.

The Committee on Dedicatory Exercises for Memorial Continental Hall decided that the President General should be the only woman participating in the ceremonies. The balance of the program would be given over to the men. Frederick Denison Owen, Chairman of the Committee on Arrangements for the Laying of the Cornerstone, was Master of Ceremonies. The planning committee proposed an ecumenical service including Bishop Satterlee, Episcopalian; Bishop Cranston, Methodist; Rabbi Mendes, Jewish; and Cardinal James Gibbons, Roman Catholic. 150 elaborate blue and white silk badges complete with a woven representation of the hall were ordered for the occasion at a cost of $120. Five hundred dollars was budgeted for decorations.

There were flags, wreaths, palms, and flowers. Every available space was draped, wreathed, or covered by some patriotic emblem. The society's great insignia hung on the west wall at center stage. Two medallions lettered in blue, one proclaiming "Home and Country" the other "Washington—Organized October 11, 1890" flanked the insignia. Below the three emblems, the names of the five women who had served the National Society as President General, Mrs. Benjamin Harrison,

Mrs. Adlai E. Stevenson, Mrs. John W. Foster, Mrs. Daniel Manning and Mrs. Charles W. Fairbanks, were inscribed on bars surrounded by laurel wreaths.

The three remaining walls celebrated events leading to the dedication day's crowning triumph. A large medallion on the south wall heralded "Desha—Flag raised Feb. 23, 1903." That on the east wall remembered "Lockwood—first turning of sod October 11, 1902," and the northern wall recognized "Walworth—cornerstone laid April 19, 1904." On this happy day the Daughters were careful to honor all three of the living Founders.

Other medallions inscribed with the names of the thirteen original states hung from the balconies, and flags of all the states and territories were posted on the floor.

The United States Marine Band played. When the President General, Mrs. Charles Warren Fairbanks, entered, they struck up "Hail to The Chief!"

In her welcoming remarks, Mrs. Fairbanks said that "the fact that a society of women erects the structure makes it unique. Its memorial feature renders it sacred and great." Quoting Henry Van Dyke, she hoped the "Doorstead" had a:

> "Lintel low enough
> To keep out pomp and pride,
> A threshold high enough to turn deceit aside,
> A door band strong enough from robbers to defend,
> Our door will open at a touch to welcome every friend."

Mrs. Fairbanks' two terms of office, 1901–1903 and 1903–1905, spanned the creation of Memorial Hall. Previously there had been an ardent desire backed by a growing fund. Under her leadership a site was purchased, the architectural competition was successfully held, and the building, although incomplete, was able to house the 14th Continental Congress. The dedication of Memorial Hall marked the crowning point and close of the Fairbanks administration. In her dedicatory address Mrs. Fairbanks assessed her term of office:

> I will unhesitatingly say that the selection and purchase of our admirable site, the breaking of the ground, the laying of the corner stone, the building and dedication of Memorial Continental Hall in the

presence of distinguished guests and during the session of the Congress of the N.S.D.A.R. must stand pre-eminent.

Much remained to be done. Mrs. Donald S. McLean, newly elected President General, went to work with a will. The Ways and Means Committee had conceived the brilliant idea of accepting contributions for specific objects. The Library, for instance, would cost $6,000. Two small domes could be had for $1,000 each; the ten portrait busts in the vestibule were $500 apiece; and the two main staircases each cost $2,000.

Memorial Portico

I hereby declare this portico dedicated to the devoted and reverent memory of the past, and to the patriotic purposes of God and our country in the future.
    Mrs. Donald McLean, President General
    1905 – 1909, April 17, 1907

Thirteen monolithic columns, fluted and ornamented, memorializing the thirteen original states and surrounding the semicircular Memorial Portico, dominate the southern exposure of Memorial Continental Hall.

Miss Mary Desha, Founder and Honorary Vice President General was appointed on February 8, 1905, "Chairman of the Committee to confer with the architect of Memorial Continental Hall as to the advisability of using marble from different States" in the columns.

Miss Desha's notes reveal the committee's discussion about what stone to use. Should the columns be marble or granite? "It is desirable the stone should be white marble. It will be more expensive than granite. Still there is marble & marble & granite & granite."

Miss Desha put the question to the architect, stating two rationales for asking the states to furnish their own marble: The sentiment of paralleling the make up of the memorial columns with that of the Continental Army, constituted of men from all sections; and the practical idea that the quarries in the several states would contribute the columns to the hall as a matter of state pride.

Edward Pearce Casey replied immediately to Miss Desha's letter:

> The various white marbles of the country are of quite different color, texture and marking . . . . after a few years weathering the difference becomes quite apparent and would be very detrimental to the appearance of the building.

She wanted to be sure. Mary Desha then wrote the State Regent of each state in question, providing a copy of the architect's comments. Within a month, eleven had replied. Unanimously they agreed with Casey. The marble should come from a single source. Further, "Delaware does not possess workable white marble quarries." The State Regent of New Hampshire could provide marble, but hesitated to "risk the marble becoming different in color and thus injuring the appearance of the building." "Connecticut does not 'grow' marble," wrote Mrs. Kinney of that state. Mary N. Putnam, State Regent of New Jersey, summed it up, "We can safely leave the matter with our excellent architect, Mr. Casey."

Mrs. A. Leo Knott of Maryland was a member of the Memorial Continental Hall Committee. Unable to attend a March 8, 1905 meeting of the committee, she sent a brochure promoting Beaver Dam Marble, quarried at Cockeysville, Maryland. The brochure stated that the marble had shown superior strength in tests made under the direction of the U.S. Government. Further promoting their product, Beaver Dam Marble company said that they had furnished 108 large blocks, each 26 feet in length, for the columns of U.S. Capitol Building and that this same superior stone was used in the construction of the Washington Monument and the U.S. Post Office Building in Washington. Mrs. Knott, promoting Maryland stone, pointed out that "it is very hard that all of the marble entering in to *our* Continental Hall should come from Vermont which was *not* one of the original thirteen States."

At a meeting of the Memorial Continental Hall Committee on April 3, 1906, a motion was made and carried that the thirteen memorial columns be made of Maryland marble.

Fully occupied at last

More than ten years elapsed from the day in 1892 that Caroline Scott Harrison, the first President General, appointed the first committee on Memorial Continental Hall until the first expenditure on behalf

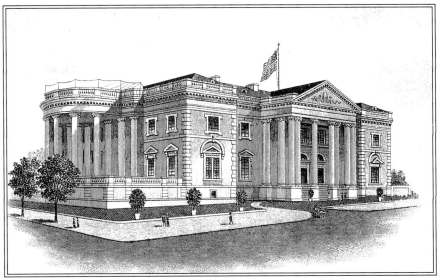

Memorial Continental Hall

of the Hall, the purchase of a site, took place in June, 1902. During that decade funds accumulated, slowly at first, then faster and faster as both membership and enthusiasm increased. Initially, underwriting for the tremendous undertaking was managed on a pay as you go basis. But once building began in earnest, the enormous sums required drained the funds as quickly as they became available and their depletion began to cause delays in construction.

By 1908 when the 17th Continental Congress convened, the permanent heating plant and ventilation system had been installed, and contracts were being let as the bank balance permitted. But the building was not habitable on a year-round basis, and the society was still renting offices for conducting its daily business.

A large sum, over $57,000, was in the bank. Still, Mrs. McLean felt strongly that financing was necessary to finish the project. The real estate holdings of the National Society, as they stood, were worth $280,000. Presenting a forceful argument for the advantages of swift completion, Mrs. McLean persuaded the Congress that it would be appropriate to bond the property for the amount necessary to complete Memorial Continental Hall immediately.

It was given to Mrs. Mary S. Lockwood to make the motion, which was acted upon favorably on April 23, 1908:

> I move that the National Board of Management be authorized, empowered and directed to enter into negotiations with such bank, trust company or other financial institution, or with such individual capitalist or capitalists as may be willing to consider the matter, with a view to securing, by means of a loan or by the issue and sale of bonds, or otherwise, such funds as may be required, not, however, to exceed the sum of . . . . to enable the Society to complete the work upon its Continental Hall, in the City of Washington, District of Columbia, in accordance with the plans and specifications heretofore adopted, and, to that end, to enter into any arrangement which, in its judgment and discretion, may be deemed for the best interests of the Society; and, further, that the Board be authorized and empowered, in the name and behalf of the Society, to execute such promissory notes, bonds or other evidences of indebtedness, and such deed of trust or mortgage of its property, as may be required to secure the repayment of such funds.

The sum to be bonded was left blank because they weren't quite sure how much they needed. Although the resolution passed, some members were quite disturbed by the omission. It is hard to imagine today's Continental Congress passing such a blank check motion. Ultimately, by unanimous consent of the house they inserted the phrase "$200,000, or such portion of that sum as might be necessary."

The plan called for Memorial Continental Hall to be ready for full occupancy on September 1, 1909. To this end, three months' notice was given to Washington Loan and Trust that the National Society would soon be moving its business offices. In matters of building completion dates, 1909 was not substantially different from 1990. At a meeting of the Hall Committee held on October 7, 1909, Mrs. Matthew T. Scott, President General 1909 – 1913, calling upon the cardinal virtue of patience, said, " . . . while we have the great joy of holding our first meeting in this magnificent apartment—almost practically the same conditions confront us which made it unadvisable to remove offices last April when the brilliant sessions of Congress were held here" [in the unfinished building]. Still, the move had been made, and the Daughters of the American Revolution were finally, proudly, lodged in "the finest building ever owned by women."

A Historic Landmark

There, from November 1921 until February 1922, the
leaders of the world's great powers assembled for the first
time in history for the purpose of consenting to disarm.
        Dr. A.R. Mortensen, Chief Historian of the
        National Park Service, April 16, 1973

Following World War I, Americans and Europeans alike longed to achieve world peace. In Memorial Continental Hall, under the leadership of Charles Evans Hughes, Secretary of State, nine nations met together at the Conference on Limitation of Armament, November 12, 1921 – February 6, 1922. The conference "produced three treaties designed to freeze and destroy armaments, to certify mutual respect for existing spheres of influence, and to recognize the independence of China." Although the "parchment peace" did not prevail, it remained a significant precedent toward disarmament.

A half-century later, in accordance with the Historic Sites Act of August 21, 1935, the United States Department of the Interior designated Memorial Continental Hall a national historic landmark. The bronze plaque was presented at Opening Night of the 82nd Continental Congress, April 16, 1973. Mrs. Donald Spicer, President General 1971 – 1974, accepted the plaque from Dr. Mortensen, administrator of the landmark program. Affixed to the north corner of Memorial Continental Hall on 17th Street, the plaque reads:

MEMORIAL CONTINENTAL HALL
HAS BEEN DESIGNATED A
REGISTERED NATIONAL HISTORIC LANDMARK
UNDER THE PROVISIONS OF THE
HISTORIC SITES ACT OF AUGUST 21, 1935
THIS SITE POSSESSES EXCEPTIONAL VALUE
IN COMMEMORATING OR ILLUSTRATING
THE HISTORY OF THE UNITED STATES
U.S. DEPARTMENT OF THE INTERIOR
NATIONAL PARK SERVICE
1973

A Complex of
Beautiful Buildings

With more than 110,000 members by 1920, the DAR was big business. For the numerous organizational chores of the large and growing National Society, a practical, modern, workhorse sort of building was wanted. Memorial Continental Hall, both in its conception and in its substance, was sublime. The rooms were furnished with fine antiques of historical significance. Wear and tear were constant concerns. Not one office was adequately equipped with up-to-date office furniture. Since sending out certificates required the use of such potentially damaging elements as paste pots and water, mailing was done from an empty room back of the kitchen. There were

Constitution Hall, the Administration Building and

insufficient restrooms for the large staff. It was hardly appropriate to subject such a noble monument to the mundane requirements of business administration.

Administration Building

It was our desire to retain for Memorial Continental Hall its chief aim and object as a sacred Memorial to the men and women patriots of the American Revolution; this was our greatest incentive toward the erection of an Administration Building which would separate the business machinery of the Society from its higher spiritual aims.
Mrs. George Maynard Minor, President General, 1920–1923, at dedication of Constitution Hall, April 19, 1928

As early as 1909, during the administration of Mrs. Matthew T. Scott, and before Memorial Continental Hall was completely finished,

Memorial Continental Hall occupy an entire city block.

105

the approaching necessity of erecting an office building was recognized. Mrs. George Thacher Guernsey, President General 1917–1920, saw and promoted the urgent need for larger quarters for the clerical staff. Plans for the new building were submitted during her term of office and accepted by the 29th Continental Congress, in 1920. It was agreed that no general solicitation of contributions would take place. Although states, chapters and members would be welcome to make gifts and furnish rooms if they wanted to, money to erect the building would be borrowed. The financial obligations could be met from regular income. Following her retirement as President General, Mrs. Guernsey was appointed Chairman of the Office Building Committee by Mrs. George Maynard Minor, President General.

On land owned by the DAR and loaned for the purpose, about 75 feet west of Continental Hall stood temporary war buildings erected to house the United States government's Council of National Defense. Following World War I, being no longer of use, they were removed by the government. There, during Mrs. Minor's term as President General, the National Society placed its two-story Administration Building. On June 3, 1921, ground was broken; on October 19, 1921, the 140th anniversary of the surrender at Yorktown, the cornerstone was laid. Mrs. Mary S. Lockwood attended the simple ceremony. Mrs. Guernsey spoke on that occasion:

> Today there are three outstanding things for which we are thankful; first, our thanks are due to our Heavenly Father for giving us this perfect day to lay the corner stone of this building; second, that our United States Senate has ratified the treaty and we are now at peace with the world; third, that we have here with us this morning to be present at the laying of the corner stone the dear little lady whom we call the "Little Mother of our Society," Mrs. Lockwood made the first resolution in any of our gatherings that we should have a building of this kind."

Architects Marsh & Peter designed the fireproof edifice of white limestone, with steps, sills, and wearing parts at the ground of granite. The wet and swampy sub-soil required special preparation of the foundations. The building was connected to Memorial Continental Hall by an underground passage from basement to basement, and through a pergola on the land between the buildings. Fire protection was upgraded and arrangements to enhance work-flow were carefully planned. The two-story card catalogue room in the center of the building provided windows and skylights for light and ventilation in accordance with Mrs. Guernsey's prediction that, " . . . the entire equipment will be devised to make of our office building a model of comfort, convenience, and efficiency, just as our Hall has been a model of beauty and dignity." An automatic push-button elevator eliminated the need to hire an operator; water bottles standing in the passages of Continental Hall were replaced by drinking fountains. An agreement with the National Society, Children of the American Revolution gave them use of a large room on the second floor for a period of ten years; at the expiration of the ten years, C.A.R. would vacate the room at any time upon 30 days' notice from the National Society.

The Library and Museum remained in Memorial Continental Hall, along with the offices of the Librarian General and the Curator General.

On February 5, 1923, without fanfare, the offices of the society were moved into the new building.

Constitution Hall

*If it will not be presumptuous in an old member of your
Society, who was its first presiding officer and who had
her part in the shaping of your beautiful first home, it will
be gratifying to tell you the deep joy with which she notes
the progress of the new auditorium that is to house the
mighty organization of today, and hopes that in her
lifetime she may see it completed.*

*Mrs. Mary Virginia Ellet Cabell, Honorary
President Presiding, letter dated April 13, 1925*

In response to a circular sent out by Mrs. Williard T. Block outlining a plan to finance proposed new construction, Mrs. Cabell pledged $5.00 and sent the first installment of $1.00 on March 21, 1924; the first contribution toward a new auditorium!

Mrs. Anthony Wayne Cook, President General 1923 – 1926, knew at the time of her election in 1923, just two months after the Administration Building had been occupied, that Memorial Continental Hall as the home of the annual Continental Congress had been altogether outgrown. The 33rd Continental Congress, in 1924, authorized a committee to report to the 34th Congress "plans, specifications, and methods of financing a building . . . contain[ing] an auditorium adequate for the future proper seating of our ever-increasing membership." Congressional attendance continued to rise so rapidly that the 34th and succeeding Continental Congresses had to be scheduled jointly at the Washington Auditorium and Memorial Continental Hall. Even this awkward arrangement was inadequate. During the 35th Continental Congress, 400 accredited delegates were forced to stand. Seats for alternates did not exist.

Mrs. Cook served as Chairman of the Committee on Plans for an Auditorium and reported on the second day of the 34th Continental Congress, in April 1925, that the architect, John Russell Pope, had furnished drawings for a "splendid structure seating four thousand persons in its auditorium," at a cost of $1.00 per cubic foot, complete. Pope's original plans included removable seats, allowing conversion of the interior of the auditorium to a ballroom or a banquet hall. The total required would be $1,825,000, but Mrs. Cook hastened to add that the cost of operating the building was "another chapter." A good salesman, she drew applause when she exclaimed, "And just think of it! Each State would have an opportunity to be responsible for a beautiful box."

She allowed three days for the members to have plenty of time to think and talk about the proposition before it came up in the order of business. Finally, on the fifth day of the Congress, the proposed auditorium was discussed. Many favored it; some did not.

Mrs. Robert N. Somerville, State Regent, Mississippi 1924–1926, opposed beginning a "stupendous undertaking" when the National Society still owed $125,000 for construction of the Administration Building. She recognized that those in attendance at Continental Congress, who authorized expenditures, had at least enough discretionary income to finance their trip. But she was concerned about the young women who had to choose between spending "their money for music lessons, a pair of skates, linoleum for the kitchen, or for joining our beloved Society . . . " She concluded, with irony, that such women were non-existent:

> All of those interested in the Daughters of the American Revolution as members or as potential members, it seems, are very rich,

clad in silk stockings and sealskin, movie-mad and working at high wages, just as high as the men.

But not everyone agreed with Mrs. Somerville. For instance, Mrs. Lynn of Oregon was excited by the proposal:

> We came for the inspiration of this meeting. . . . we who live on the rim of the United States feel that we can't bring with us as many as we should like to bring for lack of space. . . . we are going to help raise the money and try to help you build that auditorium.

Mrs. Charles Read Banks, State Regent of New Jersey, 1923 – 1926 and a Daughter after the mold of the independent-thinking Founders, Mary S. Lockwood and Mary Desha, made the telling point:

> It seems to me that one of the best arguments in favor of this proposed building is that business men of the City of Washington are opposing it. They are urging the ladies to vote against this project. These business men have in mind the fact that there is a very large business investment going into this new auditorium. It seems to me no better recommendation could be offered than the very opposition of these business men. Men don't offer a project or oppose other people's projects unless it is a source of revenue. This is a business investment. Don't let any one question that.

When all was said and done, the 34th Continental Congress approved the recommendation of the Building Committee to proceed with building a new auditorium, 444 – 292.

Although the enabling act of the United States Congress as amended in 1915 increased the limit on the Daughters' holdings to $1,000,000, a further expansion was required. On February 5, 1926, the U.S. Congress again increased the permissible real and personal estate of the National Society Daughters of the American Revolution, this time to $5,000,000.

To finance the building, a bond issue in the amount of $1,000,000 was authorized; the bonds were sold, delivered to the National Society, signed and transmitted to the purchasers. They covered a little over half the cost of the proposed facility. But the National Board of Management decided to delay construction until they had in hand an additional $1,000,000 cash. And so began the largest-ever to that time fund-raising project of the intrepid Daughters. Mrs. Alfred J. Brosseau, President General 1926 – 1929, followed Mrs. Cook's lead from the previous administration and served as the National Chairman of the Constitution Hall Committee. Mrs. Russell William Magna was appointed Finance Chairman for the committee and was expected to raise the money.

To pay for this biggest-yet project, pledges were taken to purchase state boxes, chairs, and even cubic feet of foundation dirt! By April 1, 1927, there was over $400,000 cash on hand. Every chapter in New Jersey had paid for a chair; each one would bear a little plaque in the completed auditorium. Up to 100 letters could be used in the inscription. Of the 4,000 seats in the auditorium, only 1,620 remained for subscription. Mrs. Magna said, "We have . . . become a very pulse in the nation's life." She wanted the President General empowered to go ahead with plans so that "granted that the one million dollars is assured by March, 1928," the cornerstone could be laid at the 37th Continental Congress that April. To push it all along, she adopted the slogan, *The Million by March.*

But March came and the million was not quite assured. With the cash that was already on hand and more that was promised, only $835,000 was certain. At the 37th Continental Congress that April, Mrs. Brosseau reported on developments pertaining to Constitution Hall. She said that, as instructed, she had pursued formal planning with John Russell Pope. A new library, tripling the present capacity of 15,000 volumes, had been incorporated into the plans for Constitution Hall. Concurrently, the DAR Museum would be doubled by expanding into the vacated library space in Continental Hall. Once again, word had spread that an active, flowing stream or springs existed under the DAR property. This time, a firm of engineers, Phillips & Worthington, was hired to make test borings and find out definitely. They drilled to a depth of 48 feet and were able to dispel the rumor. Perhaps the delegates to the 37th Continental Congress were a little startled to hear Mrs. Brosseau say:

> As the million is not yet in hand . . . I have made no efforts to lay the cornerstone during this Congress.

The Mesdames Brosseau and Magna were a psychologically compelling team. It is difficult to criticize their routine. If the members were disappointed by Mrs. Brosseau's announcement, at least they were well-prepared to receive Mrs. Magna's pitch:

Cartoonist Clifford K. Berryman noted the fund-raising ability of the DAR.

Members of the Congress, you have your goal in sight! We *can* put it over this morning—and we *must*. . . . You have achieved much—make it a little more. A proper slogan this morning is—"Make it a million."

They tried, but they fell short. Pledging was taken on three separate occasions that week. Each time, Mrs. Magna implored the members to make it a million. By the adjournment of Congress, the fund had grown to $891,818.70. Mrs. Magna wouldn't give up. The Daughters knew they weren't leaving Washington until the funding for Constitution Hall was assured. They went over the top the same night. At the NSDAR Congress Banquet, April 21, 1928, they *made it a million.*

Constitution Hall under construction, November 14, 1928.

On October 30, 1928 the cornerstone was set in place with full pomp. The Marine Band played. Mrs. Calvin Coolidge personally placed White House cards autographed by both herself and President Coolidge within the copper box fitted to the interior of the stone. Employing the same trowel used in laying the cornerstone of Memorial Continental Hall, Mrs. Coolidge spread the first mortar. Then, each in turn, Mrs. Brosseau, Mrs. Magna, and Mrs. Adam M. Wyant, Treasurer General, who signed the one million dollar check canceling the National Society's bonded indebtedness, spread a little mortar. To the President General, Mrs. Brosseau, was given the honor of tapping the four corners of the cornerstone with Potomac Lodge, No. 5, A.F.F.M.'s historic gavel; the same gold-tipped gavel used by George Washington in laying the cornerstone of the U.S. Capitol in 1793, and loaned by the lodge for similar rites for Memorial Continental Hall in 1904.

Less than six months later, at the close of the 38th Continental Congress, Mrs. Brosseau's final Congress as President General, April

19, 1929 at 12:00 noon, she proudly dedicated Constitution Hall and commended it "to the world for the world's best offerings, to the end that to youth may come enlightenment; to men and women who are carrying the noonday burdens of the world, stimulation and strength; and to old age rejuvenation and solace." Among the chaotic debris of construction very much in progress, the Daughters took their places and cheered as Mrs. Herbert Hoover, Mrs. Brosseau and the national and state officers entered in procession. Representing our closest neighbors, Miss Mabel Boardman, Director, brought greetings from the American Red Cross, to the north, and Dr. L.S. Rowe, Director General, spoke on behalf of the Pan American Union, to the south.

In her dedicatory remarks, Mrs. Brosseau said:

> To the mothers and fathers of the American Revolution—the complete embodiment of that great Spirit of '76—was Memorial Continental Hall dedicated. . . . The Administration Building, the next to be erected, is devoted to the purposes of a high and mighty effort; to the fulfillment of ideas conceived in a spirit of reverence and patriotism. . . . Upon this third structure, which we are today dedicating, we bestow the name Constitution Hall, in honor of that immortal document which we, too, [like Daniel Webster] regard as a fundamental law. . . . If we continue to ardently maintain those standards of Americanism to which men and women of honor can in truth subscribe, we need have no fear but that the great and eternal events will rest in the hands of God.

The 39th Continental Congress, April 14 – April 19, 1930, was the first to be held in Constitution Hall. Mrs. Lowell Fletcher Hobart, President General 1929 – 1932, presided. The building was complete. According to Mrs. Brosseau, it had "100 per cent acoustics, spacious aisles and exits, a huge venti-lighter in the ceiling which produces the marvelous sunlight effect at all hours of the day in the auditorium; and pure air which is mechanically washed and circulated."

There remained the matter of indebtedness on the new hall. Although the bonds had been recalled, to finance the building it was still necessary to borrow money. Short-term funds, pledged against the Administration Building, at lower than the six percent paid on the bonds, were utilized. When Mrs. Magna was given a rising vote of thanks for her work as Finance Chairman, she said, "I am standing here with my arms outstretched and my ears wide open to hear what you have to say to me." The "Greatest Little Gold Digger of Them All" was once again ready to take pledges.

Mrs. Magna served as Finance Chairman for Constitution Hall for six years. She worked, traveled, encouraged and cajoled. She had the light touch. She was never demanding or argumentative. But rather like the conductor of an orchestra, she addressed her instruments, the members, and lovingly, persistently, coaxed her melody—money—out of them. They were proud to respond. After she finished parting them from their funds, they rewarded her with their highest tribute. Mrs. Russell William Magna was elected President General, 1932–1935, without opposition at the 41st Continental Congress.

Constitution Hall was as good as Mrs. Hobart proudly proclaimed it to be. Although it had a seating capacity of almost 4,000, the acoustics were excellent. The appointments were elegant. The DAR decided from the opening of the hall that it would be made available to the general public. So popular did this primary auditorium of Washington, D.C. become that many people have mistakenly assumed that it was a public building. It was the convenience and popularity of Constitution Hall that

The 39th Continental Congress was the first held in Constitution Hall.

caused the most persistent problem that has ever faced the Daughters of the American Revolution. The DAR has stopped making excuses for the Marian Anderson "incident." When the great black contralto was refused use of the hall in 1939, the ensuing controversy became a "thorn in the flesh" that finds its way into print to this very day, more than 50 years later. Seeking to place the incident in its proper perspective, the DAR, in its latest statement on the subject, points out that Marian Anderson has since performed in Constitution Hall on eight occasions, including the first concert of her 1964 farewell tour. Many other black performers, black speakers, black authors and black politicians have been warmly received by delegates to NSDAR Continental Congress over the years. "Segregation was an ugly part of America's history and many of our institutions must share the blame. Such was the situation in Washington, D.C. and the country as late as 1945. It was during this period that Eleanor Roosevelt wrote in her column, 'My Day'—'I do not think one could hold the DAR alone responsible.' . . . We are unable to change what has happened. The best we can offer is that we understand."

In 1985, the United States Department of the Interior found that Constitution Hall possessed national significance in the history of the United States. As a result, on September 16 that year, the Secretary of the Interior designated it a National Historic Landmark. Thus the National Society became the only organization in the National Register of Historic Places to have two buildings, back to back, designated as National Historic Landmarks.

CONSTITUTION HALL

HAS BEEN DESIGNATED A

NATIONAL

HISTORIC LANDMARK

THIS SITE POSSESSES NATIONAL SIGNIFICANCE

IN COMMEMORATING THE HISTORY OF THE

UNITED STATES OF AMERICA

1985

NATIONAL PARK SERVICE

UNITED STATES DEPARTMENT OF THE INTERIOR

New Administration Building

During the tenure of Mrs. Roscoe C. O'Byrne, President General 1947–1950, the 57th Continental Congress, in 1948, mandated the construction of a new administration building. To answer those who complained that the timing was poor, Mrs. Rex Hays Rhodes, Treasurer General demonstrated that it was the optimum season in which to build:

> . . . plans for our present Administration Building were begun three years following World War I. Money was borrowed at six percent interest. Constitution Hall was begun at the peak of inflation following World War I, and before the Administration Building was paid for; Constitution Hall was completed the year of the depression. Over $1,000,000 at six percent was borrowed and we paid off our indebtedness so rapidly we are now able to borrow $200,000 at two-and-a-half percent on our reputation alone.

Eggers and Higgins, successor to John Russell Pope, designer of Constitution Hall, was the architectural firm chosen. Their other notable designs included the National Gallery of Art, the Jefferson Memorial and the National Archives Building. Although supplanted by Constitution Hall, Memorial Continental Hall was still being maintained as an auditorium, but fire regulations prevented maximum use. The new building plan included removing the seats, leveling the floor and eliminating the platform, and leveling the balcony floor in the older structure. Flags, portraits and insignia would remain intact, and commemorative statuary would be moved in. Locating the DAR Library, with its many memorials, in Memorial Continental Hall would be the final, best use of the historic space. Existing offices in the Administration Building would be enlarged, and a new third floor added. The building would now contain the DAR Museum gallery, well-lighted and spacious, to permit display of the remarkable variety of relics accumulated through more than 60 years of collecting. The voting room, known today as the O'Byrne Room, and a new second floor archives room, now the Americana Room, solved problems of long-standing.

In presenting the new Administration Building for dedication on April 18, 1950, Mrs. Rhodes exulted that, this time, construction was completed on schedule. Reminding the Congress that Mrs. Fairbanks, whose administration saw the completion of Memorial Continental Hall,

Evolution of the DAR Library. Top to bottom: original library, Continental Hall; second floor, Constitution Hall; auditorium, Continental Hall.

and Mrs. O'Byrne were both Indianans, she said that she had wondered if the word "Hoosier" was associated with the word "builder."

> Mrs. O'Byrne tells me that Hoosier is a word handed down from pioneer days. It seems that when the early settlers began to move into Indiana and approached the cabin of a pioneer, they would make a loud "halloo" to let the dweller know they were friendly folks. From the cabin would come an answering call "who's there?" That in time became "Who's yere" or Hoosier, and thus the dwellers in the cabins became known as Hoosiers.

Finally, she had to admit that Hoosier did not exactly mean builder, but that nevertheless, Mrs. O'Byrne's enthusiasm had spread "like a prairie fire" to reach the happy conclusion.

For her part, Mrs. O'Byrne observed that, "All of our land, as you can see, is now occupied." She was proud that the architects and builders had skillfully concealed the evidence of their work. It was difficult to tell what was new and what had been there for years. Defining the functions of the buildings she said:

> Our Memorial Continental Hall, the very symbol of the dignity and the enduring strength of the Daughters of the American Revolution has been joined by this Administration Building to Constitution Hall, our stately temple of culture. Our buildings have not lost their identities at all, but they have been united in one solid group.

Again, growth in membership and financial success created conflict with the limitations of the National Society's charter. In 1951, the U.S. Congress updated the permitted holdings, to $10,000,000. Finally, on October 1, 1976, through the efforts of Mrs. Wakelee Rawson Smith, President General 1975–1977, a definitive amendment to the Act of Incorporation allowed the DAR to hold such property "as may be convenient or necessary for its lawful purposes" and relieved the Congress of the United States of one recurring item on its agenda.

Restoration

A man builds a fine house; and now he has a master, and a
task for life: he is to furnish, watch, show it, and keep it in
repair, the rest of his days.

> Ralph Waldo Emerson, Society and Solitude:
> Works and Days

How quickly yesterday's latest fashion becomes today's old hat! The
first renovation of Constitution Hall took place during the administration
of Miss Gertrude Sprague Carraway, President General 1953 – 1956. In
addition to a face lift, the electrical system was modernized, with new
stage lighting that would "permit nearly any sort of effect," and improved
sound equipment to "equal anything in the United States" was installed.
The addition of television platforms signified the beginning of a new era
in communication. Floors were repaired, seats were reupholstered and
the stage was enlarged. In addition, much of Memorial Continental Hall
was redecorated. Surplus funds covered the expenses of the work.

Beautification of the grounds at National Headquarters, and the
dedication of the Memorial Garden on D Street took place during the
administration of Mrs. Ashmead White, President General 1959 – 1962.
Improvements at Memorial Continental Hall included sanding and
polishing, installation of floodlights, and renovation of the Banquet Hall
and clerks' lounge.

The DAR Library, occupying the space that originally formed the
auditorium of Memorial Continental Hall, contained unsightly and
unusable balconies. Structural changes could be incorporated that would
increase space available for bookstacks by fifty percent, and provide
additional reading room as well. As a "Diamond Jubilee" project, during
the administration of Mrs. Robert V.H. Duncan, President General
1962 – 1965, the 73rd Continental Congress voted to approve the
expansion. Forty steel supports and fourteen foundation piers were
added at basement level to carry the weight of the new balconies.
Railings exactly duplicating those placed when the Hall was first
constructed in 1908 – 09 were manufactured. Every care was taken, not
only to preserve the original beauty of the area, but to enhance it.

Costing over $100,000 the project was approved, funded, built and furnished within the space of one year and dedicated on April 20, 1965.

From the day its doors were opened, the Daughters made Constitution Hall available to the general public. It was the biggest, the best, the most beautiful auditorium in the city; it became the cultural center of Washington, D.C. But in the march of progress many things change. The ticket-buying population was no longer satisfied with scrubbed and ventilated air. More comfort was demanded. During the term of Mrs. William Henry Sullivan, President General 1965 – 1968, the Hall was air conditioned, to the great relief of impresarios, concert-goers and members alike. At the time of the 79th Continental Congress, in 1970, during the administration of Mrs. Erwin Frees Seimes, President General 1968 – 1971, it was announced that the indebtedness on the project had been cleared.

Membership growth continued to press the facilities of the National Society. Although the land was totally occupied, Mrs. George Upham Baylies, President General 1977 – 1980, made creative use of available space within the Administration Building. Naming the project *Building for Our Future*, she added eight offices, four on the second floor and four on the third floor, and a two-story atrium, in a previously open court area between the Assembly Room and the elevator.

Acid rain falls on the just and the unjust alike. Hopelessly damaged, the marble balusters surrounding the porticoes of Memorial Continental Hall began to crumble into tiny granular beads of impotent stone. The terraces sank as years of seepage wasted the earthen subbase. Air contamination and implacable time worked their deadly magic. The finest building ever owned by women was losing its luster. Beginning more than a decade of unremitting restoration, *A Legacy Preserved*, the project of Mrs. Richard Denny Shelby, President General 1980 – 1983, set out to restore where realistic and replace where required; rejuvenation of the stately monument was the object. The enormous task required removing the balustrades, floor tiles, and concrete slab bases of the terraces, and then leveling the subbase, pouring new reinforced concrete structural slab, and finally replacing the renewed balustrades. Crucial conservation to protect the 50-year-old Founders' Memorial Monument and repairs to the deteriorating 18th Street steps of Constitution Hall were also undertaken as part of the project.

Constitution Hall was built in 1929 with a "carriage drive" at its D Street entrance. There, arriving passengers were discharged under the protection of the glittering, glass-trimmed portico. Inexorable time passed. Ladies continued to emerge from carriages, automobiles, taxis and limousines; now delivery vans also used the drive hauling instruments, props and, later, sound and light equipment. Vehicles grew wider, taller and heavier. Curbstones were broken and displaced; walkways were damaged. The sparkling glass diamonds of the portico completely disappeared. Still, the stout D Street ramp refused entrance to no one. Although all was not well, the brave little driveway concealed most of its sufferings. It had to be completely rebuilt, making allowance for the weight and clearance requirements of today. Continuing exterior restoration of the DAR complex of buildings, the *Independence Jubilee Project* of Mrs. Walter Hughey King, President General 1983 – 1986, returned the lovely carriage drive to its original appearance, allowing for the demands of modern times. Renovation of the C Street portico, landings and steps were a smaller part of the project.

The Daughters had been collecting priceless relics and manuscripts for over 90 years. Year after year, the treasures were subjected to the rigors of the hot and humid Washington summer. There were times when mildew grew on the walls of the DAR Museum. In the damper basement storage areas, it was even worse. The ongoing project to provide climate control in Memorial Continental Hall and the Administration Building was entirely funded in Mrs. King's administration.

Now the glamorous and visually thrilling part of the restoration of DAR Headquarters was complete. But in the hidden, secret places, problems remained. The ancient galvanized iron pipes originally installed many years before were so thoroughly filled with rust and corrosion that water could not reach the third floor. All three buildings were plagued with clogged, leaking and bursting pipes. Frequently water broke through at a place far removed from where damage later occurred. It was often hard to stop a leak once it started; no one knew where the pipes and shutoffs were located. There were no comprehensive blueprints available. A "pipe survey" was taken. An entirely new system of pipes was needed; restrooms had to be modernized; a full complement of shutoff valves and a written record of their locations had to be provided. Naming the project *Pipes and Drum*, Mrs. Raymond

Franklin Fleck, President General 1986—1989, rolled up her sleeves and prepared to do what had to be done. Toting a corroded, rust-filled pipe all about the country as she fulfilled her speaking engagements, she made the mundane, necessary, very expensive project real, dramatic and even fun for the delighted membership. The kinds of restoration undertaken during her administration assured that the building was in a constant state of upheaval. The Pipes and Drum project was dirty and disruptive; but not daunting. With contagious good cheer, Mrs. Fleck declared, "Work is a blessing."

Mrs. Eldred M. Yochim, President General 1989—1992, remembered that the DAR buildings are, as Mrs. Cabell had said in 1891, a home. Her part in the restoration of the buildings would take care of "just the normal things that can go wrong with a home." Her project, *Ties That Bind*, would "tie up the loose ends" and complete the restoration of the NSDAR buildings for the 100th Continental Congress. There was plenty to do. For instance, the roof leaked. Constitution Hall now has a new, sloped, copper roof and gutters. It looks just as it always did. But finally, the floods have stopped. The new roof has been designed to provide the maximum moisture protection for the greatest length of time. The roofs of the Administration Building and Memorial Continental Hall have been brought up to grade as well. In work clothing and hard hat, Mrs. Yochim, herself, climbed a steep ladder to inspect the rebuilt skylight in Continental Hall. The windows in the buildings looked all right at a glance, but in fact they were not. Many of the locks were broken. Although a new security system was installed, there was no true security above the first floor. An enterprising second-story man could have made himself at home any evening after dark. Some of the windows were secure: they had been painted permanently shut. Each one was removed, repaired, refurbished, repainted, and replaced. Hung with gleaming brass chains and furnished with functional locks, all the windows can now be unlocked, opened, closed and relocked with ease. It is normal to repair windows in a home one loves; even in a very large home. It has been done in this home. As plaster and paint conceal all remaining evidence of the arduous restoration that has finally been completed, the DAR finds itself once again comfortably at home in the House Beautiful.

Howard Mitchell and the National Symphony Orchestra called Constitution Hall "home" for many years. Mr. and Mrs. Ronald W. Reagan were in the audience for this 1968 performance.

Part III

Service to the Nation

Mary S. Lockwood and Emily Lee Sherwood Ragan said it
well in their *Story of the Records, D.A.R.*
published in 1906:

*There has been such an embarrassment of riches to draw
from, it will not be surprising if some of the good things
worthy of mention have been inadvertently overlooked.*

The National Society in 1890 as today had three great
objectives: perpetuating the memory and spirit of the men
and women who achieved American Independence,
developing an enlightened public opinion through
education, and fostering true patriotism and love of
country. This broad commission mandated action to
occupy a legion for years to come. The account that
follows is not comprehensive, nor *can* it be in a volume of
this nature. The sketches may give some illustration of the
character and scope of the accomplishments.

*Dedication of the last Madonna of the Trail Monument
at Bethesda, Maryland, April 19, 1929.*

Historic Service

*To perpetuate the memory and spirit of the men and
women who achieved American Independence; by the
acquisition and protection of historical spots and the
erection of monuments; by the encouragement of historical
research in relation to the American Revolution and the
publication of its results; by the preservation of documents
and relics, and of the records of the individual services of
Revolutionary soldiers and patriots; and by the promotion
of celebrations of all patriotic anniversaries.*

> First of the three objectives of the National
> Society Daughters of the American Revolution

America at her birth had been called a new constellation. If the glitter had faded, perhaps it was because the story of her borning had somehow been lost or trampled underfoot by two million of America's most promising youth marching to war against each other. The great centennial celebration of 100 years of independence had helped to arouse long-dormant feelings of patriotism. However, organization and action would be necessary to effect a lasting improvement. If there were to be a general renewal of allegiance, someone must provide a spark. There must be monuments and statues and plaques; speeches and medals and parades. Quiet research and preservation combined with jubilant festivals would help focus fickle public attention on the past. Preserving that past would provide a source of inspiration for the future.

One of the resolutions passed at the organizing meeting of the National Society on October 11, 1890 read:

> Resolved, That, whereas, Hon. Mr. Sherman, M.C. from New York, has introduced a bill into the House of Representatives, arranging for the marking by the Government of historical spots of the Revolution,

we, the Daughters of the American Revolution hereby request the passage of said bill.

First Report to the Smithsonian—historical projects

The Daughters, while enthusiastically supporting Mr. Sherman's bill, had no intention of just sitting back and waiting for the government to act. They began at once, branching out in many directions. Among their earliest achievements were a multitude of historic commemorations; some modest, others elaborate. The *First Report to the Smithsonian* reported a large number of restorations, markings, dedications, fund raisings, and purchases in the various states and chapters including (among others):

Connecticut: Wayside stone, Pork Hollow; Revolutionary burial ground, Fairfield; and monuments and tablets to Fanny Ledyard, Roger Sherman, and the soldiers of Ancient Waterbury

Georgia: Monument to General Oglethorpe, Savannah; received Massachusetts Building at the Cotton States Exposition, a copy of Craigie House at Cambridge, for a chapter house, Atlanta

Illinois: Monument to George Rogers Clark, Oak Park

Kentucky: Monument to the heroic women of Bryan's Station, Lexington; and repair of the monument to Daniel Boone, Frankfort

Maryland: White marble block at the tomb of Thomas Johnson, first continental governor of Maryland; and purchase of a cemetery lot and reinterrment of the remains of Judge Thomas Beatty, who signed the declaration that the stamp act was unconstitutional; both in Frederick

Massachusetts: Tablet on the home of Paul Revere in Boston; memorial to Polly Dagett, Maria Allen and Parnel Manter, Vineyard Haven; and contributions toward the cairn in memory of Abigail Adams, the bronze tablet on the tomb of John Adams, and the bust of John Adams

New Jersey: rescue of the cornerstone of the old first court house in Somerset County

New York: Monument to the Constitution, Poughkeepsie; tablet commemorating the visit of Lafayette, Utica; tablet on the house of Gen. Benjamin Mooers, Plattsburg

Ohio: Statue of a Minuteman on Guard, Old Fort Washington; and presentation of a portrait of Gen. Nathaniel Massie, Chillicothe

Pennsylvania: Rough granite memorial stone at the place where Washington encamped on September 14, 1777 on his way to Paoli, West Philadelphia; monument at Ephrata to mark the burial place of 200 soldiers who died from wounds received, Brandywine; restoration of the old banquet room in Independence Hall in Philadelphia; ownership and restoration of the old blockhouse built by Colonel Bouquet in 1764 at the junction of the Allegheny and Monongahela Rivers; presentation of a portrait of William Penn, Pittsburgh; and a brass tablet in memory of Col. Thomas Hartly, York

Rhode Island: Bronze tablet in commemoration of the burning of taxed tea in Providence; monument to the Rhode Island soldiers who died at Valley Forge; monument to Maj. Ebenezer Adams, Kingston; and a tablet on Beacon Pole Hill, Cumberland

South Carolina: Monument to Emily Geiger in Columbia

Tennessee: Restoration of the stone at the grave of Dorothea Spotswood Henry Winston, daughter of Patrick Henry, Memphis

Vermont: Headstone in memory of Mary Brownson, first wife of Ethan Allen, Arlington; and a bronze tablet on the farm that was Ethan Allen's last home, Burlington

Virginia: Monument to Gen. Andrew Lewis, Roanoke

Washington: and many other states: Contributions toward the monument to Francis Scott Key

While the majority of markings have been accomplished by local chapters, from time to time the National Society, itself, has marked a historic site. Some of the markings of the National Society have been mentioned elsewhere or are described in detail in the following pages.

On October 19, 1931, the Yorktown Sesquicentennial, during the administration of Mrs. Lowell Fletcher Hobart, President General 1929 – 1932, two bronze tablets listing the names of the 103 American soldiers and the 132 Frenchmen who died during the siege at Yorktown were unveiled and dedicated. Hamilton Fish III unveiled the American tablet; Jean Stuart Labat, the French. Mrs. James T. Morris, who helped research the names and who spoke at the dedication said, "These names have never before been assembled. No two have ever been brought together. It is our inestimable privilege to resurrect these names from the obscurity of oblivion."

The National Society marked the grave of Dr. George Brown Goode, designer of the DAR Insignia, during the term of Mrs. James B. Patton, President General 1950–1953. An ichthyologist and Assistant Secretary of the Smithsonian Institution, Dr. Goode represented the society's strongest link with that organization. His wife, a charter member, was Chairman of the Committee on Insignia when his design was adopted on May 26, 1891. His accomplishments and honors were numerous. A former president of many prestigious organizations, including the National Geographic Society, at the time of his death on September 6, 1896, Dr. Goode was President of the Sons of the American Revolution in the District of Columbia. He was 45 years old.

On February 23, 1973, during Mrs. Donald W. Spicer's term as President General, 1972–1975, a marker "in memory of those who died in defense of their country December 7, 1941" was placed at the *USS Arizona Memorial* at Pearl Harbor. It was replaced and rededicated on February 21, 1986, in the administration of Mrs. Walter Hughey King, President General 1984–1987. The National Society also placed a number of tablets commemorating the Bicentennial of the signing of the Treaty of Paris: A marker placed at Yorktown Square, Paris, France in 1932 honoring the "Peacemakers," Benjamin Franklin, John Jay and John Adams, was refurbished and rededicated; on September 3, 1983, a tablet to the "Architects of these Treaties" was placed in front of the statue of Benjamin Franklin at Paris; on October 19, 1984, two tablets were dedicated at Yorktown, Virginia: one honoring the Treaty and one, Friendship with Great Britain.

On June 21, 1985, at St. Peters, Wolverhampton, England, a tablet was dedicated as a memorial to Button Gwinnett, signer of the Declaration of Independence. Gwinnett, born in England, was married at St. Peters in 1757.

A Friendship tablet duplicating the one placed at Yorktown was formally dedicated at #9 Grosvenor Square, London, England on May 18, 1987, during the administration of Mrs. Raymond Franklin Fleck, President General 1986–1989.

Monument to Mary, Mother of Washington

*The grave of Mary, the Mother of General George
Washington, to be sold at public auction. To the ladies
attending the Inauguration of President-elect Harrison: On
Tuesday, March 5, 1889, at 12 o'clock M., we will offer at
Public Outcry, at the Capital of the United States of
America, 12 acres of land, embracing the Grave and the
Material of the Unfinished Monument of Mary, the Mother
of General Washington.*

*Colbert & Kirtly, Real Estate Agents and
Auctioneers, Fredericksburg, Va., Washington
Post, March 2, 1889*

Just as the exclusion of women from the Sons of the American
Revolution inspired Mary S. Lockwood's famous letter, so the "terrible
advertisement" inspired Mrs. Margaret Hetzel to write the *Washington
Post* on May 6, 1889. Burning with patriotism, she penned, "How better
can the mothers and daughters of this country, in this Centennial year,
honor the memory of our Washington, who said: 'All that I am I owe to
my mother,' than by rescuing that mother's grave from oblivion and
raising the monument to her hallowed memory? One dollar is herewith
enclosed as a beginning for the woman's fund."

That particular dollar inspired the founding of the National Mary
Washington Memorial Association on February 22, 1890. Mrs. Hetzel
served as the first secretary of the association.

Mary Ball Washington died August 25, 1789. She was buried at
Fredericksburg, Virginia near her "Oratory Rock" where she was
accustomed to pray during the trying days of the Revolution.

The United States Congress immediately passed a resolution to
erect an appropriate monument over her grave. However, national
priorities necessarily came first, and the years slipped by. When
Lafayette revisited this country in 1825, an ordinary headstone marked
the place where she lay. George Washington Parke Custis, grandson of
Martha Washington, appealed for a monument in 1826. The people of
Fredericksburg had raised $2,000 when, in 1831, the cause was joined
by Silas E. Burrows of New York. Overcome with patriotism, Burrows

voluntarily pledged to erect the monument. President Andrew Jackson laid the cornerstone on May 7, 1833.

Work proceeded for four years. The base was built; the obelisk was delivered to the site. Suddenly, the project was halted, incomplete, the reasons for its abandonment shrouded in mystery. In her book, *The Building of a Monument*, published in 1903 by the then Secretary of the National Mary Washington Monument Association, Miss Susan Riviere Hetzel gives the most probable cause. According to Miss Hetzel, Burrows completely funded the project before his departure for China and subsequent death. The stone mason, Mr. Hill, "working in the hot sun, was stricken with brain fever and died." Thereafter, no one took up the contract. She said that the remaining funds may have been lost in a bank failure.

For years the monument stood, unfinished, the shaft on the ground beside it. A macabre target during the Civil War, the battle of Marye's Heights was fought within sight of it; three other engagements, Chancellorsville, Wilderness and Spotsylvania Court House, were fought from ten to fifteen miles away. Thomas Scott of the *New York Times* wrote that "within sound of that spot died over fifty thousand brave men." Ravaged by the bullets and cannonballs of both sides, serious deterioration began. In 1874, Lieutenant W.L. Marshall of the Engineer Corps, U.S. Army, pronounced the monument "an irreparable ruin." Bills to restore it were introduced from time to time, but failed to pass. And so matters remained until the shocking notice appeared on March 2, 1889.

Predictably, the advertisement raised an immediate outburst of outrage and incredulous indignation. It was charged that the land was illegally offered, a claim later upheld by the courts. In the meantime, the proposed sale had the desirable effect of pushing the public too far.

The nation was commemorating the Centennial of General Washington's Inauguration as First President of the United States. Lavish publicity promoted feelings of extravagant sentimentality. Victorian reserve was punctured by rapturous expressions of admiration; veneration of the Father of His Country approached worship.

It was the vulgar juxtaposition of wretched neglect on the one hand with profuse adoration on the other that prodded Margaret Hetzel to immediate and effective action.

As has been described earlier, at the Organizing Meeting of the National Society Daughters of the American Revolution, the first Resolution adopted pledged to support the completion of the monument to Mary Washington. With a tangible goal that appealed to both reason and emotion, the ladies set to work.

They were quickly successful. The Daughters of the American Revolution provided three-quarters of the more than $11,500 expended for the monument. The dedication at Fredericksburg on May 10, 1894 was attended by a "chaos of people of all ages and sexes."

The weather was sublime. A special train carried the government dignitaries, National Mary Washington Association members and Sons and Daughters of the American Revolution from Washington to the festivities. The Marine Band, who traveled by the same conveyance, was in place in time to play "Hail to the Chief" as President Grover Cleveland drove past in his carriage. Cleveland delivered an address of tribute. Praising Washington, the President said that, " . . . when the plaudits of his countrymen were loudest, he valued more than these the blessing and approval of his aged mother." The monument was dedicated by Mann Page, Grand Master of the Masons of Virginia.

The principal address, by Senator John Daniel of Virginia, was called the ablest oratorical effort of his life. Referencing Washington's "All that I am," Daniel said, "All that we are as a nation we owe to him. His debt is ours. Beholding this monument, we rejoice that this debt is acknowledged . . . ."

Among the other notable personages seated on the rostrum were Adlai E. Stevenson, Vice

"Mary,
Mother of Washington,
buried here, 1789"

President of the United States and Mrs. Stevenson, President General, NSDAR; Governor and Mrs. O'Ferrall; Senator Daniel; the Secretaries of State, Treasury, War and Agriculture; Chief Justice and Mrs. Fuller; Justice and Mrs. Harlan; Mrs. Amelia C. Waite, President of the National Mary Washington Association; and Mrs. Hetzel.

DAR Founder Mary Desha was present in her capacity as Vice President at Large of the N.M.W.A. Descendants of Mary Washington, including DAR Founder, Eugenia Washington, had reserved seats.

A monument to Washington in Paris

An association of American women has been formed for the purpose of presenting to France a bronze equestrian statue of George Washington, since his character symbolizes all that is most valuable in our national life.

> National Society of the Daughters of the
> American Revolution, Appeal to our members in
> behalf of the project, December 13, 1898

In token of their friendship, on October 28, 1886 the people of France dedicated the statue of "Liberty Enlightening the World," situated on Bedloe's Island in the harbor of New York, to the people of the United States. Such a compliment deserved a response.

The Washington Statue Association, an association of American women, was incorporated at Washington, D.C. in about 1887 to convey "gratitude to France for her generous aid in our struggle for national independence." Public support was sought.

The Daughters were ready to respond even before they had finished organizing. At the second meeting of the National Society, held in the home of Mrs. William D. Cabell on October 18, 1890, on the motion of Harriet Lincoln Coolidge a resolution was adopted that "a monument be erected in Paris to the memory of George Washington." The members cooperated enthusiastically.

At first, the success of the project seemed assured, but by 1898, only $20,000 of the $35,000 cost had been raised. The Washington Statue Association sent out an appeal for $15,000 to complete the work in time to present the statue at the Paris Exposition of 1900. They announced that an American sculptor, Daniel C. French, had been selected and that the model was complete, ready for casting, and "in every way worthy of its object and of the place for which it is intended."

The National Society had again voiced its support at the Congress of 1898 and established the Franco-American Memorial Committee to encourage contributions. In December of that year, the committee distributed its circular "issued in the hope that each member of our society will not only feel proud to contribute to this cause, but will interest the women in her locality in this glorious enterprise." According to the *3rd Report to the Smithsonian*, dated 1900, "The amount paid through our society as the result of this circular was $1,141.73 . . . . If all sums given by our members directly to the statue association during the thirteen years could be ascertained, our part in this memorial would probably appear larger by several thousands."

On July 3, 1900, the 125th anniversary of the date on which he took command of the American Army at Cambridge, the statue of George Washington presented by the women of America was unveiled at the Paris Exposition. Mrs. Daniel Manning, President General, represented both the Daughters of the American Revolution and the United States government, by appointment of President William McKinley. Mrs. Manning held a place of honor on the platform along with Mrs. John P. Jones, representing the Washington Statue Association. The two ladies, escorted by Major Huntington and Colonel Chaille'-Long, loosened the cords of the covering, and as Sousa's band played "Hail to the Chief," it dropped, revealing the statue beneath it.

Statue of George Washington at Paris, France

Lafayette honored by children of America

*The morning of the glorious fourth brought bright
sunshine and much heat. Bells did not ring, cannon did not
boom, the small boy was neither seen nor heard. There is
always something for which to be thankful. In the absence
of senseless hubbub, we could be thankful even for heat.*

Mrs. Sara T. Kinney, State Regent of
Connecticut, American Monthly Magazine,
September 1900

The second great event for the National Society at the Paris
Exposition was the unveiling of the statue honoring Lafayette.

Robert John Thompson, who later served as secretary of the
Lafayette Memorial Commission, originated the idea of erecting a
monument to the General at Paris. On a visit to his obscure grave in
that city, Thompson became determined to lead the children of America
to build a public memorial that would show "that America has not
forgotten the unselfish services of her French hero." Boosted by the
support of President William McKinley, October 19, 1898 was declared
Lafayette Day in the public schools. Collections taken on that occasion
produced a large amount, but not enough to pay the $100,000 cost of
the proposed statue. Subsequently, appeals by the Lafayette Memorial
Commission were sent to the various patriotic societies.

Through the Franco-American Memorial Committee of the National Society, a second circular was sent bearing the date of December
13, 1898, this one requesting each member to contribute "to this noble
enterprise." Through the National Society, members gave $1,854.14.

Sculptor of the statue was Paul Bartlett of Connecticut; architect
was Thomas Hastings. Unfinished on DAR Day, July 4, 1900, it was
represented by a plaster replica on the Square Lafayette (Carrousel du
Louvre). The Stars and Stripes appeared in great abundance; by special
permission, from the top of the Eiffel Tower. Boats in the Seine displayed
the French and American flags together; people in the streets wore bits
of red, white and blue ribbon in their lapels and carried tiny silk French
and American flags. A Frenchman was heard to say, "You Americans do
not take your holiday like the English. You are like the French, you
enjoy yourselves." Sousa's band was given permission to play American

national airs on the Place de l'Opera for the first time in the history of France. The Daughters present for the dedication received special treatment. As Mrs. Kinney reported it, "The most desirable place in the enclosure, 'Tribune B' entire, had been reserved for the Daughters of the American Revolution. It was packed. Insignia to the right of us, insignia to the left of us, insignia in front and back of us." Sousa's band played Sousa's march composed specially for the occasion, "Hail to the Spirit of Liberty." The President General, Mrs. Manning, was a speaker on this occasion. The Paris Edition of the *New York Times* praised her:

Program cover, Dedication of the Monument to General Lafayette

Mrs. Daniel Manning, as she stepped to the front of the platform, presented a charming picture. Her gown was of white crepe, trimmed with old lace, and her white hat was trimmed with white feathers and roses. Across the front of her gown she wore a broad blue ribbon, a decoration of the Daughters of the American Revolution. Her voice as she delivered her speech was perfect, and she could be heard from one side of the enclosure to the other. She talked possibly fifteen minutes, proved herself to be a past mistress of the art of speech-making, and was listened to with the greatest attention.

Mrs. Manning said, in part:

We are here today to render our homage to Lafayette—our admiration for his character, our gratitude for his help, and our attachment for the principles of civil and religious liberty which he encountered ocean, exile, and war to establish. The bells are ringing today throughout America . . . . With no spur of future emoluments nor incentive of personal ties, he came to espouse the cause of the

American people according to the principles of the Declaration, which unfolded before his eyes the consecrated standard of human rights. He crossed the ocean and offered his sword to distant, unknown fellow-men striving for liberty. And how completely his sympathy was with America is shown in a letter to his wife, when he writes: "I hope for my sake you will become a good American." . . . And thus, "with hands across the sea," America joins in this tribute to her—to our—to the world's hero—Lafayette. The friend of America, the fellow soldier of Washington, the patriot of two countries.

For her part in the ceremonies of July 3 and 4, 1900, Mrs. Daniel Manning was awarded the medal of a chevalier of the Legion of Honor.

A unique position at Jamestown

But for this aid the encroaching waters would have washed away the embankments already erected and thus obliterated all traces of the first successful settlement upon this continent.

> First Report of the Daughters of the American
> Revolution to the Smithsonian Institution, 1899

The Association for the Preservation of Virginia Antiquities was chartered at Richmond on February 13, 1889, with the main object of owning and preserving Jamestown and the old ruin and graveyard. The association failed in its numerous efforts to purchase the land; ultimately, it was presented as a gift by the owners of the island, Mr. and Mrs. E.C. Barney. The Congress of the United States appropriated $10,000 to preserve the ancient landmark. When the money ran out, the safety of the historic spot was still not assured, the tidal James River being a constant threat. During Mrs. John W. Foster's administration as President General, 1895–1896, a resolution was presented and seconded at the Fifth Continental Congress, in 1896, "That a peculiar duty rests upon the Daughters of the American Revolution to assist in its restoration and preservation, . . . that this Congress Daughters of the American Revolution appropriate a sum of money to the preservation of this historic spot which will be sufficient at least to show hearty recognition of the aims and purposes of this undertaking." Although the resolution was not voted upon, a further motion, offered by Mrs. Mary S.

Lockwood, that the DAR give $100.00 was adopted. It was felt that this token sum would show the interest and support of the DAR, and that individual members would then join the association and assist further.

To commemorate the 300th anniversary of the 1607 settlement of Jamestown, the 13th Continental Congress meeting in 1904 decided to erect a permanent memorial on Jamestown Island. The Jamestown Committee recommended a year later that the memorial be in the form of a permanent building. From a dozen plans, they chose to build, at a cost of $5,500, a replica of Malvern Hill on the James, one of the "best specimens known of early Colonial architecture. The rooms are large and convenient and the porch is unique." After completion, it would be turned over to the Association for the Preservation of Virginia Antiquities and the DAR would have no further obligation to maintain it. Although the island was bare, multitudes were expected to visit it during the coming Jamestown Exposition. In spite of the fact that the Daughters were concurrently working tirelessly to fund their own Memorial Continental Hall, they felt that this building was particularly needed. According to Lydia Pleasants Purcell, chairman of the Jamestown Committee:

> "There is no shelter there of any kind . . . . we will be the only people there to offer shelter to the world at large when they go there; and I think it puts us in the most absolutely unique position of any organization which I have ever heard of in my life."

Mr. Henry St. George Tucker, president of the Jamestown Exposition, attended the 15th Continental Congress, in 1906, with a message:

> . . . come to old Virginia. . . . as president of the Jamestown (more properly called "Jeemstown") Exposition . . . we want you to come down there and erect a building to receive the people of the world. Build it where you please. Our gates are open to you. Decorate it and adorn it as only American women can do; but let it be the centre of American hospitality for our foreigners. We ask you to do that.

On October 9, 1907, the completed "House of Rest" was confided to the keeping of the Association for the Preservation of Virginia Antiquities and received by the president of William and Mary College, the Hon. Lyon Tyler. The Virginia Daughters of the American Revolution took great interest in the house and furnished it. A tablet was erected by the Jamestown Committee that would "tell generations yet to come the story of its erection." In her dedicatory address, the President General, Mrs. Donald McLean, said "I regard this as one of the most distinctly American patriotic projects this organization could indulge in . . . .our successive generations will honor us for the unselfish patriotism we have shown."

Prison Ship Martyrs Monument

If we are victorious, and our country emerges free and independent from the contest in which she is now engaged, but the end of which we are not permitted to see, bury us in her soil, and engrave our names on the monument you shall erect over our bones, as victims who willingly surrendered their lives as the portion of the price paid for your liberty; and our departed spirits will never murmur nor regret the sacrifice made to obtain for you the blessings you enjoy.

The appeal of the prison-ship martyrs.

"A Very Dark Spot in Our Country's History" was illuminated in the November 1892 issue of the *American Monthly Magazine*. Written by Charles C. Leigh, Vice President of the Society of Old Brooklynites, the article revealed in vivid detail the horrors of British prison ships moored in Wallabout Bay during the American Revolution.

One ship, in particular, the *Jersey*, was known as "the Hell" because of its especially pestilential bearing. Its port holes were replaced with two tiers of smaller holes, each 20 inches in diameter. Crossed iron bars effectively prevented escape. Inside, "with little light and almost no fresh air, packed together like animals, poorly fed on what was sometimes spoiled and wormy food, and given water to drink that was stagnant, the prisoners, often more than a thousand at a time, died off like flies." At the end of the war, the ship was abandoned. No one boarded for fear of contagion. Soon the worm-eaten ship sank, carrying with it the records of thousands of victims, whose names had been written on its very planks.

As they died, the prisoners from the *Jersey* and the other ships were carried out by their fellow prisoners, and buried in shallow graves in the sand. There, inevitably, their bones became exposed. Although Congress was petitioned in 1803 to remedy the situation, shockingly, the bones, in greater numbers with the passage of time, lay bleaching and neglected until 1808 when a private citizen, Benjamin Ayerigg, financed their removal.

Twenty hogsheads of bones, representing over 11,500 martyred prisoners, were collected. The Tammany Society gave them a magnificent funeral on May 20, 1808, witnessed by over 30,000 persons. Thirteen large coffins were laid to rest with full military pomp. The day began with a discharge of guns from four separate locations. The grand procession, 32 sections long, was led by a trumpeter mounted on a black horse. 104 Revolutionary veterans acted as pall bearers. DeWitt Clinton, Mayor of New York City and Governor Daniel Tomkins participated.

However, the tomb was never finished, and time, once again, took its toll. By 1839 the lot, tomb, bones and all was sold for taxes.

Patriot Benjamin Romaine, a soldier in the war, bought it and built an ante chamber over the vault. Now the citizenry became aroused, and petitioned the Legislature for permission to remove the bones. However, Romaine successfully fought these attempts and at his death in 1844 he, too, was buried in the vault.

By 1873 the grave was once again in disrepair. Quietly, the city of Brooklyn placed the old, broken and defaced coffins in new boxes, and removed them to a newly built brick vault at Washington Park. Congress was petitioned, over and over again, to provide an appropriation for a monument.

Eventually, the city and state of New York promised $75,000 on condition that $25,000 be raised privately. This Mrs. Stephen V. White of Long Island undertook to do.

On November 7, 1896, Eliza M. Chandler White organized Fort Greene Chapter DAR at Brooklyn, New York to raise the funds to build the monument. She personally collected nearly $18,000. In 1899 the Prison Ship Martyrs' Association of the United States, composed of representatives of the prominent patriotic societies of Revolutionary interest, was formed to be the official vehicle for collecting the funds. The President General of the National Society was a trustee. In 1900 the United States Congress raised the ante by pledging another $100,000 on the condition that both the New York and private funds materialize. By 1904, the task was completed, and Mrs. White, feeling as Moses "must have felt when he reached the promised land and was not permitted to enter in," discovered that the public appropriations had expired after two years. Fortunately, they were renewed. At the 14th Continental Congress in 1905 a total of $202,338.63, was on hand. Mrs. White's illness and subsequent death on June 2, 1907 contributed to delays in completing the project.

The cornerstone for the monument to the Revolutionary hero-martyrs was laid on October 26, 1907. On November 14, 1908, while the bands played the "Dead March from Saul," the great flag shrouding the top of the 145-foot shaft was slowly lowered and the monument was unveiled. President-elect William Howard Taft delivered the oration. As reported in *American Monthly Magazine*, the monument was presented by Gen. Luke Wright, secretary of war; accepted by Governor Hughes of New York and talked about by the Grand Sachem of the Tammany Society. The Regent of Fort Greene Chapter, Mrs. William C. Beecher, occupied the place of honor.

The Pilgrim Memorial Fountain

The Pilgrim Tercentenary in 1920 provided the perfect occasion to honor the staunch women who, in 1620, bravely followed their husbands across unfamiliar waters to an unknown land to make a new and better life. The same 29th Continental Congress that elected Mrs. George Maynard Minor President General 1920 – 1923 voted to participate in some way in the significant anniversary. Mrs. Minor, after consulting with Mr. Arthur Lord of the Congressionally appointed Pilgrim Tercentenary Commission, presented the National Board of Management with the concept of a Memorial Fountain. McKim, Mead & White of New York were chosen as architects of the $25,000 monument; the sculptor was C. Paul Jennewein. By April, 1922, the necessary funds had been secured and several appropriate sites selected. Numerous delays plagued the project and at the close of Mrs. Minor's administration construction had not begun. She continued as chairman of the committee to erect the fountain during Mrs. Anthony Wayne Cook's administration, 1923 – 1926. Unsightly buildings were removed; a proposed parking lot was relocated. Finally on June 24, 1925 the Pilgrim Memorial Fountain at Plymouth, Massachusetts stood ready for dedication in a handsome location in the memorial park reservation on the waterfront, property of the Commonwealth of Massachusetts. Its perpetual care was guaranteed by the Department of Public Works of that state.

In her dedicatory remarks, Mrs. Minor greeted the Daughters who, she said:

> . . . gather together to do honor to the memory of the heroic women of the *Mayflower*. . . . The Pilgrims belong to no one state or section of the country; they belong to all of us, whether we come from north or south or east or west. Their spirit and ideals are the spirit and ideals of America. . . . Their names, with few exceptions are not household words on our tongues, like those of Miles Standish, or William Bradford and the rest. They figure only in the passenger list of the *Mayflower* and only as "Mary" or "Katharine," etc., wife of So and So. The family names of but few are given. . . . We may read the tragic list for ourselves. The wife of John Tilly—who was she? By what name was she called in those terrific years of sorrow and suffering? The maidservant of the Carvers—who was she? What faithfulness and courage must have been hers to follow her master and mistress into such an adventure. . . . They set the pace and blazed the trail which we have followed ever since, and, please God, we still will follow it as long as the nation shall endure.

The President General, Mrs. Cook, continued in the same vein:

> . . . The Pilgrim Fathers were a godly company of brave men and true, whose like the world seldom produces. . . . But the world has come to know that, doughty as were their souls, and firm as were their convictions, they never could have kept the faith and finished the established course, had it not been for the love, the tenderness, the sympathy and the spiritual morale of the Pilgrim Mothers. . . . It is not so much to their heroism, dauntless as it was, as it is to the ineffably sweet, sterling character of their womanhood, that we, the Daughters of the American Revolution, bow our heads in tribute today.

Further praising their example, she made an observation strangely familiar in this last decade of the 20th Century:

> We hear much in this age of new freedom and of equality among the sexes, "of finding one's self," "of living one's life," "of expressing one's individuality and of not surrendering it at marriage." In this latter connection indeed the Lucy Stoner [sic] cult would dissuade our young

women of today from assuming their husbands' names in marriage. Victims of some strange inferiority complex, they would persuade our feminists not to submerge their names and their fame at the altar. . . . Such movements as these, ephemeral as they are, constitute an attack upon the family as a unit and as an institution and upon the honor and credit of the father's name established since the time when God gave Moses the ten commandments upon Mount Sinai.

Mrs. Cook consecrated the memorial to those women of an earlier time and asked that we, the Daughters, consecrate ourselves anew, as well, to our country and our homes. The inscription on the fountain reads:

> They brought up their families in sturdy virtue and a living faith in God without which nations perish.

Marking trails

We must not allow our past to slip away from us, but talk our history, teach our history and live surrounded by its memorials.

Mrs. Charles Oliver Norton, State Regent, Nebraska DAR, 1911–1913, American Monthly Magazine, March 1909

Where foot touches earth a path is formed. Footpaths give way to wagon trails. Wagon trails give way to roads. Roads give way to highways. With the proliferation of the automobile early in the 20th century the old trails in their raw purity were doomed. They stood in mute testimony to journeys of historic significance. The trails, or at least the memory of the trails, had to be preserved.

By 1903, the DAR in Kansas had recognized the need to mark the *Santa Fe* trail. In 1909 the State Regent reported that "The material selected for the markers is of red granite from Oklahoma . . . . 95 stones are placed along the trail . . . the great Santa Fe trail is so permanently marked in the state of Kansas that the course will no longer remain a matter of conjecture." In 1906, the Missouri Daughters decided that the old trails of that state should be reblazed into modern roads, memorializing the state's pioneers. Their project, the Missouri State highway, was dedicated on October 28, 1911. The Colorado Daughters reported in 1909 that they, too, had been engaged in marking the Santa Fe trail.

Privately opened, the trail was successful in encouraging trade. In 1824, at a cost of over $30,000, the federal government made surveys and obtained concessions from the Osage Indians guaranteeing unmolested passage over 775 miles beginning on the Missouri River and traveling through Council Grove, Kansas, along the Arkansas River to Dodge City where it divided. The more direct but also more dangerous southern route went through Cimarron and Santa Fe, New Mexico; it joined the northern route at Las Vegas, Nevada.

Santa Fe Trail marker, Kansas

The Nebraska Daughters realized in 1908 that the *Oregon Trail* was in danger of being forgotten, and determined to restore it in their state. Congress introduced a bill in April 1908 providing $50,000 to mark the route and commemorate the deeds of those who established and traveled the trail.

Lewis and Clark's discovery of the Columbia River prompted John Jacob Astor, in 1811, to send the ship *Tonquin* to establish a trading post on the Pacific. A reinforcement party, headed by Robert Stuart, was sent overland following the trail of Lewis and Clark. Returning, they missed the headwaters of the Missouri River, strayed from the known trail, and following the Platte river, blazed the Oregon Trail. At first this best known trail led traders, trappers, missionaries west to Oregon. With the migration of the Oregon "Home Seekers" in 1843, it became a great national highway. The discovery of gold led to a change of perspective. Oregon became a small outpost on the "California Trail."

Before American history came to this continent, the narrow trail of the *Natchez Trace* carried travelers from the Natchez bluffs to the Tennessee Bend. 1801 saw the making of surveys, the conclusion of treaties with the Choctaw and Chickasaw, and the building of a road that brought a bond of union where isolation once reigned, from Natchez to Nashville. In 1909, Tennessee, Alabama and Mississippi Daughters set to work to rescue the memory of the Natchez Trace.

Further markings included Vermont's *Old Crown Point Road*, the *Herkimer Route* in New York, Ohio's *Harrison Military Trail*, and others along the Santa Fe trail in Missouri and New Mexico. West Virginia and Maryland were trying to locate the *Braddock Trail*.

By 1912, the Missouri DAR's concept of a *National* or *Cumberland Road* embracing Braddock's Road, the Santa Fe Trail, Kearney's Road and the Oregon Trail emerged. With the establishment of the National Old Trails Road Committee by Mrs. Mathew T. Scott, President General, NSDAR broadened its interest in roads. "The next three years may see a great National Highway stretching from the Atlantic to the Pacific and a network of historic trails through the various states as a result of our good roads' spirit," enthused Miss Elizabeth Butler Gentry, chairman of the committee.

The Century Company permitted its "Madonna of the Prairies," painted by Irish, to be renamed the *Madonna of the Trail* and to serve as the committee symbol. Miss Gentry described the Madonna: "At the front of a canvas covered prairie schooner is seen a mother 'and child, wrapped in a Paisley shawl; through the halo-like opening the strong arms of the father are seen driving toward the setting sun: a loaf of bread, a tin cup and a rifle finish the picture whose dramatic appeal grips the heart

The Madonna of the Prairie

and fires the brain." For fund-raisers red, white and blue automobile pennants and the committee pin, featuring a silver gilt Madonna of the Trail, were sold. Contagious excitement infected the Daughters of Indiana who planned to erect a monument bearing a bronze replica of the "Madonna of the Trail."

That same summer, Miss Gentry met Col. William F. Cody (Buffalo Bill) at a party where the colonel told a tale of the first exhibition of his Wild West Show in London. The Prince of Wales (later King Edward) and four European monarchs commanded a ride in Cody's "Deadwood Coach"; Cody would be the driver. After placing his guests inside the coach, the Prince took his seat with Cody and said, "You probably have never held four kings before." "Better than that, I hold four kings and the joker," quipped Cody. The witty remark earned fame and fortune for Buffalo Bill. The Princess of Wales and the royal children attended the next day's performance; requests for rides around the show ring, with Indian attack, rescue and all, poured in. Col. Cody booked royalty only; the coach was filled every night of the show's long run.

When his story ended, Col. Cody invited Miss Gentry and her friend, Miss Green, to ride in the Deadwood Coach next day. They laughingly agreed on condition that he present the coach to the DAR Old Trails Committee. Much to their astonishment, he said he *would* give a coach, not the Deadwood; that was promised to the Smithsonian. Miss Gentry received a letter from W. F. Cody dated October 26, 1912:

> Dear Miss Gentry: Am glad you have one of the original old Concord stage coaches. I have several of the old relics, but which one of them my men sent you, I don't know, until I get to the ranch. Then I'll take pleasure in giving you its history. I think the one you have was built by the Abbott Downing Company at Concord, New Hampshire, in 1863, was shipped around the Horn to California and was used on the California stage lines; finally worked its way East on the Ben Holliday over-land stage line to Old Fort Laramie; then used by Cheyenne and Deadwood Black Hills line. It has been baptized in blood many times.

The coach was placed on exhibition at the Swope Park Zoo, Kansas City, Missouri.

The National Old Trails Road Association was formed in April 1912 to "assist the National Society, DAR to carry forward its purpose of making the National Old Trails Road the National Highway." An organization of men, boasting 7,000 members in 1913 and headed by president, Judge J.M. Lowe of Kansas City, Missouri, its function was, as Miss Gentry put it, "to handle the basic and practical side of the question." She said the DAR, "handles the historic and sentimental side of the question."

They blazed their way across the nation, painting telegraph poles with the national colors, placing red, white and blue road markers, and promoting funds and enthusiasm. Mrs. Elisha E. Rogers of Connecticut, in 1914 wrote, "I am rather surprised that the Massachusetts State Highway Engineer did not recognize the *Old Boston Post Road* under that name. Why, there is a new book published with that title. Yet, after all, it is not so strange, for he may be a rather young man, and this is ancient history." *Daniel Boone's Trail*, lost for more than 100 years, was located and marked, from Salisbury, North Carolina, through east Tennessee, Virginia, across the Cumberland Gap and into Kentucky, ending at Boonesboro. Seeking the opportunity to "see America as America has never been seen before," the committee planned a DAR motor pilgrimage over the Old Trails Road to the Panama Exposition in San Francisco in 1915.

Although an Old Trails Bill was introduced in Congress by the Hon. William P. Borland in 1911, it failed to pass. Congressman Borland maintained his interest in the road. Even as the war in Europe interfered with non-military projects, the need for a National Road became ever more obvious as the railroads struggled to transport men and supplies. By 1921 the road had been completely built or re-built from Washington to within a few miles of St. Louis. The road through Illinois was under contract; in Missouri it was also assured. Kansas, Colorado, New Mexico, Arizona and California all showed progress. Concurrently, the Texas DAR was working on the *Old Spanish Trail* which ran 3,500 miles, from Florida to California; and Michigan was interested in the *Old Macinac Trail*. All across the nation, from coast to coast, from north to south, Daughters were locating and marking the pathways of the past. The DAR prepared to make a concerted effort, by letter and petition, to push the DAR Old Trails Road Act through Congress and, at the same time, to raise the funds to complete marking the 3,050-mile National Old Trails Road from ocean to ocean.

The resolution passed by the 30th Continental Congress meeting in 1921 is thorough:

Whereas, there has been introduced, and is now pending in the House of Representatives, a bill introduced by Mr. Zihlman, of Maryland (H.R. No. 2412), known as the "Daughters of the American Revolution Old Trails Act," and

Whereas, by the provisions of said bill the highway known as the National Old Trails Road is to be rebuilt as an ocean-to-ocean highway by the respective States through which it passes, and of the uniform width of 60 feet, and

El Camino Real marker, Louisiana

Whereas, said bill also provides that when that portion of said highway lying within any State has been completed according to the approved specifications of the United States Government guarantees to reimburse to such State one-half of the cost of construction within that State, and

Whereas, the construction of such a roadway over the historic trails which compose it appear to be a military and postal necessity, and

Whereas, said road when constructed will stand as the noblest monument which could be erected to the memory of those of our ancestors who as pioneers used those old trails as the gateway from the East to the West, and who by their daring and suffering gained and retained the great Northwest for our country; and

Whereas, it is believed that if the Daughters of the American Revolution will stand united in the effort to foster and increase the strong sentiment for the construction of this road which already exists, said bill may be passed at the present session of the United States Congress; now therefore

Be It Resolved, That the National Society of the Daughters of the American Revolution in Continental Congress assembled earnestly urge upon the Congress of the United States the passage of H.R. No.

2412, known as the Daughters of the American Revolution Old Trails Act at the present session of Congress;

Resolved Further, That the members of this Continental Congress now present be requested to see or communicate with their Senators and Representatives in Congress during the present week and personally urge upon them the passage of said bill;

Resolved Further, That copies of this preamble and resolution be at once forwarded to the President of the Senate and the Speaker of the House of Representatives.

The United States Congress continued to dally. At the 33rd Continental Congress, in 1924, the new national chairman of the committee, Mrs. John Trigg Moss, recognized that the original DAR plan conceived more than ten years earlier to mark the highway from coast to coast was not only excessively costly, but also that it duplicated work that had been done subsequently by the National Old Trails Association and the Automobile Associations. Under her leadership the DAR passed a new resolution:

. . . To erect in each of the twelve States through which the National Old Trails Road passes, viz., Maryland, Pennsylvania, West Virginia, Ohio, Indiana, Illinois, Missouri, Kansas, Colorado, New Mexico, Arizona and California, one marker of dignified and pretentious proportions, to cost approximately one thousand dollars, these markers to be as near alike in size and design as will be consistent with the location and surroundings, and each marker to definitely mark an historic spot or commemorate some great act of historical interest of the Revolutionary period, these markers to bear with other inscriptions the insignia of the NSDAR, and to be known as the National Old Trails Road Memorial Markers; . . .

A practical woman, Mrs. Moss decided that she would wait to select a design until after 1926, when the $12,000 had been secured. In 1927, at the 36th Continental Congress, she proposed, "a monument, not a marker—to be the figure of a pioneer mother, to be known as 'The Madonna of the Trail.'"

The Madonna of the Trail

The National Old Trails Road Association will assist your committee in the erection of memorial monuments on the National Old Trails Road by guaranteeing the expense of erection of same; and we will assist the committee in the location of the sites for these monuments.

Judge Harry S. Truman, President, National Old Trails Road Association, February 26, 1927

With funding assured, not only to sculpt and cast twelve monuments, but also to place and erect them, Mrs. John Trigg Moss presented the wax model of the Madonna, sculpted by August Leimbach, of St. Louis. Displayed was a figure of a mother, "showing fortitude, perseverance, and energy in her bearing; and the foot pressed forward, as well as the grasp of the gun, expresses firm determination. Her face is one of beauty and of strong character—the face of a Mother who realizes her responsibilities, and trusts in God." The cost of carving the statues in stone or granite was prohibitive. A composite, "Algonite stone," with qualities of density, endurance and beauty, was chosen to cast the 10-foot, 5-ton statues. With a base six feet high, and a foundation two feet above ground, each monument is 18 feet over all, weighing 17 tons.

Judge Truman addressed the 37th Continental Congress. He had traveled across the continent with Mrs. Moss, from Bethesda, Maryland to Albuquerque, New Mexico, in search of the perfect locations for the statues. He thought the Daughters assembled in congress would enjoy hearing some anecdotes about the spots chosen.

> They tell a story about a tornado in Kansas that took the tin roof off a barn, rolled it up so it was unrecognizable, and the owner sent it to a famous motor car manufacturer in Detroit. In due course he received a letter from the factory, saying that it would cost $48.50 to fix the car, but how in the world did it get in that shape?

> We found the end of the Santa Fe Trail in Missouri at every town on the Missouri River from Booneville to Kansas City and enough first schools in every State to fill a book.

Truman did more than joke, of course. As president of the organization founded in 1912 to assist the DAR, he believed in the

importance of the National Old Trails Road. He said "This great American Republic is what it is today because of your ancestors and the National Old Trails Road. . . . It is entirely right, proper and very appropriate for you to dedicate these beautiful monuments in the various States through which the National Old Trails Road runs. This road, with the railroad which followed along it, was the artery for the pioneer settlement of the whole West."

The sites selected for the monuments were Bethesda, Maryland; Washington County, Pennsylvania; Springfield, Ohio; Richmond, Indiana; Wheeling, West Virginia; Vandalia, Illinois; Lexington, Missouri; Council Grove, Kansas; Lamar, Colorado; Albuquerque, New Mexico; Springerville, Arizona; and Upland, California. The statues were transported from their point of manufacture, St. Louis, in a great cradle of sand. The first was dedicated in Ohio on July 4, 1928; the second in West Virginia on July 7; and the third in Kansas on September 7. Altogether, ten were erected and dedicated in 1928. February 1, 1929, saw the 11th monument dedicated in California, with the final link, at Bethesda, Maryland, dedicated during the 38th Continental Congress on April 19, 1929.

Twelve Madonnas of the Trail, one in each National Old Trails Road state, testify to the fortitude and perseverance of the pioneer mothers.

Preserving historic relics

Preserving relics of the lives and service of the men and women who achieved American Independence is part of the first objective of the Daughters of the American Revolution. The first exhibition of those relics took place at the Columbian Exposition at Chicago in 1893. When Congress chartered the DAR in 1896, it gave the National Society the privilege of depositing its relics in the Smithsonian Institution or the National Museum, on its own terms. The members were delighted to have a safe repository for their family treasures. One of the colorful features of the early Continental Congresses was the presentation of these historic gifts.

At the 23rd Continental Congress, on April 24, 1914, during a general revision of the Constitution of the National Society, the office of Curator General was created. "It is proposed to add, 'and a Curator General,' which means an officer in charge of the museum." The change was put forth by the Revolutionary Relics Committee to allow the museum to "develop better, be more dignified . . . ." At the time, the museum occupied a passageway in Continental Hall. The most valuable relics were hidden away; there was no suitable space in which to display them. The adoption of the motion elevated the museum to a position equal with the library and prepared the way for today's modern DAR Museum with its well-lighted gallery and movable displays.

The first major loan exhibit in the DAR Museum was mounted during the administration of Mrs. Richard Denny Shelby, President General 1980 – 1983. Titled "The Jewish Community in Early America," the exhibit was initiated by John L. Loeb, Jr., Ambassador to Denmark, to honor his late grandmother, Adeline Moses Loeb, a DAR member in New York. The gala opening attracted such luminaries as former President Gerald Ford and Postmaster General William Bolger.

Record keeping

On January 15, 1892 the Historian General was directed to condense into the form of the "year book" the life histories contained in the files of application papers. The first *Lineage Book of the Charter Members of the Daughters of the American Revolution*, edited by Mrs. Lockwood, was subsequently published in 1895. For almost 50 years, a valiant effort was made to condense the information and print the books. The membership always increased faster than the volumes could be published. At any one time, half, at best, of the application papers had been processed. Ultimately, 166 volumes of lineage, 1,000 application papers per volume, and as many as ten volumes per year, had been filled when the task was discontinued in 1939.

The Act of Incorporation signed by President Grover Cleveland in 1896 required that the National Society should report its proceedings annually to the Secretary of the Smithsonian Institution. The Secretary would then pass pertinent portions along to Congress. It was understood that the report to Congress would be in printed form. Since the official Proceedings of the early Continental Congresses were voluminous, a special condensed report was transmitted to the Smithsonian and printed by the Government Printing Office at government expense. The *First Report to the Smithsonian Institution,* edited by a special committee and published in 1899, covered the first seven years of the National Society. Subsequent reports were compiled annually by an Assistant Historian General until 1914 when that office was renamed Director General in Charge of Report to Smithsonian Institution. The Constitutional revision of 1919 recorded a further name change to Reporter General to the Smithsonian Institution. When the National Society was notified in 1974 that it would have to pay the cost of having the report printed, an alternative was sought. It was found that the annual proceedings of each Continental Congress, edited by the Recording Secretary General and published by the DAR, would meet the provisions of the Act of Incorporation. Therefore, the 77th Report to the Smithsonian Institution, covering the years 1973 – 74, was the last. Although the office was not abolished, the title was changed to Reporter General and other duties were assigned. The proceedings of the first 18 Continental Congresses were incorporated in *American Monthly Magazine.* Every year since 1909, the National Society has published a separate volume of its annual proceedings. The *Proceedings of the 100th Continental Congress* will appear in 1991.

A Resolution passed during Mrs. Russell William Magna's administration in 1933 urged the members to press their legislators to provide funding for the preservation, restoration and photostating of early census records, particularly those of 1800, 1810, and 1820, which were in danger

Researcher studying French language account of the "Adresse du major-general Jackson a son armee" in L'Ourmier de la Louisiane, published at New Orleans, January 25, 1814.

of destruction because of constant handling. Many had been removed from circulation because of their shabby condition. Dutifully the Daughters wrote their letters, and one particular Daughter, Mrs. Lue R. Spencer, wrote persuasively, to President Franklin D. Roosevelt twice, the Librarian of Congress, and others. She was able to report to the 43rd Continental Congress in 1934 that 221 volumes of 100,826 pages had been photostated and rebound on "almost indestructible" paper. Another nineteen volumes were restored; the original volumes with their "pages of quaint handwriting" would be "preserved and cared for with the reverence they deserve."

Over the years, hundreds of thousands of pages of genealogical records have been located in unpublished sources, assembled, typed, bound and placed in the DAR Library, helping to make it one of the most outstanding genealogical reference libraries in the nation. Supplementing the DAR Library, the Seimes Microfilm Center was established during the administration of Mrs. Erwin Frees Seimes, President General 1968–1971. Filmed and placed there were copies of all DAR application papers. In addition, the Center contains unpublished, non-copyrighted records of the Genealogical Society of the Church of the Latter Day Saints, Federal and State censuses, and state, regional and family records.

Valley Forge Memorial Bell Tower

*I have made special efforts for several years to dispose of
our property at Valley Forge to those who would preserve
it for its historic associations and hallowed memories. Not
meeting with any encouragement, I am now obliged to
make a sale at the earliest possible date, regardless of what
use the purchaser may make of the property. If the
"Historic Hills of Valley Forge" should fall into the hands
of those who would use them for speculative purpose, it
will be a source of deep regret to many.*

> J.B. Carter, letter to Mrs. Benjamin Harrison,
> October 5, 1891

Carter's lightly-veiled threat to sell his property at Valley Forge,
Pennsylvania, to the first bidder was reminiscent of the Mary Washington Monument episode at Fredericksburg, Virginia, in 1889. Stepping
up the pressure, Carter sent Mrs. Harrison a second letter on October
12 and a third, October 15. Each communication suggested that he
would be forced to sell to speculators who were eying the property. He
distributed a circular that stated that the land provided "A splendid
location for a large Summer Hotel," and that it was "a good location for
general manufacturing purposes." Mrs. Harrison's reply of October 18
bore the news that the DAR board had received the October 5th letter
and that a committee had been appointed to "consider the feasibility of
making the purchase." But "some facts have come to the knowledge of
the ladies: viz. that the headquarters and the surrounding grounds of
ten acres have already been purchased by another society. . . . I have
heard some express the fear that the ownership by two societies might
provoke considerable friction."

Carter denied that the land had been sold. The evidence suggests
that he may have been confused by the existence of two societies with
similar names. Each time he wrote to Mrs. Harrison, he addressed her
as President of the Society of the Daughters of the Revolution. Perhaps
J.B. Carter was unknowingly conducting negotiations with two organizations at once. Be that as it may, the DAR did not undertake the project.

In 1893, the Pennsylvania Legislature purchased about 475 acres as a public park and historic landmark.

Over the years, a number of monuments were placed and dedicated to the memory of soldiers who died in the camp. In 1903, Dr. W. Herbert Burk began to dream his dream of a wonderful shrine, comprising a chapel, a carillon, and more. Commemorating the sesquicentennial of American Independence, the Star Spangled Banner National Peace Chime was dedicated at Valley Forge on July 4, 1926. The thirteen bells representing the original thirteen states, funded largely through the DAR, formed the nucleus of the National Carillon, which was housed in a temporary wooden tower.

Time passed and the tower deteriorated. The carillon, now consisting of 49 bells, one for every state in the Union and a National Birthday Bell, was not only insecure, it was unsafe. Rev. John Robbins Hart, Chaplain at the Washington Memorial Chapel at Valley Forge, began actively seeking funds to build a permanent home for the bells. In that patriotic summer of 1941 his plan for an imposing stone tower seemed within easy grasp. With the bombing of Pearl Harbor on December 7, support evaporated as American interests were, of necessity, directed toward war in the Pacific. Frantically, Dr. Hart tried to press the project on the National Society. When Mrs. William H. Pouch, President General 1941 – 1944, brought Dr. Hart's proposal to the attention of the executive committee of the National Society, it was politely turned down. The DAR was already deeply involved in financing the bells for the carillon and did not want to assume another obligation. Dr. Hart called it a "staggering blow" and responded with a letter of such emotional force that by the 51st Continental Congress, meeting at Chicago May 4 – 7, 1942, he appeared as an invited guest to address the Daughters on his project.

> The faith of General Washington is our faith. We believe in God and man, and the liberty for which Americans have always been willing to work, fight and die will be proclaimed from this magnificent tower, erected as a memorial to a free American people by a free American people.

Dr. Hart was successful. The National Society pledged to help raise $75,000 to build the tower and on April 13, 1944, Mrs. Pouch laid the cornerstone. However, although the National Society agreed to help,

*The Valley Forge Memorial Bell Tower,
dedicated April 18, 1953.*

the timing was wrong; further, the terms of the project were not satisfactory. It was difficult to raise money when the war effort so obviously came first. Mrs. Frank Edgar Lee, Historian General in the administration of Mrs. Julius Young Talmadge, President General 1944–1947, suggested that the DAR pay for the tower partly with War Bonds, to be held until the close of the war. Dr. Hart did not accept the plan. And he expected to have the authority to change specifications without notice. Moreover, costs were rising. In spite of so many difficulties, Mrs. Lee was able to galvanize the members into pledging $119,859 for the tower. Construction during the administration of Mrs. Roscoe C. O'Byrne, President General 1947–1950, brought the base of the tower, called the Memorial Room, almost to completion. Funds raised by the close of her term totalled over $250,000; much more than the early request for $75,000. But there was disagreement over the name of the building. Dr. Hart's accession to the National Society's insistence that it would be called the Valley Forge Memorial Bell Tower solved the difficulty. During Mrs. James B. Patton's tenure as President General, 1950–1953, the decision was made to complete the building. A day-long train pilgrimage to the site by more than 400 Daughters on the Sunday before the opening of Congress in 1952 increased enthusiasm and helped bring the project to its moment of dedication on April 18, 1953.

This Tower is dedicated by the National Society, Daughters of the American Revolution, to those patriots of the Revolutionary War whose faith and courage won and established American Freedom, and to those heroes of World Wars I and II who defended and preserved that blessed heritage.

Cornerstone inscription, Valley Forge Memorial Bell Tower

Frank P. Law, Carillonneur, gave the dedicatory carillon recital. Main speaker for the day was the Hon. Ivy Baker Priest, Treasurer, United States of America. Mrs. Patton dedicated the Bell Tower and presented it to the Rector, Church Wardens and Vestry of the Washington Memorial Chapel. Rector, Dr. John Robbins Hart, accepted the Bell Tower, considered to be the finest of its kind in the world.

During the administration of Miss Gertrude Carraway, President General 1953 – 1956, all portions of the project were completed. A total of over $500,000 had been expended, a far cry from the early estimate of $75,000. The great achievement included the following: the 114-foot high stone Bell Tower, 24 feet square at the base, consisting of Memorial Room, Carillonneur's Room and Belfry; a full seven octave carillon of 56 bells; the Rose Window, made by the D'Ascenzo Studios in Philadelphia, portraying General Washington kneeling in prayer, surrounded by the symbols of the four evangelists, Matthew, Mark, Luke and John; the eight-foot, four-inch stone statue of George Washington, sculpted by C. Paul Jennewein of New York City (who also sculpted the Pilgrim Memorial Fountain in 1925); Jennewein's four-panel stone bas relief illustrating what Valley Forge means to the nation; electrification of the Carillon; bronze memorials; 64 patriot stones; honor rolls on the walls naming 8,678 veterans, floor blocks naming 59, and 218 special inscriptions on bronze; several thousand other inscriptions of state and national officers' names, chapter names, and other friends; 6 bronze gates and 15 stained glass windows.

When all was said and done, $25,000 remaining in the National Society's project account was transferred to the Investment Trust Fund and, having completed its mission, the Committee for Erection of the Memorial Bell Tower at Valley Forge was discharged.

Promoting celebrations

The Founders of the Daughters of the American Revolution went all the way back to the beginning of American history and gave birth to their society on the anniversary of the day the continent was discovered by Christopher Columbus. In 1890, with the Quadricentennial of the great explorer's first voyage clearly on the horizon, and in anticipation of the Columbian Exposition soon to be held at Chicago, the DAR modestly chose to perpetuate that particular day of all others because, "It was the sacrifice of her jewels by a woman that furnished the means that enabled Christopher Columbus to discover America." Founders' Day for the DAR is October 11, the day Columbus sighted land in the New World. Today, the National Society promotes October 12 as Columbus Day, as does most of the rest of the world, with the exception of the United States government, which has its own reasons for designating the second Monday in October.

One hundred years ago, George Washington was still held in a nearly sainted regard. The First Continental Congress, at the Church of Our Father in Washington, D.C., on February 22, 1892, commemorated the great man's birthday. Every year thereafter, Congress was held during the week of George Washington's Birthday until it was finally conceded that winter weather would usually prevail in February. Then it became apparent that if Continental Congress were going to promote the celebration of a patriotic anniversary, one occurring during a milder season would receive the honors. The 13th Continental Congress, in 1904, was the first to be held in the spring of the year. Since that time, with three notable exceptions during World War II, it has almost always been held during the week in which the 19th of April falls, and commemorates the Battle of Lexington, April 19, 1775, at Lexington, Massachusetts. George Washington's federally-approved birth date has become the third Monday in February. It is impossible for Washington's real birthday, February 22, to fall on a third Monday. The Daughters, who still hold the Father of His Country in the highest esteem, promote the celebration of February 22 as George Washington's Birthday.

By 1893, the National Society was hitting its stride by calling, on June 14th, for members to fly the United States Flag on Independence Day. The following year, they urged that June 14th, the anniversary of the adoption of the Flag, be designated Flag Day and that the flag be flown on that occasion, too. Soon the prominent display of the Star-Spangled Banner was a routine part of every patriotic celebration.

A Constitution Day observance was recommended as early as the 29th Continental Congress, in 1920. It was Miss Gertrude Carraway, President General 1953 – 1956, who suggested that a week-long observance was appropriate. The Continental Congress on April 21, 1955, agreed, by resolution. The following June 7, as the Executive Committee of the National Society presented a flag to the United States Senate, the subject was discussed. Senator William F. Knowland of California was able to introduce Senate Concurrent Resolution 140 one week later, on Flag Day, authorizing and requesting President Eisenhower to proclaim September 17 – 23 as Constitution Week. The legislation passed; Eisenhower issued his proclamation on August 19, 1955. Owing to the success of the celebration, on January 5, 1956, Senator Knowland introduced a Senate Joint Resolution to have the President designate September 17 – 23 annually as Constitution Week. The resolution was adopted on July 23 and signed as Public Law 915 on August 2, 1956. To show its appreciation for his help, the National Society presented an Award of Commendation to Senator Knowland in April, 1956.

The Governor of Kentucky first proclaimed February as American History Month at the instigation of Mrs. William H. Noel, State Chairman of Americanism. During the administration of Mrs. Frederic A. Groves, President General 1956 – 1959, an American History Month Committee was authorized. The celebration has been popular and successful, but has received less legislative success than Constitution Week. Although 1967 and 1968 were proclaimed American History Month by the U.S. Congress and the President, a permanent designation remains to be achieved in the future.

The National Society has enjoyed commemorating its own anniversaries, too. In July 1915 a gala reception honored Mrs. Mary Smith Lockwood, the Pen Founder of the DAR, on the 25th anniversary of her historic letter to the *Washington Post*. The Golden Jubilee commemorating the 50th anniversary of the organization took place from October 1940 to April 1941. In 1965, the 75th Birthday of the National Society was celebrated as the Diamond Jubilee. The Centennial of the National Society Daughters of the American Revolution was officially designated to take place between October 11, 1990, the 100th anniversary of the organizing meeting, and October 11, 1991, 100 years after the historic Regents' Meeting of October 1891, and 100 years after the rolls of Charter Membership in the organization closed.

The most recent edition of the *DAR Handbook* states that the following dates should be observed: New Year's Day, Martin Luther King's Birthday, January 15; American History Month, February; Lincoln's Birthday, February 12; Washington's Birthday, February 22; American's Creed Day, April 3; Battle of Lexington and Concord, April 19; Armed Forces Day, May (3rd Saturday, usually); Memorial Day, May 30; Flag Day, June 14; Independence Day, July 4; Constitution Day, September 17; Constitution Week, September 17 – 23; Founders' Day, October 11; Columbus Day, October 12; Veterans Day, November 11; Thanksgiving Day, Fourth Thursday in November; Bill of Rights Day, December 15; Christmas Day, December 25. It also records that "Birthdays of States and of notable patriotic persons may be appropriately observed whether or not they are legal holidays."

Educational Service

To carry out the injunction of Washington in his farewell address to the American people, "to promote, as an object of primary importance, institutions for the general diffusion of knowledge," thus developing an enlightened public opinion, and affording to young and old such advantages as shall develop in them the largest capacity for performing the duties of American Citizens.

Second of the three objectives of the National Society Daughters of the American Revolution

If the DAR has been misunderstood, its position on education as a developer of American citizenship has been largely the agency of the confusion. The National Society examines the America of the Founding Fathers and attempts, through education, to preserve it. As there are on the Supreme Court of the United States both liberal interpreters and strict constructionists, the DAR is a strict constructionist of Americanism. This position is not always popular. It can require courage to maintain such a point of view. For 100 years, the DAR has "voted its conscience," taken positions, and worked industriously to uphold its objectives. DAR opposition to communism, a proud case in point, created amazing resentment, criticism and unwelcome publicity beginning in 1918 and continuing until the world-wide collapse of communism in 1989 – 90 confirmed its judgment.

The dawn of the second century of DAR service reveals a strong program in the public and private schools of America. The American History Essay Contest for grades five through eight, and the American History Scholarship competition offering an $8,000 first place award to high school seniors, encourage thoughtful knowledge and continuing study of American history. Junior American Citizens clubs, targeting preschool through eighth grades, educate and encourage children to live as good citizens, while Citizenship Medals recognize outstanding qualities among elementary, junior and senior high school students. The DAR Good Citizen award is annually presented to thousands of top student leaders across the nation. The first DAR scholarship was given in 1892 to maintain a student at Miss Berry's School; precursor of a wealth of financing for worthy young people. ROTC Medals have been awarded by the DAR since 1967 to student cadets of outstanding ability and achievement in secondary school, junior college, college or university programs of the Army, Navy, Air Force, and Marine Corps. Annual awards to U.S. Service Academies began in 1908 with an award at the United States Naval Academy and are now given at eight institutions: The United States Naval Academy; the United States Military Academy; the United States Coast Guard Academy; the United States Merchant Marine Academy; the United States Marine Corps at Quantico, Virginia; the United States Air Force Academy; the Officer Candidate School, United States Coast Guard at Yorktown, Virginia; and the United States Naval Educational Training Center at Newport, Rhode Island.

Educational activities are directed toward DAR members, too. The National Defense Committee, established in 1926, strives to bring pertinent information to the attention of the members, thus assisting them in their efforts to develop an enlightened public opinion. The committee advocates a strong national defense, and faithful adherence to the United States Constitution. Also working to keep members informed, the Resolutions Committee meets the week prior to Continental Congress to consider resolutions received from State Societies, chapters and members. Only those adhering to the stated objectives of the Daughters of the American Revolution can be considered. Not more than twelve resolutions, plus a rededication resolution and a reaffirmation resolution are presented to the Continental Congress for action. Resolutions become the policy of the National Society once they have been acted upon favorably by the Continental Congress, and remain in effect until rescinded.

First Report to the Smithsonian—educational projects

Educational projects of the National Society reported in its first seven years included essay contests, publishing ventures, book donations, and activities in and about the schools of the nation, including (among others):

California: Published an account of ceremonies attending the planting of a sequoia as a symbol of liberty in Golden Gate Park, San Francisco; published a volume of historical sketches

Connecticut: Donated 100 volumes on historical subjects to public library in Ansonia; published historical sketches in Norwich; published forgotten songs and ballads of the Revolution in *New England Magazine*, New Haven; published a patriotic calendar, New Milford; each new member at Derby contributed one book, amounting to 300 by 1897; prizes in the high school at Stamford, first for the best essay on "Representative men of Connecticut during the Revolution," and second for the best examination in American history; cooperatively established a "Bureau of exchange of historical papers" to save time and labor

Georgia: Exhibited Revolutionary relics during the 1895 exposition, Atlanta; petitioned the State legislature in behalf of coeducation, Augusta; raised funds to house their library, Griffin

Illinois: Managed exhibit of Revolutionary relics at 1893 World's Columbian Exposition, Chicago; provided home where children of Bohemian parentage could spend evenings, and started a small school, Evanston; books of history and biography presented to Harlem settlement where many German immigrants lived, near Oak Park; worked among children of Bohemian immigrants, Bloomington; protested dismissal from government service of Miss Elizabeth Key, granddaughter of Francis Scott Key, Moline; provided library and encouraged children of foreign immigrants to spend time there, also presented medal for best essay on "Surrender of Cornwallis," Highland Park

Iowa: Supported a lecture course in American history, Clinton

Kentucky: Presented 5,000 copies of the national songs to the public schools, and gave prize for the best essay on a Revolutionary subject, Louisville; offered a prize for the best essay on "The spies of the Revolution," Richmond

Louisiana: Began collection of a library of history as annex to Howard Library and offered three gold and silver medals for essays on Revolutionary topics, New Orleans

Maryland: Exhibited relics, Baltimore; medal offered by State Regent for best essay on Maryland history from 1634 or earlier to the present date

Massachusetts: Published a paper called "Tea Leaves," Boston; chapter at Wakefield circulated petitions throughout the state to prevent demolition of Faneuil Hall; prize in grammar school for best essay on battles of Revolution commemorated by the names of the city streets, East Boston; prizes for best patriotic essays, Cambridge; prizes to senior class for essays on "The part taken by Massachusetts in the Revolution," Springfield; prizes for best essays on history of Easthampton during Colonial or Revolutionary periods

Minnesota: Published three volumes of historical papers, St. Paul

Missouri: Began fund for an alcove of American history in library, Kansas City

New Hampshire: Gave 51 volumes of American history to high school, Manchester; researched the cruiser *Reprisal*, Newport

New Jersey: Awarded prize for best essay on "Township organization and government" and topics of American history in public schools, and induced school commissioners to appoint Friday of each week for study of United States history and singing of patriotic songs, Bound Brook; last Friday of each month to be observed with patriotic exercises in all public schools, and prizes awarded for patriotic essays, Montclair; established museum of relics in restored Wallace house (George Washington's headquarters in 1778–79) at Somerville by chapters, Trenton; restored first and second floors of Wallace house, Somerville; presented prizes for study of history, New Brunswick; gave prizes for best essays on battles of Trenton and Princeton, Trenton

New York: Awarded prize for best essay on "Revolutionary struggle in the Mohawk Valley," Little Falls; worked to keep education out of politics, Buffalo; exhibited books written by chapter members to Tennessee Centennial Exposition of 1897, from Brooklyn; medals and replica liberty bells as prizes for essays on Revolutionary subjects, Poughkeepsie; gave American history books as prizes for essay on "Ratification of the National Constitution by the State of New York," Fishkill; presented prizes for historic essays, Albany; gave 150 volumes to NSDAR library from Sing Sing; Revolutionary calendar published, also exhibited historic relics and published catalog, and endowed chair of American history at Barnard College, New York City; prizes awarded in public schools at Utica, also restored name of Lafayette to a city street; prizes for best examination in American history, Cazenovia; state records presented to town library, Seneca Falls; historical pageants, Saratoga Springs; prize for best essay on "Sullivan's Raid," Geneva; American history books for town library, Ogdensburg; awarded prize for best essay on American history, Binghamton; enlarged department of American history in Vassar College library, Poughkeepsie

Ohio: Encouraged patriotic essays and books for children of Dayton; published history of pioneer women, Piqua; gave prize in eighth grade for best essay on a colonial subject, Cleveland

Pennsylvania: Donated prize for best essay on "The part taken by Pennsylvania in the Revolution," Harrisburg; gave a library, Allentown; presented prizes for best essays on "Fort Necessity," Pittsburgh; gave many prizes in the public schools for patriotic essays, donated prize for the best essay on "Benjamin Franklin," Wilkes-Barre

Rhode Island: Gave $40 for the best essay on American history to a student in the graduating class of the Woman's College at Brown University and raised funds for the same institution, Providence; supported a national university at Washington, D.C., East Greenwich; gave $500 for the Woman's College at Brown, Pawtucket

South Carolina: Influenced State endowment of chair of American history at Peabody State Normal School, Nashville; supported relics exhibition at Tennessee Centennial, Knoxville

Texas: Raised funds to endow a chair of history at the University of Texas

Vermont: Began historical library, Rutland; funded a State historical museum of relics near Bennington

Virginia: Gave $100 to the State to preserve county records, Norfolk; held instructive loan exhibit, Richmond; published historical sketches, Roanoke

Washington: Awarded prize for essay on "Why Washington refused to be king," Tacoma

Wisconsin: Prize for best essay on "Battle of Lexington," Janesville

DAR Magazine

It is a woman's work and bears the womanly
characteristics—it is pure, enthusiastic, imperfect, aspiring
and persistent.

> Ellen Hardin Walworth, Founding Editor,
> American Monthly Magazine, at Congress of
> Representative Women, Chicago, May 19, 1893

On May 7, 1892 the Board passed a resolution "That the Board of Management publish a monthly magazine which shall contain the report of the proceedings of the Continental Congress, and from time to time the proceedings of the Board of Management, and such reports as may be sent from the respective chapters, all to be under the charge of Mrs. Ellen Hardin Walworth, subject to the supervision of the Board of Management."

The First Continental Congress created an immediate need to publish. An investigation into the costs of printing and distributing the report of the Congress, added to the existing expense of communicating with the members, resulted in the provocative discovery that if the Proceedings were serialized, a monthly magazine answering all these needs and more could be issued at little or no additional net expense. Mrs. Walworth set to work at once and produced the first handsome issue of *American Monthly Magazine* with a cover date of July 1892.

For $1.00 members were urged to subscribe to a magazine "progressive in matter and in style." Volume 1, Number 1, embellished with a handsome portrait of "Caroline Scott Harrison, President General of the Daughters of the American Revolution," as a tissue-protected frontispiece, included articles of historical, educational and patriotic content. Setting a precedent that was followed for years, the lead story after a prospectus of the magazine and a statement of the principle of organization of the National Society was a biographical sketch of a prominent Daughter; for the debut issue, the preeminent Daughter, Mrs. Harrison. The 112-page magazine included an article about the memorial building the young organization planned to erect, a poem written by the editor and entitled "Our Spinning," notices, and the first installment of the Proceedings of the Continental Congress. It billed itself as *The American Monthly Magazine*, Historical and Literary.

But *American Monthly Magazine* was not the first publishing venture of the National Society.

The lamented Mrs. Flora Adams Darling had a nephew, Francis A. Adams, who edited the *Gotham*, a New York-based magazine of small circulation which could be modified to serve the National Society. The minutes of the Executive Board for November 20, 1890 show that "The By-Laws then being considered by the Committee, ... It was moved and seconded Article XVI be amended by striking out the words 'The Gotham' and substituting the words 'Adams Magazine.' Carried." The first Constitution and By-Laws of the National Society state that the *Adams Magazine* shall be the official exponent of the society.

The first issue of *Adams Magazine* appeared in January 1891. The familiar seal of the Daughters of the American Revolution, the dame seated at her wheel over the motto, "Home and Country," appeared on the cover. It was satisfactory in many ways. However, as Mrs. Darling became embroiled in controversy she tried to use the magazine to put forth her personal point of view. The third issue appeared with a cover date of July 1891. In it, Mrs. Darling aired her grievances and sowed the seeds for a new organization. By the time she resigned from the National Society Daughters of the American Revolution, *Adams Magazine* no longer carried the seal or the name of the National Society. Volume 1 No. 4 of her magazine appeared in October 1891 with a similar but subtly altered seal. The dame, in identical attitude, had been redrawn. The name on the seal was that of Mrs. Darling's newly created society, Daughters of the Revolution; the motto displayed had not changed. Many a member of DAR, receiving her copy of the editorially redirected *Adams Magazine*, was upset or confused by the war waged on its pages. By Volume 2, which began to appear in January 1892, the dust had more or less settled. *Adams Magazine* continued to be published that year. It was called *Magazine of the Daughters of the Revolution* from 1893 – 1896, when it ceased being published.

In the course of 99 years of continuous publication, *American Monthly Magazine* has evolved into the *Daughters of the American Revolution Magazine*. The first name change, to *Daughters of the American Revolution Magazine*, took effect with the July 1913 issue. In December 1937 the well-known author, Frances Parkinson Keyes, who wanted to make her own mark, changed the name to *National Historical*

Magazine just one month after she was announced as the new editor. After Mrs. Keyes' tenure had become past history, by vote of the 55th Continental Congress, in 1946, the name, *Daughters of the American Revolution Magazine,* was restored.

There have been 16 different editors of the magazine, from "alpha," Mrs. Ellen Hardin Walworth, to "omega," Miss Mary Rose Hall. Other notable editors have included Mrs. Mary Smith Lockwood, Founder, the second editor; and Presidents General Mrs. Grace L. H. Brosseau, whose editorship began 28 years after her retirement as President General, and Miss Gertrude S. Carraway, who retired as magazine editor following her election as President General in 1953.

From 1892 to 1909, the magazine published the Proceedings of each Continental Congress in monthly increments throughout the year. Recognizing that the verbatim transcript, of limited interest, was squandering valuable space, following the move of the DAR business offices to Continental Hall, and beginning with the 19th Continental Congress, the Proceedings were published as a separate book and the magazine, with a more public character, continued in the broad-interest niche it had carved out for itself.

The National Society has published a magazine continuously since 1892.

Harriet Lothrop's dream

Good citizens cannot be made suddenly. They must grow and absorb the proper elements in their youth, and the work of the public schools in that direction should be popularized by a patriotic society that will be expressly for the children and youth of the entire country.

> Mrs. Daniel Lothrop, First
> President, National Society of the
> Children of the American Revolution

Harriet Stone Lothrop

Her father, architect Sidney Mason Stone, was opposed to women writing for publication. Undaunted, his talented, dreaming daughter chose a pen name and submitted her short stories about brave, wholesome youngsters with unquenchable good spirits to the children's magazine, *Wide Awake*. The first, "Polly Pepper's Chicken Pie," appeared in 1877. Curious, Daniel Lothrop, her publisher, made an unannounced visit to the budding author, Margaret Sidney. They were married on October 4, 1881, and lived out her fantasy in the historic house they bought, the Wayside, formerly the home of the Alcott family and, later, of Nathaniel Hawthorne. There she wrote her famous series of books about *The Five Little Peppers*. Two million copies were sold in her lifetime.

Harriet Mulford Stone Lothrop had been a widow for three years when, as Regent of the Old Concord Chapter, of Concord, Massachusetts, she gave the official response to the President General's welcome at the Fourth Continental Congress on February 19, 1895:

> I would even say that the time is propitious for us convening here to form a young people's society to be called Children of the American Revolution . . . .

Each day, the business of the Congress consumed more than its allotted time. Two days were spent on elections. Finally, on the last day, February 23, the President General, Mrs. Adlai E. Stevenson, called upon Mrs. Lothrop who offered a resolution that "the Society of the Children of the American Revolution shall be organized and adopted by the Daughters of the American Revolution." Miss Ella Lorraine Dorsey endorsed Mrs. Lothrop's plan, resolving further that " . . . the youth of the country are the material from which the power of the State is drawn, and that the Children of the American Revolution be adopted in name and purpose by the Congress." Mrs. Donald McLean had the final word, seconding everything and adding that " . . . it be placed in charge of Mrs. Lothrop . . . who proposed and originated it." The motion carried unanimously.

By July, *American Monthly Magazine* boasted a new "Children's Department." There news of the rapidly organizing C.A.R. societies was promulgated along with Mrs. Lothrop's editorials and poems and stories of interest to young people. Her first article said:

> . . . We are first and last and always a *live* organization. We must remember that. Now we have come to the reason why we form such a Society as this . . . . Is it . . . to look back to the early history of our country . . . winning honor and fame that we may bask in and proclaim to the world? No! . . . Is it because we . . . feeling all the while no one but those like us who had ancestors winning this honor and fame, can possess patriotism and good citizenship? No! No! Is it because we . . . have and hold all the various delights and advancements coming to us through our Society to ourselves and ourselves alone? No! No! No!

> . . . Look back, . . . upon those brave and broad-souled men and women who made and kept this country. . . . They proclaimed a liberty that was for all men . . . and thus shoulder to shoulder for the best good of all did they fight. God was with them and they knew it, . . . not for themselves alone, but for their country—for America— to make it the land of the free!

> . . . And so this National Society, Children of the American Revolution was formed that we may help forward to patriotism and good citizenship, not only those who are eligible to membership in it, but also all those who are not eligible.

Mrs. Lothrop envisioned a society that would harness the natural energies of childhood as a force for good for the whole community. A year later, at the Fifth Continental Congress, she was able to report 812 enrolled members with "2,915 young people working like Trojans to fill out their papers." She reported that the Society was self-reliant and self-supporting. Work against the desecration of the American flag had been undertaken, along with the effort to preserve the American Sabbath. She suggested that perhaps, in the future, control of the C.A.R. should be shared with the Sons of the American Revolution and the Sons of the Revolution, however she was not convinced. Still, the suggestion had been made.

The National Society Children of the American Revolution was incorporated as a separate organization on April 11, 1895, and reincorporated on April 2, 1919 with perpetual incorporation. Members in good standing of the Daughters of the American Revolution, the Sons of the American Revolution and the Sons of the Revolution may serve as senior officers. Headquarters for the N.S.C.A.R. is at 1776 D Street, N.W., Washington, D.C., in a suite of rooms in the buildings of the National Society Daughters of the American Revolution.

Patriotic education

> *And then the mountain school work . . . it is immensely*
> *valuable. It is a great work. Now, girls, I want you to go*
> *on. You are doing a most patriotic work—the best that has*
> *ever been done in the world for any government, and as a*
> *good man said in Congress: "If you stir us up too much*
> *you can break up this government, but you will have the*
> *Daughters of the American Revolution left."*
>
> Mary S. Lockwood, Founder and Chaplain
> General, 18th Report to the Smithsonian
> Institution, 1916

The work of patriotic education was already well under way in the various states when Mrs. Charles W. Fairbanks, President General, appointed Mrs. J. Heron Crosman as chairman of the national committee in 1903. The Children and Sons of the Republic clubs for children of foreign-born parents had begun in Cincinnati in 1901. When she reported to the 14th Continental Congress, in 1905, Mrs. Crosman cited "short and pithy patriotic lectures" that had been translated into foreign languages, "clubs among the 'hoodlum' elements to prevent lawlessness and viciousness," and "elevating the souls and minds" of boys and girls by giving them "wholesome, healthful pastime." The special task she envisioned was to promote good citizenship. "Are we not 50,000 in membership, and cannot 50,000 American women, descended from the patriot makers of the nation do *anything?*"

By 1915 little girls of foreign parents were being trained in domestic economy. They were "Girl Home Makers" sewing dresses, making jelly, going to market, and serving tea. "The first lesson is how to wash the little hands and faces, begrimed with the soot of the unspeakable neighborhood." In the gentlest way possible, the clubs instilled patriotism along with household skills. Prizes were given to encourage good grades in United States history. 29 southern mountain schools received assistance. Included were the Berry School, founded at Floyd County, Georgia by Miss Martha Berry in 1902 and the Women's Christian Temperance Union Settlement School, at Hindman, Kentucky. The fee for an eight-month term at the Berry School was $62.

This busiest of all DAR committees comprised at various times Americanism, Manual for Immigrants, Welfare of Women and Children, and Better Films, and was itself, at one time, a part of the National Defense Committee. By 1932, in an effort to avoid duplication, the work had been sorted into several committees: Americanism, Approved Schools (after 1960, DAR School), National Defense, and a little later, Motion Picture. In the meantime, Children and Sons of the Republic metamorphosed into Sons and Daughters of the Republic, followed by Sons and Daughters of the U.S.A., and, finally in 1937, to Junior American Citizens.

Miss Martha Berry spoke to the 17th Continental Congress on April 22, 1908. She made the delegates laugh when she reported that:

> . . . in a log cabin, I started with a few children from the mountains in a little school. I asked them if they had brothers and sisters. I found out that the chief asset of each family were brothers and sisters.

Her aim was to uplift. Her strategy was to teach the simple things of everyday life. $50 paid the expenses of one boy for one year. Admitted on the basis of merit, the boy was expected to help farm, split rails, cook, wash, scrub and run the dairy in return. She told of one mother who had made great sacrifice to send her son to school:

> She had done without milk and butter; she had lived principally on just corn bread and coffee and meal; she had sold her only cow to keep her boy there. She could not have been more than forty-five years old, yet she looked so old and worn, she had been forgotten all these years. She wore a plain calico dress and a sun-bonnet, and she looked so tired and worn. I watched her very carefully as her boy came down the aisle to receive the gold medal. . . . When she saw her boy come up before that assembly her face changed; there were tears in her eyes and from being the homeliest face in that audience, I thought her face was most beautiful, because it was filled with that fadeless light, that beautiful light of mother-love, because her boy was receiving this honor.

The Congress reacted enthusiastically to Miss Berry's address. A resolution to take up a collection was adopted, but before it could be implemented, there was objection to setting such a precedent. Reconsidering the resolution, they decided to pledge scholarships instead. Within the space of a few minutes, fourteen boys had been guaranteed places in the school for the coming term.

In 1919 South Carolina proudly reported that "our mountain industrial school, Tamassee, . . . is an actual fact." The following year it received $1,000 from DAR outside of its home state. To criticism that schools should be supported by the states in which they are located, the chairman replied:

> Each and every section is responsible for all. All that tends to sectionalism is dangerous. Patriotic education erases the hyphen. To speak of Southern Daughters, or Western Daughters, or Northern Daughters, or Eastern Daughters, is as absurd as to call certain citizens German-Americans, and others Irish-Americans. The hyphen does not exist in either case.

Children and Sons of the Republic clubs were thriving, too. "States on the border report these clubs as comprised of Mexican youth, while Illinois, Georgia, Florida and other States report interesting clubs of Negro boys under the name of Booker T. Washington Clubs and of Negro girls under the name of Sojourner Truth Clubs."

Alabama announced the establishment of Kate Duncan Smith DAR

School to the 33rd Continental Congress, meeting in 1924. Its purposes and plans would be "purely altruistic and patriotic." The new school was named for Mrs. J. Morgan Smith, State Regent of Alabama for ten years, and Honorary Vice President General when it was brought into being. The Alabama Daughters sought and expected national support for their ambitious project from the very beginning:

> . . . as the school has above the entrance "Daughters of the American Revolution" . . . members of the organization everywhere will feel an especial pride and interest in this undertaking and will give, not only of their sympathy, but of their treasuries as well. . . . I ask and appeal to you for help in this school. It is your school; because this school is absolutely and unconditionally controlled by the Daughters of the American Revolution. It will diligently and earnestly teach the high principles on which our society is founded and upon which the very life of this government depends.

Certainly, the DAR has been faithful in its trust to the schools. It no longer tries to support as many as it did once upon a time. Six schools, the "DAR Schools": Kate Duncan Smith DAR School in Grant, Alabama; Tamassee DAR School in Tamassee, South Carolina; Berry College in Mount Berry, Georgia; Crossnore School in Crossnore, North Carolina; Hillside School in Marlborough, Massachusetts; and Hindman Settlement School in Hindman, Kentucky, benefit from the passion for patriotic education of the National Society Daughters of the American Revolution.

Kate Duncan Smith and Tamassee, built by Daughters, have held a special place in the hearts of the Daughters. One committee, the Junior Membership Committee, comprised of members between the ages of 18 and 35, dedicates the proceeds of *all* of its fund-raising activities to them. Among the buildings provided to these two schools by the National Society have been the Talmadge auditorium-gymnasium, honoring Mrs. Julius Young Talmadge, President General 1944–1947; the Allene Wilson Groves Cottage for little girls at Tamassee, honoring Mrs. Frederic A. Groves, President General 1956–1959; the Doris Pike White auditorium-gymnasium at Kate Duncan Smith, honoring Mrs. Ashmead White, President General 1959–1962; and the Adele Erb Sullivan Administration Building at Tamassee, honoring Mrs. William Henry Sullivan, Jr., President General 1965–1968.

Over the years, the schools have been the recipients of tens of millions of dollars of support as loving gifts. The 99th Continental Congress, in April 1990, reported one year's giving to DAR Schools: $591,590.98. In addition, DAR endowments to the six schools provide over $250,000 annually.

Special publications

The National Society has published a multitude of books and pamphlets in addition to regularly scheduled periodicals. Many are of great genealogical and historical value, but of limited interest beyond these specialized areas. Others have general appeal. A few are described here.

When Lewis Barrington was doing the research for his volume, *Historic Restorations of the Daughters of the American Revolution*, published by Richard R. Smith, New York in 1941 with the cooperation of the Daughters, he said that although the DAR "has never avowedly included the preservation of historic houses, the Society has done more in this field than any other organization." Barrington documented 210 restorations, both exclusively DAR projects and cooperative ventures. In her foreword, Sarah Corbin Robert, President General 1938–1941, said "To the extent that historical buildings remain a demonstration of the spirit which has made a people, to that extent their restoration is justified."

Mrs. Robert V.H. Duncan, President General 1962–1965, urged a vigorous "Know-Do-Tell DAR" attitude. Her "Diamond Jubilee" project, *In Washington, the DAR Story*, was published in 1965. So popular did the book become that it became the first of a trio of handsome four-color books the National Society published about the DAR. *In Washington* and the follow-up volumes, *Washington Landmark*, 1976, and *Pillars of Patriotism*, 1985, were extremely effective in bringing the beautiful buildings of the DAR National Headquarters into the living rooms of Daughters all over the nation and the world. Of interest to the general public, the books show many details of the DAR Museum and thirty-three State rooms. Mollie Somerville researched and compiled the three books.

During the Bicentennial of the American Revolution, it became apparent that the record of DAR-owned houses was out of date. *Historic and Memorial Buildings of the Daughters of the American Revolution* was published in 1979, during the administration of Mrs. George Upham Baylies, President General 1977–1980. An earlier Bicentennial publication, *Women and the American Revolution*, appeared in 1974 as a project of the Spicer administration.

During Mrs. Richard Denny Shelby's term as President General, 1980–1983, *The Wide Blue Ribbon*, short essays describing the administrations of each President General during the first fifty years of the existence of the Daughters of the American Revolution, was published. A cookbook, *A DAR Sampler*, also appeared at that time.

Robert Ewell Greene's *Black Courage 1775–1783*, published in 1984 during Mrs. King's administration provided important references to black participation in the American Revolution. Further, it pointed up the need for continuing research. The first volume of a series focusing on Black and American Indian service researched and compiled by staff genealogist, Elisabeth Schmidt, *Minority Military Service* appeared in 1988 during Mrs. Fleck's administration. Prepared as a membership aid to encourage minority participation in the programs and projects of NSDAR, it dealt with Rhode Islanders who supported the cause of the American Revolution. A second book, on Connecticut, also appeared in 1988. During Mrs. Yochim's administration, the Massachusetts volume appeared in 1989, followed by Maine in 1990 and New Hampshire-Vermont in 1991. Further installments of the series are planned.

A catalogue of the DAR Museum collection, *The Arts of Independence*, by Elisabeth Donaghy Garrett, appeared in 1985. This colorful coffee-table volume documents the treasures of the DAR Museum.

Improved conditions for women and children

*Prophetic souls among us believed the time had come for
an aggressive movement of the Daughters of the American
Revolution against the industrial system which encourages
or even permits the employment of children under the age
of twelve or fourteen years in mills, factories, shops,
stores, furnaces, or mines, or in agricultural pursuits
except under favorable conditions. We are against all night
labor for all minors and for shorter hours of labor and the
best hygienic and sanitary condition of work and housing.*

> J. Ellen Foster, Chairman of Committee on
> Child Labor, 17th Continental Congress, April
> 20 – 25, 1908

A crucial change has occurred over the past 100 years in the
situation of children. In the late-19th and early-20th centuries, children
were an asset, vital to the economy. When America was primarily an
agrarian society, the labor of children beside their parents on the family
farm often meant the difference, not merely between poverty and
affluence, but between starving and eating. The family that could spare
a son in apprenticeship to a trade was providing for the son and making
an investment in his future. This was fair, give-and-take, an even
exchange.

Even as the industrial revolution ushered in a new age of boom
and plenty, it perpetuated peripheral horrors, populated primarily by
child laborers, victims of poverty and misery trapped in positions of
near-slavery, characterized by low wages and inhumane conditions.
Greed placed children in untenable situations from which there was no
escape. This was exploitation.

In 1906 the Daughters voted at the 15th Continental Congress to
"endorse the bill authorizing the secretary of commerce and labor to
investigate the industrial, social, educational, moral, and physical conditions of the women and children of the United States." They followed
up the next year by establishing a Committee on Child Labor, and in
subsequent years, a Committee on the Welfare of Women and Children.
They were concerned with questions of infant mortality, the birth rate,
juvenile courts, dangerous occupations and diseases of children, and

were instrumental in the passage of the law creating the Children's Federal Bureau, established to investigate and report upon all matters pertaining to the welfare of children.

They worked with women and children, providing clothing, education, and even a home and income at times. By 1914 the DAR sponsored a National Charity Officer who personally distributed major humanitarian relief, all voluntarily contributed, and directed a corps of local charity officers as well.

One crippled child, so deformed that she had to crawl, received four operations through the auspices of the National Society. Ultimately, the woman who had donated the funds adopted the child. In another case, a young shop clerk performed unsatisfactorily at her job. The charity officer tried to become better acquainted, and took her to lunch. The girl, who was disfigured by the loss of an eye, confessed that she was embarrassed by her appearance. Within two weeks, the DAR had provided a glass eye. Her morale improved so dramatically that one month later, she was promoted to the head of her department. The officer reported, "She now has self-confidence, and is pushing her way right along." A particularly successful example of "rescue work among young girls" was reported as typical: A desperate young woman was sent to a hospital for unwed mothers where, three months later, she delivered her baby. Special nurses were provided "when the baby was with the mother, to prevent the mother from smothering it." The charity officer located the responsible man, encouraged him to marry the girl, and reported that the "little mother is now happy. They both seem fond of the little boy baby."

In 1917 the Welfare of Women and Children Committee proposed that it serve as a "lookout" committee to perform a kind of DAR triage. If the committee identified a legislative need in the community, it would be referred to the Legislative Committee. The charity officer would be informed of deplorable economic conditions and educational needs or problems would be forwarded to the Patriotic Education Committee. As it happened, the largest part of this work, although worthy, did not fall within the objectives of the Daughters of the American Revolution. By 1918, the Patriotic Education Committee directed the work and the charitable efforts of the National Society emphasized war relief.

Expositions

A discovery will be made equal, perhaps, in its effect on the world to that of Columbus, for half the population of the world hitherto holding a subordinate and too often a slavish position are suddenly elevated and set free. This is no figure of speech, for official recognition means an entrance into the affairs, the business, and the history of the world. Such recognition, developing more and more each day, is given to women in the World's Columbian Exposition.

Ellen Hardin Walworth, Founder, American Monthly Magazine, February 1893

Mary Smith Lockwood, also a Founder of the National Society, and outspoken exponent of equality for women, was a lady manager of the World's Columbian Exposition held at Chicago 1893. It was she who pressed the First Continental Congress to sponsor an exhibit there. But the infant society, while congratulating itself on its first year of accomplishment, was nevertheless fearful of taking the great step implied by committing itself to the Chicago venture. Mrs. Lockwood was bitterly disappointed to be rejected. Betraying an uncharacteristic anger, she complained, "I will not have it go out to the public that you have voted my motion down. I, therefore, ask the privilege to withdraw my motion and bring it before the Board of Management, and I will take great pleasure in sending you some literature on the subject." Mrs. Lockwood's motion was withdrawn; the literature she supplied must have been persuasive. The Second Continental Congress, representing 2,746 members, confidently decided that it would, indeed, be represented at the Exposition later that year.

Mary Virginia Ellet Cabell, President Presiding, circularized the members, writing:

So excellent an opportunity for noting what has been done by our sex, and of considering the probable issues of that remarkable phenomenon known as the "Woman's Movement," was never enjoyed before, and will probably not be so comprehensively presented in this generation again.

She urged every chapter in the United States to send as large a representation as possible for "our day," May 19, 1893, because no society should be more "largely and worthily represented than the three thousand Daughters of the American Revolution, who have based their organization upon a sentiment—the true and grand sentiment of patriotism—which must ever form the foundation of our national life and supremacy."

Participation by women in the Women's Congress of the Columbian Exposition did advance, not merely the cause of women's rights, but also the perception of American women as sophisticated and politically adept. If the exhibits shown and the 330 papers presented turned out to be primarily women preaching to women, still they were reported in the press; men were becoming aware of a new force loose in the nation. Mrs. Walworth said that recognition in the exposition set women free. She may have overstated the case. However, if women thought that their position was one of slavery, freedom was surely in the air. One aim shared by such diverse organizations as the American Woman's Suffrage Association, the Women's Christian Temperance Union, and the Daughters of the American Revolution, as well as others, was the enfranchisement of American women. Although they were frustrated by the interminable years of work required to gain the vote, from a historical perspective the passage of the 19th Amendment to the Constitution was only a few short years after the World's Columbian Exposition in 1893 and the founding of the National Society Daughters of the American Revolution in 1890.

The World's Columbian Exposition was only the first of many to which the Daughters bent their energies. At the Cotton States International Exposition, at Atlanta, in 1895, Miss Janet Richards read Miss Eugenia Washington's paper on the history of the Daughters of the American Revolution. The National Society had every reason to be proud of its exhibition at the Paris Exposition of 1900. The Grand Prix it received was the highest award obtainable, and demonstrated the extraordinary achievement of the organization, then not quite ten years old. Mrs. Sara T. Kinney's report on the exposition for the *American Monthly Magazine*, appearing in the September 1900 issue, pointed out that "The American Revolution means something to the French people . . . " Included in the honored exhibit were bound volumes of *American*

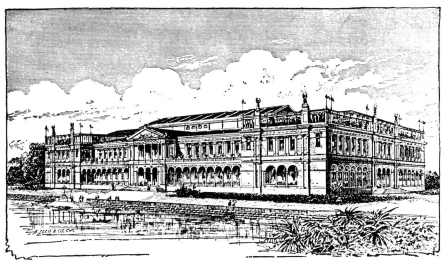

The Women's Building of the Columbian Exposition held at Chicago, Illinois. DAR Day was May 19, 1893.

Monthly Magazine, portraits of the Presidents General, samples of the DAR Insignia, spoons, stationery, historic china, application papers and certificates and a copy of the national charter issued by the Congress of the United States.

There were others, each with its special DAR Day: Tennessee Centennial Exposition, Nashville, Tennessee, 1897; Trans-Mississippi Exposition, Omaha, Nebraska, 1898; Pan-American Exposition, Buffalo, N.Y., 1901; South Carolina Inter-State and West Indian Exposition, Charleston, South Carolina, 1901 – 02; Louisiana Purchase Exposition, St. Louis, Missouri, 1904; Jamestown Tercentenary Exposition, Jamestown, Virginia, 1907; Alaska-Yukon-Pacific Exposition, Seattle, Washington, 1909; Appalachian Exposition, King's Mountain, Tennessee, 1910; Panama-Pacific International Exposition, San Francisco and San Diego, California, 1915; Sesquicentennial Exposition, Philadelphia, Pennsylvania, 1926; Sesquicentennial in Hawaii, 1928.

The National Society secured two rooms in the Social Science Building for the Century of Progress Exposition at Chicago in 1933. The walls were painted powder blue "to match the blue in the colors of our Society." Hanging on the walls were an electric DAR sign, a picture of

George Washington, pictures of DAR Headquarters in Washington, D.C. and a graph of DAR activities. Furnishings were of the Revolutionary period. The Central Division of the society furnished two hostesses a day for the duration of the exposition. DAR Day was June 14, 1933, when the State Society of Illinois and the President General, Mrs. Russell William Magna, served as hostesses. In a first-time-ever departure from established routine, the National Board of Management held its June meeting at Chicago. Three companies of the 6th Infantry, U.S. Army, preceded by the Infantry Band, escorted a parade from the "Blue Ribbon Casino," through the Science Building, to the steps of the Federal Building. Sixty-one pages, clad in white and carrying the Flag of the United States of America, the DAR Banner and the flags of the forty-eight states marched behind the escort, followed by past State Regents of Illinois, Illinois state officers, and the members of the National Board. As official hostess, the State Regent of Illinois, Mrs. Julian G. Goodhue, immediately preceded the President General and her pages. Then came other members of the National Society. The roll of the drum announced the beginning of the outdoor patriotic exercises; then they paraded again, to the Hall of States, for the balance of the program.

DAR Day and special festivities also accompanied DAR participation at: Texas Centennial Exposition, Dallas, Texas, 1936; Golden Gate International Exposition, San Francisco, California, 1939; New York World's Fairs, New York, New York, 1939 and 1964; Expo '67, Montreal, Canada, 1967; World's Fair, Knoxville, Tennessee, 1982; and the Louisiana World Exposition, New Orleans, Louisiana, 1984.

A nursing scholarship

The Philippines Chapter, organized in Manila January 4, 1913, left a legacy that endured long after the chapter itself ceased to exist. Citing extremely high infant mortality rates in the Philippine Islands, Philippines Chapter worked for years to establish a Philippine Scholarship Endowment Fund, to provide medical training for Filipino girls. Under the energetic leadership of Mrs. Caroline E. Holt, who traveled to Continental Congress year after year to report on and encourage the cause, $20,000 was set aside. The income was to provide medical scholarships to help Filipino girls through their hospital training. Nurses were educated in the United States for a number of years, returning to Manila prepared to train more nurses. In 1945, in spite of the shambles existing in the Islands because of the war, the chairman of the Caroline E. Holt Scholarship Fund Committee was able to state, "In the years since 1913 we have had the satisfaction of seeing infant mortality greatly lessened."

Although the shattered Philippines Chapter was unable to survive the war, its work and that of Mrs. Caroline E. Holt live on in the NSDAR nursing scholarship that bears her name.

The first Americans

The 30th Continental Congress, in 1921, devoted much of the third evening's program to the American Indian. Speakers included DAR member, Congressman Alice M. Robertson of Oklahoma; Mrs. Mary W. Roe, wife of a missionary to the Indians, also a member; and Mr. Thomas L. Sloan who described the bravery of several Indians during the World War and then introduced Princess Tsianina as the greatest singer in the Indian race.

Princess Tsianina was the first girl west of the Mississippi to respond to General Pershing's call for entertainers to go over seas to entertain the American Expeditionary Forces, and the first girl to sing on the Rhine after the armistice was signed. An honorary member of the Second Division of the American Expeditionary Forces and a member of the American Legion, she found an enthusiastic audience for her selections which included: "Invocation to the Sun God" and "From the Land of the Sky-blue Water." Following her rendition of a piece called "Canoe Song" the Princess described how it came to be written. Dining with the composer in New York, she said to him: "I wish you would write an Indian Opera and have a song in it in which I could tell the white race what they have done to my people in a nice way." The Daughters responded by demanding an encore.

Mrs. Roe narrated some of her experiences as a missionary. She said that she was wearing an Indian dress belonging to Princess Tsianina, "in order that you may recognize me, not only tonight, but . . . in these days that are still before us in this wonderful Congress. My blood is white; my ancestry is New England, but my beating heart is Indian."

She was especially concerned about the effects of peyote. "If any man should come into this city of Washington and pass around a dangerous drug . . . and use it for a whole night, and then with the passions and with the mind inflamed, should call this religion, if a man tried that in the city of Washington you would run him out of the city." She urged that an anti-peyote bill be passed. She also spoke out for adjudication of Indian claims through the courts. Reaching her main point, she spoke in support of improved educational opportunities for Indians. Urging the Daughters to do more, she said, "I want to know why it is that we have a scholarship even for the Filipino and not for the North American Indian?"

The Daughters, who evidently had been listening, passed a resolution on the fifth day of the Congress endorsing the American Indian Institute at Wichita, Kansas and placing it on the list of authorized schools and colleges, thus assuring it of their interest and support. The resolution also urged Congress and the State Legislatures to enact statutes to prohibit the importation and sale of peyote.

DAR interest in American Indians, as demonstrated by this early example, continued. The dual focus emphasized educational assistance

Costumed young visitors to Constitution Hall read the program of the 56th Continental Congress, held in 1947.

to Indian youth, and informing DAR members about such needs. In 1936, a subcommittee on American Indians was authorized as a part of the Americanism Committee. It was transferred to the Conservation Committee in 1937 and became a national committee in its own right, the American Indians Committee, in 1941. Today the National Society sends support to Bacone College in Oklahoma and to the Chemawa Indian School in Oregon and over $70,000 annually in scholarships to American Indian students.

Promoting good citizenship

As early as 1895 DAR chapters reported that they had "memorialized" their state legislatures to have citizenship taught in public schools.

Beginning in 1934, a committee called DAR Good Citizenship Pilgrimage recognized "Good Citizen Girls." State winners were given a trip to Washington, D.C., where they received recognition at Continental Congress, and toured the Nation's Capital. By 1948 the pilgrimage had been discontinued, and a cash award was sent in its place. A new name in 1952, DAR Good Citizens Committee, confirmed the change, but the winners, all female, continued to be known popularly as Good Citizen Girls.

As the prestige of the little round lapel pin extolling the virtues of dependability, service, leadership and patriotism increased, the unfairness of awarding it only to female good citizens became apparent. Since 1975, boys have participated in the contest on an equal basis with girls. Since the DAR Good Citizen award is annually presented to only one member of the senior class in each high school, it is a reliable barometer of truly outstanding youth. In the 57 years since the DAR began recognizing good citizens on a national basis, thousands of young men and women have been named DAR Good Citizens. Monetary awards often accompany the honor. The National DAR Good Citizen receives a $5,000 scholarship.

A more recent innovation was the Good Citizenship Medal awarded under the auspices of the National Defense Committee. This award, intended as an encouragement, may be given freely, as appropriate, in elementary schools and in junior and senior high schools. The criteria are honor, service, courage, leadership and patriotism.

Mrs. William A. Becker, President General 1935–1938, emphasized youth in her administration. "I have made it my special plea with you this year that the boys and girls of America shall not be friendless," she said, "that faith in the brotherhood of man and devotion to the free spirit of America may be kept alive in the coming generation." She developed a network of assistance for needy and deserving young people. "Becker Boys and Girls" received homes, work, clothing, music lessons, carfare: whatever they needed to enable them to continue their education. "How did Mrs. Becker ever know about me?" asked one young Becker Boy in Illinois. Concurrently, Junior American Citizens clubs developed from the Sons and Daughters of the U.S.A. clubs, growing from a total membership of 49,218 active members in 1,549 clubs in 1936 to 2,370 clubs enrolling 81,417 members by the end of Mrs. Becker's term of office. The program has remained so popular that in 1990, 230,579 JAC members were reported in 1,869 clubs teaching the principles of good citizenship, its privileges and responsibilities, loyalty to the United States of America, respect for its flag, and the history of our country and government to youngsters in kindergarten through high school.

Heirs of Liberty

In its heyday, network radio saw itself as a promoter and defender of Americanism and American values. Almost every announcement, it seemed, included parenthetical support for the right, the good, and "our boys." It is not surprising that the DAR had access to the airwaves at a time when even the commercials exuded patriotism.

"Heirs of Liberty," a series of radio broadcasts featuring historical sketches of the founding fathers and bringing to the microphone living descendants of American patriots, was broadcast in the autumn of 1941. Sponsored by the Committee of Revolutionary and Colonial Societies (Patriots' Committee) with the assistance of the U.S. Department of Justice, the 15-minute programs were broadcast nationwide over NBC's Red Network.

The Patriots' Committee, chaired by Mrs. William H. Pouch, President General 1941–1944, included representatives from, in addition to the Daughters of the American Revolution, the Daughters of the

Revolution, the Sons of the American Revolution, the Sons of the Revolution, the U.S. Daughters of 1812, the Children of the American Revolution, and the General Society of the War of 1812.

The 13 founding fathers scheduled to be portrayed in the series were George Washington, Thomas Jefferson, Patrick Henry, Benjamin Franklin, Alexander Hamilton, John Adams, James Monroe, Edmund Randolph, James Madison, Francis Scott Key, John Marshall, George Mason and Andrew Jackson. Each weekly broadcast began, of course, with the announcer's statement. Then, leading actors of the day starred in the historical sketch, followed by an interview with a descendant of the patriot cameoed in the sketch. With the exception of George Washington, whose collateral descendant, the Rev. F. Bland Tucker, a great, great, great grand-nephew, appeared on the show, all representatives were lineal.

Each member organization of the patriotic committee sent, in turn, a representative. For the third broadcast of the series, the DAR provided a great, great, great granddaughter of Patrick Henry, junior member Mrs. H. Harold Mays. Mrs. Mays was elaborately costumed for the occasion. "I wish you could see her," said the announcer, who then explained that she was dressed in a Colonial costume of brocaded old blue taffeta, worn by a member of her family at the George Washington Centennial Ball. With admiration, he told of the large cameo brooch pinned at her neck; the brooch that came down to her from the granddaughter of Patrick Henry, Sarah Shelton Aylett Fontaine.

In her remarks, Mrs. Mays, a descendant of both the eldest and the youngest daughters of Patrick Henry, said, "Today America offers the only living hope of a way of life under which men can enjoy individual liberty and freedom." Quoting her famous ancestor when the thirteen colonies were threatened with disunity on September 5, 1774, she concluded her speech with Henry's memorable, "The distinctions between Virginians, Pennsylvanians, New Yorkers, and New Englanders are no more. I am not a Virginian, but an American." Concluding with her own words, Mrs. Mays said, "Let us stand together and share alike the blessings and responsibilities of carrying forward a democratic government for free men! We are all Americans!"

Service women from Somerset, Pennsylvania, Chapel Hill, North Carolina and Huntington, West Virginia pose beside a Red Cross truck, gift of the District of Columbia DAR during World War II.

Patriotic Service

*To cherish, maintain and extend the institutions of
American freedom, to foster true patriotism and love of
country, and to aid in securing for mankind all the
blessings of liberty.*

Last of the three objectives of the National
Society Daughters of the American Revolution

It was, in part, the tragic, obvious, visible erosion of the natural love of country that inspired the organization of the National Society. For the Founders of the Daughters of the American Revolution, history and education were the means to an end. That end was patriotism.

The Civil War and its aftermath left the country so bitterly divided that the glories of 1776 were but rapidly retreating memories. The Revolutionary patriots had departed from the scene. Those eye-witness accounts that had not yet been told were lost forever. However, the sons and daughters of the Revolutionary warriors, and a few widows, who had thrilled to hear at first hand the tale of Independence dearly bought, were living still. Whether they resided in the North or the South, they knew the value of the nation so recently preserved. And knowing so well the dearness of America, they felt allegiance.

Clearly, anyone who failed to love America was uninstructed in America's history. Knowledge would inspire allegiance where ignorance caused contempt. Thus was born a noble work. The Daughters took upon themselves the task of educating a rapidly changing, widely diverse population in the special meaning of liberty for all as secured by the Constitution of the United States of America. The seed would be sown wherever the need could be shown—especially among the young. Cultivation by way of education in American history and ideals would follow. A pure patriotism was to be the harvest.

First Report to the Smithsonian—patriotic projects

*We claim this to be in no sense an aristocratic
organization. It is a patriotic organization.*
    Mary Desha

This classic work of early DAR history cited numerous instances where the fledgling organization set forth to foster true patriotism. It also effectively showed that the Daughters of the American Revolution recognized the importance of conservation from its earliest days. So important did the National Society consider tree plantings and husbanding of other vital resources, that the Conservation Committee was established in 1909, and has maintained an unbroken record of service since that time. A representative sampling of patriotic activities, including tree plantings, as reported in the *First Report*, while far from complete, includes:

California: Planted a historic arch of trees, one from each of the thirteen original states and planted a "liberty" tree, a sequoia, in soil imported from historic battlefields, in Golden Gate Park, San Francisco

Connecticut: Supported a Real Daughter, Simsbury; presented its *first* state flag to the state, Groton; encouraged patriotic books and songs, Willimantic; raised funds for monument to Francis Scott Key, Ansonia; sent a seedling of the Charter Oak to California, Norwich; published a history of "Our Flag," New Haven

Delaware: Sent a maple seedling to California

Georgia: Worked to promote a harmonious and patriotic spirit in the South

Illinois: Presented each child in the public schools with a small flag, Evanston; presented a flag to Harlem settlement, Oak Park; 12-foot flag and framed copy of Declaration of Independence to Boys' Club and 25-foot flag and 110-foot flag pole to the town, Highland Park; flag to Women's Club, Princeton

Indiana: Presented "loving cup" to battleship *Indiana*, Lafayette

Iowa: Chapters united to cause a bill to be presented to State legislature enforcing display of American flag on all public school buildings in the state; large flag to Lucas County, Chariton

Kentucky: 5,000 copies of the national songs to public schools of the city, Louisville

Maryland: Sent a mulberry tree to California, Frederick; raised funds to erect monument to the Maryland Line, Baltimore

Massachusetts: Placed framed lithograph of the flag in 200 public schools, Boston; provided for a Real Daughter, Taunton; sent an elm from the old North Bridge at Concord to California, Springfield

Minnesota: Chapters cooperated to secure order from State board of education that American flag be displayed on all school buildings during school hours; petitioned State legislature to prohibit raising of foreign flags on public buildings, St. Paul

Missouri: Placed patriotic pictures in public schools, St. Louis

New Hampshire: Influenced public schools in patriotic observances, Milford; chapters cooperated to send a rock maple from homestead of General Stark to California

New Jersey: Induced school commissioners to appoint Friday each

Junior Members practice conservation by planting a tree — 1959.

week for singing patriotic songs, Bound Brook; flag raised over school on ten important anniversaries, Montclair; sent linden tree from Washington's Headquarters to California, Somerville; supported a Real Daughter, Newark

New York: Chapters cooperated to send white oak from battlefield of Saratoga to California; presented flag to the University, Rochester; sent birch sapling to historic grove at Tacoma, Washington, Yonkers; asked board of education to set aside one afternoon each month for patriotic observances and to raise flag over school buildings on patriotic anniversaries, Poughkeepsie; presented flags to the Sons of the American Revolution, to Morristown, New Jersey Chapter, and a "gigantic" flag pole for General U.S. Grant's tomb, New York City; two trees to California, Saratoga Springs; had the salutation of the flag adopted in the public schools, Geneva; sought permission to introduce pledge to the flag in morning sessions of public schools, Binghamton; annual commemoration of the burning of the city by the British and the flight of the women and children, Kingston

Ohio: Encouraged patriotic books, Dayton; placed copy of the Declaration of Independence, Wilmington

Pennsylvania: Presented 20-foot flag to school board of Longswamp and sent earth for Liberty Tree to California; presented a flag bearing DAR Insignia to the State, Philadelphia

Rhode Island: Copies of Declaration of Independence in 13 post offices and all public schools in city, Bristol; induced citizens to display flag on patriotic anniversaries, East Greenwich; contributed to silver service of U.S. gunboat *Newport,* Newport; chapters cooperated in sending white birch from birthplace of Nathanael Greene to California

Tennessee: Contributed earth for Liberty Tree in California, Memphis; celebrated Tennessee Centennial Exposition, Wautauga

Virginia: Arranged celebration in city schools and presented portrait of Washington to each, Norfolk; paid transportation for furnishings for duplicate of Mount Vernon at Chicago World's Fair, Charlottesville

Washington: Contributed to Columbian Liberty Bell and planted grove of historic trees, Tacoma

Wisconsin: Secured legislation against desecration of the flag

Correct use of the Flag

Never in the history of our country has our flag been so
widely honored as in the past year.

> Mrs. Daniel Manning, President General
> 1898 – 1901, at Eighth Continental Congress,
> February 20, 1899

The only resolution adopted at the First Continental Congress was offered by Mrs. George Shields, and stated that:

Whereas the Flag of our Country is the emblem of our Nation, and deserves the homage of every true American citizen; and

Whereas the only distinctive national song we have is the "Star Spangled Banner"; be it therefore

Resolved, That we, the First Continental Congress of the Daughters of the American Revolution, earnestly request all American citizens, native born and adopted, whenever that song is sung or played in their presence, to show their respect and love for our country by rising and standing until it is finished.

Resolved further, That we also respectfully and earnestly recommend that the song be sung at least once a week in all the public schools of the United States, so that all American children may learn the words of the song, and learn to honor the Stars and Stripes.

As has been noted elsewhere in the text, a motivating factor in the establishment of the National Society was the idea that women were peculiarly adapted to heal the deep divisions that still existed in the United States 25 years after the end of the War Between the States. Aware of their differences, these women felt that their similarities should be emphasized. Symbolic of the rift was the *national* symbol, the Flag of the United States of America. No rule but the rule of the heart protected its dignity. No code but the code of honor existed to suggest when or how it should properly be flown. In the North, if there was no particular regard for the flag, neither was there any ill regard. In the South, readoption of the Stars and Stripes as the unifying emblem waited in uneasy abeyance. Of greatest distress to the Daughters was the flagrant disrespect shown to the flag.

In a tribute given in memory of Mrs. John W. Foster, third

President General of the National Society, at the 32nd Continental Congress, in 1923, Mrs. Amos G. Draper said:

> It was owing to the Daughters of the American Revolution that the flags of the United States were unfurled for the first time in many a southern town. When I read history and hear about all the wonderful union of the North and South, and that it is attributed to this and that, I agree, but I know that the greatest incentive, the biggest contributing factor, was the conduct of the Daughters, the leaders of the Daughters of the American Revolution in the southern states that has made that union possible.

At the Chicago World's Fair (Columbian Exposition) an incident occurred on August 21, 1893 that found its way into the *American Monthly Magazine.* A reception was given to West Point cadets in the California Building. A forty-foot flag was laid on the stairs as a carpet. A Daughter saw it, gathered it in her arms and attempted to carry it away, but was stopped by a woman in charge who put it down again. Two cadets, arriving to attend the reception "came and saw the flag, and as they must walk on it if they went up, one said to the other: 'We are taught by this Government to keep the flag afloat, not under foot.' And to the honor of both, they left the building." Recalling Nathan Hale's story of "The Man Without a Country," who suffered a terrible punishment for speaking disrespectfully of the flag, the reporter asked, "What would Mr. Hale have written of a woman who deliberately took the flag of her country and threw it down for the feet of every passerby to trample?" When an army officer was asked if the cadets were obeying an army regulation by refusing to walk on the flag, he answered:

> Army regulation! I should think not. There are some things which need no laws and regulations. There is nothing in the military law against an officer and a gentleman's right to throttle his mother or to stamp upon his children.

However, good things were happening, too. On Flag Day, June 14, 1893, the National Board of Management had recommended that all members display the National Flag upon their homes on the coming Fourth of July. The colorful display brought favorable comments. The custom began to spread. In June, 1894, at a National Board meeting, Mrs. A. Howard Clark offered a resolution that all Daughters of the American Revolution celebrate the anniversary of the adoption of the

The freshman art class of E.C. Glass High School, Lynchburg, Virginia, painted these posters of historic American flags for the 1958 Flag Day celebration.

flag, June 14, as Flag Day, and commemorate it by displaying the flag in their homes. This, too, was a popular move resulting in much favorable publicity. On February 27, 1897 a "memorial and bill" was presented to the Continental Congress by Mrs. Frances Saunders Kempster, to prevent misuse, mutilation or improper use of the flag. Predictably, it, too, was adopted. A flag committee was appointed with Mrs. Kempster as chairman. The resolution was presented to United States Congress, December 18, 1897. Congress, however, was not yet prepared to act.

By 1902, Mrs. Kempster was reporting with some frustration that her bill had been before Congress for five years. Still, if legislation had not passed, many improvements could be recorded. There was a time when the flag had been used to advertise liquors, tobacco, food, clothing, handkerchiefs, napkins and door mats. Education had virtually eliminated such occurrences. She said that schools all across the country were teaching reverence for the flag, and that 19 states had adopted flag laws.

Borne on a wave of enthusiasm, on March 12, 1904, the Flag Bill was passed in the Senate and hopes were high. But still it was unable to win approval in the House of Representatives.

There were proud moments, too. In 1907 the Daughters of the American Revolution presented a silk flag to the United States naval authorities and General Horace Porter, chairman of the John Paul Jones Committee, to enshroud remains of the famous hero when he was brought home from France for burial.

A clipping from the *Boston Advertiser* stated that "The silk flag that Commander Perry planted at the North Pole was the one presented to him by the Daughters of the American Revolution on July 6, 1908, just before the *Roosevelt* hoisted anchor for her long trip northward."

On June 14, 1923 a United States Flag Code was adopted by the National Flag Conference meeting in Memorial Continental Hall. The President General, Mrs. Anthony Wayne Cook, was a member of the conference. By April 22, 1925, the DAR Committee on Correct Use of the Flag was able to report that over 200,000 Flag Code pamphlets had been sold. Finally, on June 22, 1942, in the patriotic heat of the war, the 77th Congress passed Public Law No. 623, The Flag Code.

The Daughters of the American Revolution has traditionally provided the flag for the Speaker's rostrum in the House of Representatives and in the United States Senate.

For almost 50 years, the Flag Code codified "Flag Etiquette" and provided a citable reference for corrections pertaining to the flag. In the 1990's the Flag of the United States of America was again under attack. Once again certain elements in American society sought to misuse the flag for their own purposes. The Supreme Court found that the Constitution protects the individual's right to express himself in such a manner. However, 50 years of educating with the authorized Flag Code have yielded positive results. Popular opinion is firmly behind the "correct use of the flag." The Flag Code is still popular, in demand and widely distributed. Children and adults, today as never before, request and use information about the Flag of the United States of America.

Portrait of Caroline Scott Harrison to the White House

. . . this gratified Mrs. Harrison and her family, and seemed in every way appropriate as a national gift to the nation from a National Society, whose aims are so closely allied with the preservation of the government.

              American Monthly Magazine, Volume II, No. 3, March 1893

The idea of placing her portrait in the White House was first thought of as an acceptable way to demonstrate gratitude to Mrs. Benjamin Harrison, the President's wife and the first President General of the National Society, for her fidelity to the young organization through its early growing pains. When she died in office on October 25, 1892, these tentative plans were quickly confirmed as the most appropriate tribute to her memory the DAR could provide. A life-sized, full-length portrait costing $2,500 was commissioned from well-known portraitist, Daniel Huntington. Several of Huntington's other works already hung in the White House. His great work, the "Republican Court" showing the first reception given by President and Mrs. Washington, and filled with accurate historic likenesses, was there and had drawn praise from the President of the Metropolitan Museum of Art of New York.

    The unveiling took place at the Third Continental Congress, at 7:30 p.m., February 22, 1894, at the Church of Our Father. An eye witness states that the President General, Mrs. Stevenson, looked "somewhat pale" but "very lovely in a walking gown of black velvet, with bonnet of lace and pearls." The "flag so dear to us all" covered the "beloved form" in the portrait. As Miss Maud Morgan and her Lenox Choral Society, of New York, sang the Star-Spangled Banner, the spell-bound audience watched Mrs. Judge Putnam of Saratoga draw the flag aside. In her remarks, Mrs. Ellen Hardin Walworth, Treasurer of the Portrait Fund emphasized that the funds for the portrait had been contributed as a free-will offering from the members. No "fairs, entertainments, or other devices" had been necessary. Huntington donated $1,000 of his usual $3,500 fee because of the "historic character of this work and the objects of this Society." Describing Mrs. Harrison, she said:

She represents . . . a type of the ideal American woman of the future. . . . A woman unlike those on the one side who are radical, aggressive, and mannish, or those on the other side who are pining, sentimental, and clinging, but a woman self-reliant, intelligent, and modest, active and independent, a competent citizen of the United States, yet womanly and gentle.

The DAR Hospital Corps

The year has been the most notable in the career of our organization.

> Mrs. Daniel Manning, President General
> 1898 – 1901, addressing Eighth Continental
> Congress, February 20, 1899

The National Society was founded by patriotic women with a sense of mission. Throughout its earliest years, they worked industriously in furtherance of their stated goals; always, in the background, lurked the question, "What do you do?" On April 21st, 1898 the United States declared war on Spain and the Daughters stepped forward to answer that question by performing noble service to the nation they loved.

Dr. Anita Newcomb McGee was an organizing member, first Librarian General of the National Society, and a practicing physician. She had discussed with General George M. Sternberg, Surgeon General of the Army and husband of another prominent Daughter, the readiness of the DAR to compile a roster of approved nurses in case of war. Not until after the declaration of war did the United States Congress recognize the wisdom of such a step. Dr. McGee, with General Sternberg, worked out the requirements to certify the nurses. They must be graduates of a recognized training school, between 30 and 50 years of age, healthy, with character recommendations, and able to take the oath of allegiance of the United States.

Dr. McGee was appointed Director of the DAR Hospital Corps. Miss Mary Desha and Mrs. Amos G. Draper were appointed Assistant Directors. From all over the nation, patriotic women wrote to President William McKinley and Secretary of War Russell Alger begging to serve. The majority had no training. Beginning on May 3, batches of such letters were sent to the DAR Hospital Corps from the War Department almost daily. From that date until September 1898 the committee examined the applications of over 5,000 nurses. All letters were answered; where some indication of eligibility was given, follow-up questionnaires were sent. Ultimately the DAR Hospital Corps certified 1,081 thoroughly trained women for service at the front and provided a dozen aprons each for their kits. There was, during that time, no other official organization or head of the army nurses. The role of the DAR, which was to screen applications and locate suitable nurses, ended once the applicants were processed.

Dr. McGee was appointed Acting Assistant Surgeon, U.S.A., in charge of army nurses, on August 29, 1898. In her official capacity, she was empowered to organize the Army Nurse Corps. After the war, in 1900, when the Army Reorganization Act was being written, Dr. McGee, at

The Dr. Anita Newcomb McGee Award to the Army Nurse of the Year.

General Sternberg's request, prepared the Army Nurse Corps section of the act which was not changed until 1947. Because Dr. McGee was a physician and she had recommended that the Superintendent of the Corps should be a nurse, she resigned from her position on December 31, 1900.

Since 1966, at the invitation of the Secretary of the Army, during the annual Continental Congress the National Society has presented the Dr. Anita Newcomb McGee Award to the Outstanding Army Nurse of the year. The two organizations recognize their close ties with mutual pride.

The work with the DAR Hospital Corps actually occupied relatively few members; however, interest in the Spanish-American War effort was intensely supported by the more than 23,000 members across the nation. Nearly $300,000 of money and supplies were sent to the hospitals. The hospital launch *D.A.R.* for transporting the sick and wounded from shore to ship was presented to the government hospital ship *Missouri*. In her report to the Congress, Mrs. Manning said, "Wherever it went it gave comfort and peace and joy, and the Daughters will always feel glad that it was their privilege to succor in that way."

Army nurse and wounded veterans of the World War I era.

World War I

*We would in some practical way show our appreciation of,
and our sympathy with, the great fight that France is
waging in behalf of democracy, human freedom and
civilization, and if there is one way rather than another in
which we may prove our faith by our works we will gladly
avail ourselves of that privilege.*

> *Mrs. Matthew T. Scott, Honorary President
> General, Chairman of National Committee on
> War Relief Service to His Excellency, J.J.
> Jusserand, Ambassador of France, May 3, 1917*

As the world prepared to go to war, the Daughters of the American
Revolution prepared for peace. In 1912, Mrs. Matthew T. Scott,
President General 1911 – 1913, appointed a Committee on International
Peace Arbitration. Its first duty was to promote the celebration of the
Centennial of the signing of the Treaty of Ghent on December 24, 1814,
which closed our second war with England. From there it would proceed
to "foster, especially among the children and the youth of the land, a
sentiment opposed to the 'organized murder' which Sir General Baden-
Powell characterizes as war." Members were asked to cooperate with
peace organizations, to support prominent peace speakers, and to
promote peace through legal and peaceful means. The methods invented
by the Founders of the Republic, wherein the Supreme Court settled
difficulties between one state and another, could be applied to settling
difficulties between one nation and another. The election of Mrs.
William Cummings Story, President General 1913 – 1917, seemed to
signal a change. However, in 1914, at the 23rd Continental Congress,
the chairman of the Peace Arbitration Committee, Mrs. Joseph H.
Dearborn, was still repeating such slogans as, "Our country is the world,
our countrymen all mankind."

That was one opinion. Speaking for the majority at the same
congress, Mrs. Mary S. Lockwood introduced a resolution that was
carried enthusiastically by a rising vote:

> RESOLVED: That the National Society of the Daughters of the
> American Revolution give notice to the Government of these United
> States, through the Secretary of War, that we hold ourselves in

readiness, collectively and individually, for any services our country may require of us in this dilemma of war.

Mrs. Story wrote the President, placing the National Society at his service. In 1915, Miss Mabel Boardman, National Secretary of the American Red Cross, appealed for financial aid. A Red Cross Fund was immediately established. Up to April 1917, total contributions to the American Red Cross were $19,241.48 and to the Belgian Relief, $148,615.99. In addition, hospital garments and surgical supplies were provided in great quantities.

The declaration of war on April 6, 1917, just days before the opening of the 26th Continental Congress, shifted the National Society into high patriotic gear. The Daughters were in the war and determined to do their part. Secretary of War Baker, seeking the use of Memorial Continental Hall by the Red Cross, had said:

> You are talking about patriotism all the time; now there is one immediate and practical thing you can do.

The motion, "that at the close of our Continental Congress, after due consultation with the Red Cross as to what they most need in the way of more room for their work, and in order to render what immediate and practical assistance we can, we offer to them the use of all the space in this building we can possibly spare," was put after very little discussion and unanimously carried. The proceedings of the meeting reflected the excitement with which the delegates realized that, "I know perfectly well that we could clear out our kitchen on the third floor, and also offer the use of the banquet hall," and "Kentucky would feel very proud to have her room used for that purpose, for immediate use."

With the encouragement of a new President General, Mrs. George Thacher Guernsey, 1917–1920, the society loaned the land behind Memorial Continental Hall to the government, where a two-story temporary building of 100,000 square feet was ready for occupancy by November 1, the same year. Designed by Waddy B. Wood, the building for the Council of National Defense was the first temporary war building erected in Washington, D.C., and was completed in less than sixty days. It was a handsome structure, under the circumstances, with a classical facade at the entrance, "heated by steam, lighted by electricity, and supplied by ample toilets, with offices as well ventilated and arranged as they would have been in a modern office building." Its six long wings provided office space for 600 people.

Mrs. Scott, who had worked so hard to preserve the peace, was appointed chairman of a permanent War Relief Service Committee and went immediately to work. With a staff consisting of two vice chairmen, a secretary, and Mrs. William Henry Wait as director of publicity, Mrs. Scott was able to inspire the members, inform them, and maintain meticulous records of their contributions. Mrs. Wait distributed a series of forty-four instruction bulletins, reports, questionnaires and other literature. The response was overwhelming. Members prepared "331,686 surgical supplies, 296,268 knitted garments," filled buddy bags, sent Christmas gifts, drove ambulances, purchased bonds, and more. One member outfitted 26 aviators and provided lunches to six trainloads of soldiers; a chapter in the desert met each troop train and served lemonade. Vehicles were purchased: 16 ambulances, one automobile, three field kitchens, and one truck. Contributions were sent to every kind of organization engaged in war relief; to name a few: the Young Men's Christian Association, the Young Women's Christian Association, the Salvation Army, Knights of Columbus, Jewish Relief, American Library Association, and the War Camp Community Service. Speakers were provided for Red Cross and war rally meetings. Performers entertained. Writers wrote. 206 members went abroad for war service. There they worked in hospitals, canteens, and wherever they were sent; most remained in France, but some went to England, Italy, Turkey, Greece, Siberia, and with the army of occupation to Germany. They all did what they could.

With the armistice in 1918 came the task of rebuilding. A sub-committee on French War Orphans was established. After conferring with Ambassador Jusserand, Mrs. Scott authorized him to send the names of 2,000 fatherless children for "adoption" by the DAR. A few of the 2,000 were shared with other organizations, such as the Order of the Eastern Star, and the Children of the American Revolution, but most became the responsibility of the Daughters. The cost per child was $36.50. After sending the cash, the chapter or the individual Daughter was sent the name and address of "her" child. Almost always, clothing and other gifts were sent in addition to the financial support. In two years, $135,708.85 was raised, providing for 3,655 children.

The little village of Tilloloy, France, situated on the French side of the front line from 1914 to 1918, was twice ravaged by the invading German armies; its 400 citizens were completely displaced. Houses, chapel, all were ruined. A letter from Tilloloy, written on June 8, 1917, said:

> My father, Monsieur d'Hinnisdal, is the Maire of the village. He is putting up a tiny wooden shack where he will go to live, and will do all he can to help the people. If we can collect the money to rebuild the houses and to furnish them; to give the farmers tools and to buy some live stock, we can put these people on their feet again. . . . If only someone will help us? It is terrible to see all this suffering, and to be unable to relieve it.

They longed, not for welfare, but for a new start. It had been the intention of the Daughters of the American Revolution, when Tilloloy was brought to their attention in 1914, to restore the village. It was estimated that $45,000 could finance the task. Unfortunately, the second

The DAR War Work Committee pin.

Rebuilding after World War I included such tasks as Mending Day at Camp Custer, 1919.

destruction, in 1918, was worse than the first. A notice from the July 29, 1919 edition of the Paris paper *Temps*, said:

> But the most cruel loss of all is that of the beautiful church of Tilloloy, a jewel of the Renaissance. Built of red stone and brick, with perfect care and taste, both inside and out, it offered a unique example of this style in its richest and most adorned application. . . . only part of the walls has been left standing.

Shells so maimed the land that 900 acres of cultivated fields were reduced to 60 acres. Nearly 100 wells about 90 feet deep had supplied the village. Almost all were destroyed or contaminated. Furthermore, the French government had taken responsibility for rebuilding the village. Still, the Daughters wanted to redeem their pledge to Tilloloy. $42,365.84 had been designated for its relief by April 1919, when Mrs. Wait made a full report on the accomplishments of the War Relief Service Committee to the 28th Continental Congress. The decision of the DAR to install a water works system gave exactly the constructive kind of assistance that was needed.

Mrs. Wait's report showed that an enormous amount of work had been done on which no "price" had been placed, such as the making of 23,903,104 surgical supplies, 379,114 hospital garments, and 194,812 knitted garments for the Red Cross, using Red Cross materials; the provision of 48,346 box lunches; and 20,429 scrap books. No value could be placed on hospitality. But it added up: 42,398 men in service had been house guests of Daughters; 96,329 had dined in their homes; 50,109 had been entertained at public restaurants. The total value of cash and priced gifts from the National Society, which at that time numbered 102,223 patriotic women, was $3,730,385.60. There were, in addition, Liberty Loans, Thrift and War Savings Stamps taken by Daughters amounting to $37,032,732.81 and the NSDAR Liberty Loan of $100,000. Total documented war expenditures by Daughters was $40,863,118.41. Further, they *sold* war investments to others, $52,019,379 worth. As to sharing space with the Red Cross, the report tersely states: "Use of entire building given to Red Cross."

As Mrs. Wait said:

> We have been true to our trust: we have stood in the second-line trenches of Home Service. The Daughters of the American Revolution have made no "Drives" for the benefit of our War Work. We are *not* included as beneficiaries in the United Work Campaign Fund. We have *not* received from the Government any supplies for our war work as an organization. We had *no* "franking" privileges, for use of the mails, express or telegraph. We ourselves have financed all our own expenses incurred by the war.

The $100,000 Liberty Loan had an important life of its own. Interest on the fund provided pensions for needy Real Daughters. Later, when there were only two surviving Real Daughters, the interest paid pensions for Spanish-American War nurses whose service had ended just short of qualifying for a United States government pension.

Forty rooms at DAR National Headquarters were given to the war effort.

World War II

The matter of Citations by the United States Treasury and "Awards for Meritorious Service" bestowed by the Army, Navy and the American Red Cross upon states, chapters and individuals would alone comprise a separate volume.

> Grace Lincoln Hall Brosseau, Honorary President General in Record of War Work of the National Society during the World War II from April 1941, to May, 1946

Two requests of every member of the Daughters of the American Revolution were made by newly-elected President General, Mrs. William H. Pouch, in April 1941: Each one was asked to enlist in some branch of military or civil defense, and to pause each day at noon, Washington time, for a moment of silent prayer.

By the time Pearl Harbor was attacked on December 7, an elaborate duplicate card index was in place showing the potential strength of DAR service: originals were filed in the National Defense office at headquarters, copies were held by Chapter Regents.

That building space would be

contributed was a foregone conclusion. First, the corridors of Constitution Hall, with ample room for 100 workers, were offered to the American Red Cross of the District of Columbia. As the need increased, more and more space was given. Antiques and museum pieces were stored; every room that could be spared was given to the Red Cross. In Memorial Continental Hall, a War Service Center entertained service men six days a week. The Prisoners of War office of the American Red Cross occupied 23 rooms, supplying food, clothing and medicines to American and Allied soldiers in foreign prison camps. The National Board room was used by the Pan American Sanitary Bureau. A cheerful, youthful note was added by the day nursery operated in four rooms in the basement of Constitution Hall for children of enlisted men whose wives were now working. Daily, the children romped in the outdoor playground established there for them. War relief entertainments were held, without cost to the sponsors, in the auditorium of Constitution Hall. The National Officers' Club room provided training space for American Red Cross workers. In all, 40 rooms were given to the war effort.

With war activity completely established in DAR Headquarters, a change in plans for Continental Congress was inevitable. Four congresses were held out-of-town. One, the 54th, in 1945, was canceled, at the request of the Office of Defense Transportation. Mrs. William H. Pouch, President General 1941 – 1944, never presided at a congress held in Constitution Hall. The 51st Continental Congress convened on May 5, 1942 at Medinah Temple, Chicago, Illinois; the 52nd, April 17, 1943 at Taft Auditorium, Cincinnati, Ohio; and the 53rd, April 16, 1944, at the Commodore Hotel, New York, New York. Mrs. Julius Young Talmadge, President General 1944 – 1947, was forced to "sit out" what would have been her first congress, in 1945. Faced with the dilemma of record-keeping, the decision was made to compile and publish the reports of National Officers, Committee Chairmen, and State Regents just as if a congress had taken place; in the records of the National Society, the *Proceedings of the 54th Continental Congress* in 1945 holds its place among all the others. Mrs. Talmadge presided over the 55th Congress, May 20, 1946, at the Marlborough-Blenheim Hotel, Atlantic City, New Jersey. By 1947, the war-time guests had departed, and although the Congress convened late, on May 19, the Daughters were finally able to return to Washington, D.C.

The sponsorship of four L.C.I. (Landing Craft Infantry) ships' crews by the combined chapters of greater New York inspired the Amphibious Forces to request that each state, and the Children of the American Revolution, take over one ship. The 53rd Continental Congress unanimously endorsed the project. Ultimately, 89 L.C.I.'s were sponsored, along with two "L.S.T.'s" and two "L.S.M.'s" and one Liberty Ship.

The honor roll of war service showed that 75,642 members and men in members' families, served. Included in the count were W.A.C.S., Waves, Spars and Nurses. The greatest number, 6,507, came from the District of Columbia.

The amount of money, goods and services contributed by members

Miss Edla S. Gibson, New York State Regent, accompanied by 14 regents from New York City, presents a "Victory" wagon and a mobile canteen to the Staten Island Chapter, American Red Cross.

of the National Society from April 1941 to May 1946 staggers the imagination:

For the Red Cross: $392,646.16 was given to the Blood Plasma Fund; 13,119 members donated blood; 91 mobile units and 15 plasma centers were given; $1,279,848.33 was contributed to the Red Cross; 112,554 DAR members worked 26,236,388 hours making 3,058,409 articles.

War bonds and stamps were purchased in the amount of $206,619,715.16. $187,832.41 was contributed to the War Projects Fund; $344,761.26 to War Services, which also received 16,773,355 volunteer hours. 962 members worked with the blind; $18,146.82 was contributed for that work. 196,901 Buddy Bags with a dollar value of $386,426.94 were given.

As they did in World War I, states, chapters and individuals made numerous imaginative contributions in addition to the statistics offered in Mrs. Brosseau's report: hundreds of thousands of magazines and books; tons of tin, paper, fat and scrap metal; Victory Gardens; Christmas gifts; entertainments; slippers; convalescent supplies; trees planted honoring service men; portable "Victrolas" with records; cookies and cakes; seeds for beautifying camps; Seeing Eye dogs; flags; eye glasses; athletic equipment; Braille books; canes; wheel chairs; funds for artificial limbs; fur coats for fur for seamen's jackets; afghans; portable altar Triptychs; cod liver oil; British, Greek, Russian and Chinese relief; pipe organ at Newton D. Baker Hospital; radios; and thousands of acts of individual kindness.

"Foreign" chapters experienced more direct involvement. Eleven members remained in China during the war. Four were interned by the Japanese, two of whom were over 80 years of age. 12,237 hours of war work were reported in Cuba; in England, an American ambulance was presented; members in France raised 1000 goats for wool for the government; members in Germany were active in Red Cross work. The Philippine Islands reported that "We did well to live." 18 members there were interned at Santo Tomas prison for three years; one starved to death. In Rome, too, they worked under adverse conditions; four members were carried off by force by the Germans.

The Daughters were proud to include the war work of the Children of the American Revolution in their report. Vehicles purchased by the

C.A.R. included one ambulance, one clubmobile, one jeep, and five scooters. The *U.S.S.-LCI (L) 617* was sponsored by the society; War Stamps and War Bonds totaling $5,000,000 were purchased; the C.A.R. Board Room was turned over to the Red Cross; $1,000 was contributed to feed five foreign children (from Holland, France, Italy, Belgium and Germany); hours were contributed in USO Centers; thousands of afghans were knitted and crocheted.

A large number of members, 637, gave military service during the war.

Mrs. Brosseau, in her report, said:

> The whole story can never be told because so much individual effort was expended in so many ways which do not appear upon the records of time.

On active duty in Vietnam

In January 24, 1968, just before the "Tet offensive," Mrs. William Henry Sullivan, President General 1965 – 1968 arrived in Saigon to visit the U.S. Armed Forces in the combat area and in the evacuation hospitals in Vietnam. Traveling by Army plane and helicopter, escorted by members of General W.C. Westmoreland's staff, she visited a number of medical facilities, both native and American; for example, the Khanh Hoa Province Hospital, a 289-bed Vietnamese hospital receiving United States assistance, and the 93rd Evacuation Hospital at Long Binh. A photo caption in the *DAR Magazine* says that when the troops at Pleiku heard that the President General of the Daughters of the American Revolution had arrived, they quipped, "Mom is here!" Progressing from field to hospital to embassy, occasionally in sight of artillery fire, she presented DAR Americanism Medals to servicemen chosen by their commanding officers. Mrs. Sullivan made the decision to present General Westmoreland with one of the 47 medals that were bestowed during the trip. Mrs. Sullivan reported that morale was high, but that "Their greatest wish is more support from the American people on the home front." Relatives of service personnel receiving the Americanism Medal were grateful and proud. One mother wrote:

> May God's blessings be ever present upon you and all your loved ones, upon all the 186,000 American women, for the loving and

dedicated works of loyalty given our wonderful country. . . . My husband and I salute you and each and everyone of your members for your great and marvelous works. . . . Our daughter was selected for this honorable Daughters of the American Revolution Americanism Medal. . . . I am so happy you were there to see her, and giving us the very nearness of her, through you. We had not heard from her in two months.

Another mother, a DAR member, had written her son the previous year assuring him that the DAR stood fast behind our fighting forces. "Little did I know it would be affirmed at such a personal level! . . . sincerest 'thanks' as only a mother can be grateful."

Working with veteran-patients

Interest in veteran-patients can be traced to the Spanish-American War when the DAR Hospital Corps provided the nucleus of the Army Nurse Corps. Daughters have provided necessities and comforts for such patients ever since. DAR established a special committee, DAR Service for Veteran-Patients, in 1968. After placing volunteers in 45 Medical Centers, the National Society became a member of the Veterans Administration National Advisory Committee (VAVS) during the administration of Mrs. Donald Spicer, President General 1971 – 1974. At this writing, DAR members actively serve in 160 VA Medical Centers, at the patient's bedside, in laboratories, pharmacies, clinics and offices, reception areas, libraries and chapels.

The entrance to America

No woman will quarrel with another when she is being
shown how to make something pretty for her baby, and so,
in the simplest way in the world, fighting ceased and now
peace reigns in the detention room.
Mrs. Alfred J. Brosseau, President General
1926 – 1929, National Chairman, Ellis Island
Immigrant Aid Committee, DAR, 1923 – 1926

Dominating the entrance to the harbor of New York City is Frederic Auguste Bartholdi's colossus, Liberty Enlightening the World. For millions of American immigrants, the Statue of Liberty has raised her "lamp beside the golden door" in her solemn but sincere gesture of welcome. Directly in her shadow, at least as important if not nearly as apparent as the giant statue, for 62 years the cluster of buildings on Ellis Island bore within them the key to the future for the hopeful ones who arrived daily.

Those who were fortunate came with everything in order; they were quickly passed through to their new life in the land of the free. Others were detained. Known criminals, prostitutes, the mentally ill, or those suffering from contagious diseases could be denied admission. Those awaiting deportment or appeal of their cases were detained on Ellis Island. Because they were segregated by sex, families were separated. In many cases, detainees spoke and understood only their native tongue.

Fear, bewilderment, mental strain and idleness, all compounded by the language barrier, created resentment, suspicion and sorrow among the immigrants held in the Women's Detention Room at Ellis Island. Fighting was common. In a pamphlet prepared in about 1927, Mrs. Brosseau said, "When quarreling failed of its effectiveness these women resorted to their fists and confusion reigned . . . augmented by orange peelings that were thrown hit or miss . . . " In 1923 the federal government permitted the Daughters of the American Revolution to begin occupational work there, the only society to sponsor such work on Ellis Island. According to Mrs. Brosseau, "Then came a great change." Being given cloth, yarn, crochet cotton and embroidery materials, the women were able to pass the wearying wait more easily, and make necessities and luxuries for their families at the same time. One woman, detained for a year before being finally released, said she was going "to join the Daughters of the American Revolution so she could come back and help us with our good work."

The success of the DAR in calming the situation in the women's room was so marked, that a year later, they were asked to extend their activities to the men, including those in the "warrant case" section. The warrant cases were those who had offended United States law in some way. Perhaps they had crossed the Canadian or Mexican borders illegally; or had been recently released from prison in their native land; some had stolen passage aboard ship; others had run away from sea service. As Mrs. Brosseau said, "There we encounter human nature in all its infinite variety, . . . Princes and other men of title rub shoulders with criminals and stowaways. We also find the same avidity for work that the women have displayed." For men, as well as women, enforced idleness was the great enemy. Useful activity was the antidote to the mental depression caused by uncertainty and boredom. Materials and instructions were provided for the male detainees to embroider and bead women's handbags, crochet belts and neckties, and hook rugs and large mats. They made shirts, trousers, underwear and pajamas. A favorite activity was the weaving of woolen scarves on small homemade looms. Asked why gray wool was usually rejected in favor of bright colors, one man replied, "Our lives are too drab now and we need the brightness to give us courage."

Courage the DAR supplied, generously. Over the years at Ellis Island and its western counterpart, Angel Island in San Francisco Harbor, approximately $230,000, 21,000 boxes of supplies, and sewing machines, looms and carpenter's tools, as well as trained workers to distribute the supplies and give instructions in their use, were contributed from 1923–1940.

On January 2, 1934, at the request of the United States government, the Daughters established occupational therapy at the Marine Hospital on Ellis Island. The hospital, operated by the Public Health Service, was originally an immigration hospital for detainees ill enough to need it. Tuberculosis and other chronic diseases were treated there, as well as psychiatric cases. As immigration decreased owing to the establishment of government quotas, beds at the hospital were also made available to the regular beneficiaries of the Public Health Service: merchant seamen from American ships, United States Coast Guard, light-house keepers and others. Three full-time workers, two therapists and a craft teacher, were employed by the DAR. Their salaries were paid by a five cents per capita contribution from each member. Chapters were asked to send additional money for supplies: $15.00 would warp a loom for a year; $6.50 would purchase a leather hide for tooling. Or they could send pearl cotton, crochet cotton, rug wool, rayon bias, linen thread, silk or scrap leather.

During World War II, Ellis Island became a Coast Guard receiving station. The DAR was asked to continue occupational therapy among the Coast Guard and Merchant Marines recovering at the hospital there.

By the end of the war, the DAR had added a new hospital on Staten Island to its work at Angel and Ellis Islands. DAR involvement at Ellis Island ended when the facility was abruptly closed in 1951 by the United States government.

The restoration of the Statue of Liberty in preparation for its centennial in 1986, and subsequently, that of Ellis Island, received the enthusiastic support of the National Society Daughters of the American Revolution. During the administration of Mrs. Walter Hughey King, President General 1983 – 1986, the DAR proclaimed February 14, 1985 as "Liberty Love Day," for receiving contributions toward the Lady's restoration. Ultimately, members contributed over $500,000. During the administrations of Mrs. Raymond Franklin Fleck, President General 1986 – 1989 and Mrs. Eldred Martin Yochim, President General 1989 – 1992, $250,000 was contributed to the restoration of Ellis Island.

DAR gave over $500,000 toward the 1986 restoration of the Statue of Liberty.

DAR Manual for Citizenship

*. . . America for Americans. By American I mean any man
or woman who puts the Old World and its prejudices
behind them, and takes upon them the oath of a broad
democracy and a pure patriotism.*

          Mary S. Lockwood, Founder, in American
          Monthly Magazine, December 1895.

As President Franklin Delano Roosevelt pointed out when he
addressed the 47th Continental Congress in 1938, "Remember that all
of us, you and I especially, are descended from immigrants and
revolutionists." For more than 250 years most immigrants to America
shared similar backgrounds. The 1880's saw the beginning of a tremendous influx of foreigners of varying cultures. Established Americans often
resented the threat they perceived as old and new clashed. At the 30th
Continental Congress, meeting in 1921, Mrs. George Maynard Minor,
President General 1920 – 1923, said that the National Society should
take the lead in establishing better relations. She said:

> We were among the first to put into practice an attitude of
> friendliness toward them in place of the almost hostile attitude . . .
> which has too often characterized America's treatment of them in the
> past. A friendly, human sympathy should characterize our intercourse
> with these strangers whom we need and who need us.

Calling the attention of the delegates to a "Guide to the United
States for Immigrants" published many years previously in Connecticut,
she suggested that the National Society should finance a manual of
information containing "the Constitution of the United States, The
American's Creed, the pledge to the flag with rules for the correct use
of the flag, an address of welcome from this Society, and all practical
information concerning our laws and government; . . . everything in
short which he needs to know in order to lead the life of a law-abiding
American citizen." The Congress accepted her plan and voted that it
should be given free to immigrants at Ellis Island and other ports of
entry. The *Manual of the United States for the Information of Immigrants and Foreigners*, which had been awaiting approval went to
press. The first year English, Spanish, Hungarian, Yiddish and Polish

New citizen studies DAR Manual for Citizenship. Foreign language editions continued until 1952.

editions of 50,000 each were printed. There were 75,000 in Italian. The word came in that the *Manual* supplied a "long-felt need." Year by year its popularity increased. In 1928 almost 500,000 were provided. After that time, distribution decreased proportionately as did immigration. By 1952, the *DAR Manual for Citizenship* was printed in 19 foreign languages plus English. That year, the foreign language editions were discontinued at the request of the United States government. The 10,000,000th manual was presented during Mrs. Richard Denny Shelby's administration at the 92nd Continental Congress on April 23, 1983. The National Society continues to encourage men and women to, as Mrs. Lockwood said so many years ago, "put the Old World and its prejudices behind them, and take upon them the oath of a broad democracy and a pure patriotism," and distributes approximately 35,000 free manuals per year to help them.

Independence Hall

In January 1971, during the administration of Mrs. Erwin Frees Seimes, President General 1968 – 1971, the Rose Garden in Independence Hall Park, Philadelphia, Pennsylvania, was formally presented to the United States Park Service. A major project in Independence Hall, itself, the first *Bicentennial* project of the National Society, was authorized in Mrs. Donald Spicer's term as President General, 1971 – 1974, by the 81st Continental Congress in 1972 and dedicated on July 4th that year. On the day of the ribbon-cutting, 26,032 people viewed the rooms. As a very generous and significant "Gift to the Nation," the DAR agreed to underwrite the cost of furnishing the Governor's Council Chamber and the Committee of the Assembly's Room on the second floor of Independence Hall, Philadelphia, Pennsylvania. Years before the Bicentennial Celebration finally succeeded in rekindling the long-banked fires of patriotism among the general public, the DAR, as always, remained faithful. The Daughters' $200,000 gift to America ensured that the furnishings selected for the cradle of our Independence were authentic 18th century articles. The *New York Sunday News* of December 30, 1973 reported that, "Charles Dorman, the curator at Independence Hall, says he would have committed hara-kiri if it hadn't been for the DAR."

The Governor's Council Chamber, Independence Hall, 2nd floor, furnished by the National Society in 1974.

Martha Washington portrait

*We . . . hung the picture in the original place, and we
like to think, on the original nail.*

> Mrs. Lowell Fletcher Hobart, President General
> 1929 – 1932, letter to C. Powell Minnigerode,
> Secretary and Director of the Corcoran Gallery
> of Art

In commemoration of the George Washington Bicentennial, the 40th Continental Congress voted to present a copy of the 1757 Woolaston portrait of Martha Washington to Arlington Mansion. The original portrait was painted before the marriage of the widowed Martha Dandridge Custis to George Washington. Owned by George Washington Parke Custis, it hung at Mount Vernon and later at Arlington. Finally, the picture was bequeathed to Washington & Lee University by Miss Mary Custis Lee.

Mathilde W. Leisenring, a Washington artist, painted the faithful replica. It was dedicated on October 26, 1931 and accepted for the government by Colonel F.H. Payne, Acting Secretary of War. Mrs. Hobart called the presentation of the portrait the "crowning event" of her administration.

Allyn Cox murals in the United States Capitol

Sixteen major paintings, dramatizing pivotal moments of American history, grace the ceiling of the central east-west corridor of the House wing of the United States Capitol, the "Great Experiment Hall." Each work depicts a turning point in the American experiment. The 16 moments immortalized are: The Mayflower Compact, 1620; The Albany Congress, 1754; The First Continental Congress, 1774; The Declaration of Independence, 1776; The Constitutional Convention, 1787; The First Federal Congress, 1789; Washington's Inauguration, 1789; Washington's Farewell Address, 1796; The Monroe Doctrine, 1823; Lincoln's Second Inaugural, 1865; The Smithsonian Institution, 1855; The Library of Congress in the Capitol, 1800 – 1897; Steam Powered Amphibious Boat, 1804; Iron Foundry, circa 1850; Theodore Roosevelt circa 1904 [speaking]; and Women's Suffrage Parade, 1917. Each painting is amplified by vignettes on either side shedding further light on the depicted event. Created by the well-known muralist, Allyn Cox, they were painted, in position, in oil on canvas glued to the plaster panels in the Capitol corridor. The 84th Continental Congress, during the administration of Mrs. Wakelee Rawson Smith, President General 1975–1977, authorized the commission as the National Society's *Bicentennial Tribute to the United States of America*. The tentative plans for the project were made during the brief administration of Mrs. Henry Stewart Jones, President General 1974–1975, who died in office on April 7, 1975. Funded during Mrs. Smith's term of office, the works were completed over a period of several years and dedicated in 1982, shortly before the artist's death. A full-color catalog of the Bicentennial Tribute paintings was published jointly in 1986 by the National Society Daughters of the American Revolution and the United States Capitol Historical Society. The book also shows the murals in the eastern north-south corridor of the House wing of the Capitol, the Hall of Capitols. Those paintings, completed by Allyn Cox in 1974, tell the story of the U.S. Capitol and were sponsored by the United States Capitol Historical Society.

A Women's Suffrage Parade, 1917, painted in the United States Capitol by muralist, Allyn Cox, as one of his immortal moments in American history.

The Second Century
of Service

May time always be merciful, to the end that the hour shall never strike and quell the fine exuberance of spirit and the generous outpouring of rich gifts when need makes a sacrificial demand upon the Daughters of the American Revolution. The response always has been—and always will be—akin to that made by the forefathers and foremothers when answering the call of 1776.

*Grace Lincoln Hall Brosseau, President General
1926–1929, in DAR Magazine, October 1940*

Much has changed in the 100 years since the National Society Daughters of the American Revolution was organized on October 11, 1890. However, the National Society remains today, as it was then, focused on three great objectives: historic preservation, educational activities, and patriotic endeavor. It may well ask itself, as did Mrs. William D. Cabell, Vice President Presiding, on February 22, 1892, "What is your object; what do you propose; what good will you do; what is the use of such an organization?"

DAR, the first, the largest and the longest-lived of the women's patriotic organizations based on lineal descent, has served the nation devotedly for a century. The direct and indirect results of its efforts are part of the fabric of American society. The flag has been saved; the House Beautiful has been built; historic places have been marked. Ellis Island has completed its task of processing immigrants; welfare of women and children is thoroughly overseen by the federal government; and the nation is criss-crossed by a network of exceptional highways. Communism is fading; capitalism and democracy are the bright hope of the future.

With so much accomplished, what, indeed, is the use of such an organization as the Daughters of the American Revolution today?

The objectives of the DAR were valid in 1890; they remain valid today. America needs, as she has always needed, knowledgeable citizens, aware of the sacrifices required in the past, the present, and the future to preserve freedom; enlightened citizens, familiar with the great treatises and documents that define and guarantee our American way of life: The Federalist Papers, the Declaration of Independence, the Constitution of the United States, and, lest we forget, the Bible; patriotic citizens, who respond to the sacrifices and the guarantees with faith, love and dedication.

All the work of the National Society in furtherance of its three objectives is important. What has been won must be defended. What has been built must be maintained. What has been saved must be preserved.

There is, however, one area that stands out. The key to the future is education. A new crop of young Americans is produced every year. So long as bright-eyed youngsters embark on their careers of learning, so long must they be taught the doctrines and practices of good citizenship. Knowledge of our American heritage is not automatic; it must be learned. Training in Americanism and recognition of good citizenship is just as important as ever.

There is also in America a group that has been left behind. Illiteracy destroys the fabric of our nation as does nothing else. Its chief dangers are two: illiterate adults lack the tools to answer their own questions; and they are besieged with hearsay information of uncertain reliability. In addition, adults who cannot read lead, at best, haphazard existences, at worst, lives of secret shame. Eradication of illiteracy is a challenge that must be met.

The colossus still lifts her lamp beside the golden door. The clamor to enter and participate in the American dream continues unabated. From 1871 to 1890, 87% of immigrants came from Europe, another 10% from Canada and Newfoundland, 2% from Asia, and fewer than 1% from Central and South America. Because they usually spoke some language other than English, they were perceived as "different." However, in actuality they were more similar to resident Americans than they were dissimilar. From 1971-1980, immigration statistics showed an important change: 17.8% European, 35.2% Asian, and 44.3% Hispanic. The granting of permanent resident status to formerly illegal aliens in 1989 skewed the figures for that year: 9% European, 27% Asia; almost 62% Hispanic. Many of today's immigrants differ, not only in language, but also in cultural background, ethics and attitudes. It is critically important for everyone that they achieve a productive and satisfying position in American society. To do so, they must understand and accept what makes America great. They must adopt American ways as their ways. They must become Americans.

The three great tasks that face the nation and the DAR in the area of education are: Citizenship training of our youth; eradication of illiteracy in our adults; and Americanization of our newest citizens. These tasks, undertaken in a spirit of historical perspective, will go far toward encouraging that same pure patriotism that was the ultimate aim of the Founders of the National Society.

In her Centennial message to the members of the National Society Daughters of the American Revolution, Mrs. Eldred Martin Yochim, President General 1989 – 1992, said that the Centennial Administration sought to inspire the members "to make a lasting difference." She continued:

> Within our Society, we have the creative talent, the organizational resources, and, above all, the commitment to expand and extend our service to "God, Home and Country." With your support, the National Society will move forward confidently into a second century of service: Perpetuating the memory and spirit of the men and women who achieved American independence, developing an enlightened public opinion, and fostering true patriotism and love of country.

Appendix 1

THE WASHINGTON POST, SUNDAY, JULY 13, 1890—SIXTEEN PAGES.

WOMEN WORTHY OF HONOR
THE PATRIOTIC SPIRIT OF '76

Something for the Sons of the Revolution to Read—Hannah Thurston Arnett

RECENTLY the first regular meeting of the Washington branch of the newly-organized society, "Sons of the Revolution," was held in this city. Prof. G. Brown Goode explained the object of the meeting, "that it was purely historical in its purpose, and was to perpetuate the memory of the men who achieved American independence." The South and the North joined hands on a common platform, and good speeches were from all sections. So far we say amen.

Senator Sherman was the presiding officer. There were sixty persons present, and twenty of these were women. In the opening remarks the Senator said "he approved of any movement that would perpetuate the memory of the heroes of the Revolutionary war, and hailed with pleasure the organization composed of men and women of the descendants of Revolutionary sires. The women might not have done any of the fighting, but they took an equally important part in looking after the homes, that the men might absent themselves in their country's cause."

If this is the case why do men and women band themselves to commemorate a one-sided heroism? If these were true, patriotic women, why is not the patriotism of the country broad and just enough to take women in, too? It is a noble act for the descendants of the Revolutionary sires. But were there no mothers of the Revolution? Were these sires without dams? I trow not.

I have heard of a man who had a dam by a mill site, while he had "no mill by a dam site," but I have yet to hear of a man who had a Revolutionary sire without a dam by the home site. This is an opportune time to bring forward some of the women of "'76" lest the sires become puffed up by vain glory. I will begin with a true story of the Revolution, which can be backed by scores more of equal patriotism.

The days were dark and hopeless, the hearts of our forefathers were heavy and cast down. Deep, dark despondency had settled upon them. Defeat after defeat had followed our army until it was demoralized, and despair had taken possession of them. Lord Cornwallis, after his victory at Fort Lee, had marched his army to Elizabethtown, N.J. and there encamped. This was in that memorable December, 1776. The Howe brothers had already issued their celebrated proclamation, that offered protection to all who would seek refuge under the British flag within sixty days and declare themselves British subjects, and take an oath binding themselves to not take up arms again against the mother country or induce others to do so.

In one of the many spacious homes of the town, there had assembled a goodly number of the foremost men of the time to discuss the feasibility of accepting the proffered proclamation. We are much inclined to the belief that enthusiasm, bravery, indomitable courage and patriotism were attributes that took possession of our forefathers and held on to them until they became canonized beatitudes, upon which the sires alone had a corner; but we find on close scrutiny that there were times when manly hearts wavered and to courage was added a prefix, and this was one of them.

For hours the council went on, the arguments were sincere, grave but faltering. Some felt that the time had fully come to accept the clemency offered—others shook their heads, but the talk went on until every soul in the room had become of one mind, courage, bravery, patriotism, hope, honor, all was swept away by the floodtide of disaster.

There was one listener from whom the council had not heard. In an adjoining room sat Hannah Arnett, the wife of the host. She had listened to the debate, and when the final vote was reached she could no longer constrain herself. She sprang to her feet and, throwing open the parlor door, in her majesty confronted that group of counsels.

Picture a large room with a low ceiling, furnished with the heavily-carved furniture of those days, dimly lighted by wax candles, and a fire in the huge fireplace. Around a table sat a group of anxious, disheartened, discouraged-looking men. Before them stood the fair dame in the antique costume of the day. Imagination will picture her stately bearing as she entered into their august presence. The indignant scorn upon her lips, the flash of her blue eyes, her commanding figure and dignified presence brought every man to his feet.

Consternation and amazement for the moment ruled supreme. The husband advanced toward her, shocked and chagrined that his wife had so forgotten herself; that she should come into the midst of a meeting where politics and the questions of the hour were being discussed. He would shield her now. The reproof he would give later on; and so he was quickly at her side, and, whispering, said to her:

"Hannah! Hannah! this is no place for you. We do not want you here just now."

He would have led her from the room.

She was a mild, amiable woman, and was never known to do aught against her husband's wishes, but if she saw him now she made no sign, but turned upon the astonished group.

"Have you made your decision gentlemen?" she asked. "I stand before you to know: have you chosen the part of men or traitors?"

It was a direct question, but the answer was full of sophistry, explanation, and excuse.

"The case was hopeless; the army was starving, half clothed and undisciplined, repulses everywhere. We are ruined and can stand out no longer against England and her unlimited resources.

Mrs. Arnett, in dignified silence, listened until they had finished, and then she asked: "But what if we should live after all?"

"Hannah! Hannah!" said her husband in distress. "Do you not see that these are no questions for you? We are doing what is best for you—for all. Women have no share in these topics. Go to your spinning-wheel and leave us to settle affairs. My good little wife you are making yourself ridiculous. Do not expose yourself in this way before our friends."

Every word he had uttered was to her as naught. Not a word had she heard; not a quiver of the lip or tremor of an eyelash. But in the same strangely sweet voice she asked: "Can you tell me if, after all, God does not let the right perish, if America should win in the conflict, after you have thrown yourself on British clemency, where will you be then?"

"Then," said one, "we should have to leave the country. But that is too absurd to think of in the condition our country and our army is."

"Brother," said Mrs. Arnett, "you have forgotten one thing which England has not, and which we have—one thing which outweighs all England's treasures, and that is the right. God is on our side, and every volley of our muskets is an echo of His voice. We are poor, and weak, and few, but God is fighting for us; we entered into this struggle with pure hearts and prayerful lips; we had counted the cost and were willing to pay the price, were it in our hearts' blood. And now—now because for a time the day is going against us, you would give up all, and sneak back like cravens to kiss the feet that have trampled upon us. And you call yourselves men—the sons of those who gave up home and fortune and fatherland to make for themselves and for dear liberty a resting-place in the wilderness! Oh, shame upon you cowards!"

"Gentlemen," said Mr. Arnett, with an anxious look on his face, "I beg you to excuse this most unseemly interruption to our council. My wife is beside herself, I think. You all know her, and know it is not her wont to meddle into politics or to bawl and bluster. To-morrow she will see her folly, but now I pray your patience."

Her words had already begun to leaven the little manhood remaining in their bosoms, but not a word was spoken. She had turned the light of her soul upon them, and in the reflection they saw photographed their own littleness of purpose or want of manly resolve.

She still talked on: "Take your protection if you will; proclaim yourselves traitors and cowards, false to your God! but horrible will be the judgment you will bring upon your heads and the heads of those that love you. I tell you that England will never conquer. I know it, and feel it in every fiber of my heart. Has God led us so far to desert us now? Will He who led our fathers across the stormy, wintry sea forsake their children, who have put their trust in Him? For me, I stay with my country, and my hand shall never touch the hand nor my heart cleave to the heart of him who shames her."

While these words were falling from her lips she stood before them like a tower of strength, and, turning toward her husband, she gave him a withering look that sent a shock through every fiber of his body. Continuing, she said: "Isaac, we have lived together for twenty years, and through all of them I have been to you a true and loving wife; but I am the child of God and my country, and if you do this shameful thing I will never own you again as my husband."

"My dear wife!" answered Isaac, excitedly, "you do not know what you are saying. Leave me for such a thing as this?"

"For such a thing as this?"

"What greater cause could there be?" answered the injured wife. "I married a good man and true, a faithful friend, and it needs no divorce to sever me from a traitor and a coward. If you take your protection you lose your wife, and I—I lose my husband and my home."

The scornful words uttered in such earnestness; the pathetic tones in which these last words were spoken; the tears that dimmed her sad blue eyes, appealed to the heart of every man before her. They were not cowards all through, but the panic sweeping over the land had caught them also.

The leaven of courage, manliness, and resolution had begun its work. Before these men left the home of Hannah Arnett that night every man had resolved to spurn the offered amnesty, and had taken a solemn oath to stand by their country through good days and bad, until freedom was written over the face of this fair land.

There are names of men who fought for their country and won distinction, afterward, who were in this secret council, but the name of Hannah Thurston figures on no roll of honor.

Where will the "Sons and Daughters of the Revolution" place Hannah Thurston?

Mary S. Lockwood
Washington, July 12

Editor's Note:

Hannah Arnett's correct name was Hannah White Arnett. Hannah McLaren Shepard Wolff, a great-grand-daughter of Mrs. Arnett, wrote *The Washington Post* on July 19, 1890 stating that the name, Thurston, was in error.

Mrs. Wolff was present on July 29, 1890 at the first informal meeting toward organizing the National Society Daughters of the American Revolution, held in the home of Mrs. Louise K. Brown. Mrs. Wolff became a charter member, but did not attend the organizing meeting on October 11, 1890.

Mary S. Lockwood was a professional writer, a member and at one time president of the Women's Press Club. She was capable of pointed and persuasive original prose, as exemplified by the first four paragraphs of her letter to the *Post*; she was also expert at succinct re-writing. Such was the case with the story of Hannah Arnett.

"Hannah Arnett's Faith," a centennial story written by Henrietta M. Holdich, another descendant of Hannah Arnett and charter member of the National Society, first appeared in the New York *Observer* in 1876. It is the same story related by Mrs. Lockwood in 1890, but without the touch of the professional writer. The Lockwood version, faithfully following the outline of the original, is completely rewritten, tighter and more dramatic.

Curiously, William O. McDowell, whose formal call to organize the National Society Daughters of the American Revolution appeared in the Monday, July 21, 1890 edition of the *Post* in the same column with Mrs. Wolfe's letter, was also descended from Hannah White Arnett, but he did not spot the error in Mrs. Lockwood's use of the name, Thurston, nor had he previously heard or read the Hannah Arnett story.

Mary S. Lockwood freely acknowledged that the inspiring tale told in her letter to the *Post* was a retelling of an old story, but the fact that the letter appeared in print without credit to the original author caused some comment. Mrs. Wolff, in her own letter, dryly said, "I am at a loss to understand why the contributor to *The Post*, in copying Mrs. Holdich's article, should have introduced the name of 'Thurston' . . . ."

We have been unable to locate any evidence that Mrs. Holdich objected to providing the raw material, as it were, for Mary S. Lockwood's memorable opus. It is fair to state that although Mrs. Lockwood became exceedingly popular and respected in the National Society, she was not universally admired, especially in the earliest days. Mary Smith Lockwood's immortal letter to *The Washington Post* ignited the spark that founded a mighty organization, but it set *her* off on the wrong foot.

Appendix 2

Minutes of the Organizational Meetings of the National Society Daughters of the American Revolution

Minutes, October 11, 1890

A meeting for the organization of the National Society of the Daughters of the American Revolution was called by Mrs. Flora Adams Darling, and held at the Strathmore Arms, 810 12th Street, Washington, D.C., at half past two o'clock in the afternoon of Saturday, October 11, 1890.

Mr. W.A. [*sic*] McDowell called the meeting to order and made an interesting historical statement.

Upon the motion of Mrs. Cabell, Mr. McDowell was elected Chairman of the meeting and Miss Desha was chosen Secretary pro tem.

The Constitution was then read by Mr. McDowell.

It was moved and seconded that the Constitution be adopted, subject to revision by a committee appointed to consider it. The motion was carried.

Mrs. Darling, Mrs. Cabell and Miss Desha were appointed on this committee.

On the motion of Miss Pauline McDowell the following officers were nominated and unanimously elected:

President General: Mrs. Benjamin Harrison.

Vice President General in Charge of Organization: Mrs. Flora Adams Darling.

Vice Presidents General: Mrs. David D. Porter, Mrs. William D. Cabell, Mrs. H.V. Boynton, Mrs. A.W. Greeley, Mrs. F.A. [*sic*] St. Clair, Mrs. G. Browne Goode, Miss Desha, Mrs. William C. Winlock.

Secretaries General: Mrs. E.H. Walworth, Mrs. William Earle.

Treasurer General: Mrs. Marshall McDonald.

Registrars General: Miss Eugenia Washington, Mrs. A. Howard Clarke.

Historian General: Mrs. M.S. Lockwood.

Surgeon General: Miss Barton.

Chaplain General: Mrs. Teunis S. Hamlin.

Executive Committee: Mrs. William D. Cabell, Miss Desha, Mrs. Walworth, Mrs. MacDonald, Mrs. Mary S. Lockwood, Miss Eugenia Washington, Mrs. Hetzel.

Advisory Board: Mr. G. Browne Goode, Chairman; Prof. W.C. Winlock, Mr. William A. McDowell, General H.V. Boynton, General Marcus J. Wright, Mr. W.L. Gill, Secretary.

It was then moved, seconded and carried that the election of National Board of Managers be deferred to adjourned meeting.

It was moved, seconded and carried that the following resolutions be adopted.

(See pages 15, 16, 17, 18, 19 for Resolutions Entire)

The button worn by Mr. McDowell was presented by him to Miss Eugenia Washington amid the applause of the Association.

Mrs. Ellen Hardin Walworth then gave an account of the Monument at Saratoga and the marking the Battle Field at Bemis Heights with tablets.

(See Pages 4,5,6,7 of COPY for Resolutions)

The date of the Annual Meeting was discussed, but the subject was left open for further consideration. October eleventh, February the twenty-second and other dates were considered.

The Constitution was then signed by those present, and the Association then took a recess till October 18 at half past four.

Signed by

Mary Desha

(Secretary pro tem)

by S.P.B.

(See following page for Resolutions)

Resolutions Adopted at Meeting for Organization of National Society of Daughters of the American Revolution.

I. RESOLVED, That this our organization meeting, we initiate that important part of our work—the securing and preserving of the Historical spots of America, and the erection thereon of suitable monuments to perpetuate the memories of the heroic deeds of the men and women who aided the Revolution and created Constitutional Government in America,—by undertaking to do what we can towards completing the monument to the memory of Mary Washington, mother of George Washington; and we hereby, call upon every patriot to send in a contribution, large or small, to our Treasurer, Mrs. M. MacDonald, 1514 R Street, Washington, D.C., for this purpose.

II. RESOLVED, That the ribbon of our badge and rosette be red with white edges.

III. RESOLVED, That a Committee on Insignia and Seal be appointed as follows: Miss Breckinridge, Mrs. Cabell, Mrs. Goode with power to act.

IV. RESOLVED, That, whereas, Hon. Mr. Sherman, M.C. from New York, has introduced a bill into the House of Representatives, arranging for the marking by the Government of historical spots of the Revolution, we, the Daughters of the American Revolution hereby request the passage of said bill.

V. Whereas, It was the sacrifice of her jewels by a woman that furnished the means that enabled Christopher Columbus to discover America, and

Whereas, It was this fact that occasioned the calling of the meeting for the organization of the Daughters of the American Revolution on the anniversary of the successful result beyond the hope or expectation of the discoverer; be it,

RESOLVED, That the Eleventh of October shall be the permanent anniversary or meeting day of the Society.

VI. Whereas, There will be celebrated one of the greatest events in the World's history—namely, the 400th Anniversary of the Discovery of America—in 1892 and 1893, the greatest feature of which is expected to be the Exhibition in Chicago, and

Whereas, The Management of the Chicago Exhibition has placed a large responsibility in connection with the Exhibition in the hands of a Board of Lady Managers; be it,

RESOLVED, That we hereby request that a special building or space be set aside for the exhibition of relics and other things illustrative of the period of the American Revolution, under the care of the Lady Managers; and we urge that this historical exhibition be afterwards brought to, and continued permanently in the City of Washington under the care of a Board of Managers in which this Society shall be represented.

VII. RESOLVED, That the thanks of this Society be tendered Mr. W.A. McDowell for his enthusiasm which has contributed so largely to the creating of that interest which has resulted in the formation of this Society, and for his counsels which have been of so great value to us.

VIII. RESOLVED, That we hereby elect Mrs. Flora Adams Darling a life member of this Society in recognition of her loving interest and labors, which have resulted in this Society of the Daughters of the American Revolution.

IX. RESOLVED, That official note of the organization of this Society be sent to the National Board of Officers of the Sons of the Revolution, and of the Sons of the American Revolution with expressions of good will and of hopes and pledges of cordial cooperation in the work we have in hand.

X. RESOLVED, That greetings be extended to the Queen Isabella

Association, Chicago, Illinois, and a copy of this resolution be forwarded to the President of that Association.

Minutes, October 18, 1890

The second session of the meeting for organization of the National Society of the Daughters of the American Revolution was held at the residence of Mrs. William D. Cabell, on October 18, 1890, at half past four o'clock, being adjourned from the meeting of October 11, 1890, at Strathmore Arms.

The meeting was called to order by Mr. William O. McDowell, Chairman of the meeting of October 11th, who then conducted Mrs. Cabell, Acting President General to the chair and also the Secretary General, Mrs. Ellen Hardin Walworth, to her place.

Mrs. T.S. Hamlin then read from the Scriptures and offered an eloquent prayer in behalf of the objects of the Association.

Miss Desha, secretary of the meeting of October 11, 1890, read the minutes of meeting and also the Constitution.

The Secretary General read a letter addressed to the Vice President in Charge of Organization from Mrs. Benjamin Harrison accepting the office of President General; also a letter from General Wm. Seward Webb, President of the Sons of the American Revolution, offering congratulations, and assistance to the Daughters of the American Revolution; also a letter from Mrs. Roger Pryor and one from Mrs. Bolt.

On motion of Mrs. Clark it was resolved that the letters of Mrs. Harrison and General Webb be spread upon the minutes, which letters are as follows:

Executive Mansion
Washington
"My dear Mrs. Darling:
"Many thanks for your kind note, and Mrs. Harrison desires me to say that she will accept the position as Honorary President General of the Society and thanks you and the other ladies for their cordiality in the matter."
"(Signed) Mrs. Dimmick"

National Society of the Sons of the American Revolution
Office of the President General
New York, October 15th, 1890
Miss Mary Desha
Secretary of the Meeting of the
Daughters of the American Revolution
218 North Capitol Street
Washington, D.C.
"My dear Madam:
"I beg leave to acknowledge receipt of your letter containing resolutions passed at your meeting October 12th and hasten to assure you that I shall bring the resolutions to the notice of the Board of Managers at their next meeting.

"I may in advance assure you of our cordial sympathy and cooperation in the field of patriotic work."

"Yours truly,

"W. Seward Webb

President General"

By direction of the President, the Constitution was taken up for consideration. Several members took part in a discussion on Article II, concerning eligibility for membership.

On motion of Mrs. Hamlin the Constitution was referred to the Executive Committee for revision.

The Chairman of the Committee on Seal and Insignia reported that the colors of the rosette should be blue and white. A discussion ensued on this clause of the report between the advocates of red and white and those of blue and white. Upon a call for the question, it was

RESOLVED, That the colors be blue and white.

The Committee further reported that the design for the Seal be the figure of Abigale [sic] Adams in the costume of 1776 seated at a spinning wheel. This was received with favor, and it was suggested that a cradle be added with the motto: "The hand that rocks the cradle rules the world." A decision was deferred, and the whole subject was left with the Committee for further consideration.

On motion of Mrs. Lockwood, it was

RESOLVED, That after this Association has assisted in the completion of the monument to Mary Washington, the next effort shall be to provide a place for the collection of Historical relics which will accumulate at the World's Fair, and for all other relics which may come to the Society, and for historical portraits, pictures, etc. This may first be in rooms, and later in the erection of a fire-proof building.

On motion of Mrs. Lincoln, it was:

RESOLVED, That the blank forms of application for membership now in use are the authorized forms of this Society.

Mr. McDowell delivered an interesting address, after which the officers and members were presented with copies of the Constitution and By-Laws of the Mary Washington Society.

The meeting then adjourned to November 11, 1890.

Minutes, November 11, 1890

The third and last session of the meeting for organization of the National Society of the Daughters of the American Revolution, was held at the residence of Mrs. Wm. D. Cabell on the evening of November 11, 1890, at half past seven o'clock, being adjourned from the meeting at the same place on October 18, 1890.

Mrs. Wm. D. Cabell, the Vice President General presiding, called the meeting to order, and stated that it was by special request of the President General, Mrs. Benjamin Harrison, who was present, that she was presiding over the Society.

The Chaplain General, Mrs. Hamlin, read a portion of the Scriptures, and then offered a prayer.

The Secretary General, Mrs. Walworth, read the minutes of the last meeting. No objection being made, the Presiding Vice President General declared the minutes approved.

The Secretary General was then instructed to read the Constitution as reported from the Executive Committee to whom it had been referred for revision.

The Constitution was read and on motion of Miss Washington, seconded by Mrs. Clark, it was accepted and adopted.

The Committee on Seal and Insignia reported that the Seal of the Society should be two and three eights of an inch in diameter, charged with the figure of a dame sitting at her spinning wheel: The legend to be: "Daughters of the American Revolution." Two mottoes were suggested: "Libertas et Patria" and "Amor Patriae."

A motion was made and carried to accept the report of the Committee in regard to the Seal, and the legend and to adopt the motto "Amor Patriae."

On motion of Mrs. Coolidge, the sympathy and cooperation of this Society was extended to the Association of which Mr. Field is President, for the presentation of a gift to the people of France, in commemoration of their generous assistance to our country in the Revolutionary War.

The Historian, Mrs. Lockwood, read two letters from Mrs. Sinclair of Virginia, presenting to this Society valuable relics of the last century.

The Vice-President, Miss Desha, on behalf of Wimodaughsis offered to the Daughters of the American Revolution the use of parlors and desk-room in the house of that Society.

On motion of Mrs. Hetzel the thanks of the Society were expressed for the kind offer.

On motion of Mrs. M.S. Lockwood the daughter of Mr. W.O. McDowell was admitted as one of the Daughters of the American Revolution.

The Vice President in Charge of Organization read a statement of the progress of the work of organization in the different States of the Union.

After consultation with members of the Advisory Committee, a motion was made by one who had voted for it, to reconsider the clause of the Constitution which related to eligibility. A reconsideration was agreed to.

A motion was then made and carried that the words: "as the mother of such a patriot," should be added to the eligibility clause.

A large number of names were nominated for charter members.

The Vice President General Presiding announced that the next meeting would be on December 11, 1890.

The meeting was then adjourned.

Minutes, November 20, 1890

A meeting of the Executive Board of the National Society of the Daughters of the American Revolution was held at Mrs. Walworth's house, 1111 17th Street, November 20, 1890, at seven o'clock, the Chairman presiding.

After the meeting was called to order by the Chair, the minutes of the preceding meeting were read and approved.

The proof sheets of the Constitution of the Society were laid before the Committee, and compared by them with original Constitution.

It was moved, seconded and lost that Art. III, Section 6 of the Constitution be amended by inserting words to the effect that five should constitute a quorum of the Executive Board. (See Robert's Rules, p. 112)

It was moved, seconded and carried that Art. V, Section I be amended by adding the sentence: "The annual meeting of the local chapters for the election of officers shall be held on October 11, unless that date fall on Sunday, in which case, the meeting shall be held on the following Wednesday."

The By-Laws then being considered by the Committee, it was moved and seconded that Articles V and VII, referring to Secretaries and Registrars General be amended by changing those words from singular to plural form wherever they occur. Carried.

It was moved and seconded Article XVI be amended by striking out the words "The Gotham" and substituting the words "Adams Magazine." Carried.

Moved and seconded that the motto be changed from "Amor Patriae" to "Home and Country." Lost, the Chairman voting.

The circular prepared by Mrs. Walworth was then laid before the Committee. Moved and seconded that specific information be added to the circular.

Bibliography

Aikman, Lonnelle. "The DAR Story." *National Geographic Magazine*, Vol. C, No. 5, November, 1951. pp.565–598.

Americana Collection and Archives. Washington, D.C.: National Society Daughters of the American Revolution.

Darling, Flora Adams. *Founding Daughters*. Washington, D.C.: 1901.

Daughters of the American Revolution Magazine and forerunners. Washington, D.C.: National Society Daughters of the American Revolution, July, 1892–October, 1990.

Desha, Mary. *The True Story of the Origin of the National Society of the Daughters of the American Revolution*. Washington, D.C. 1891.

Duncan, Mrs. Robert V.H., ed. *In Washington: The National Society Daughters of the American Revolution*. Washington, D.C.: National Society Daughters of the American Revolution, 1965.

Earhart, Lida B., PhD. "The Founding and the Founders of the National Society of the Daughters of the American Revolution"; "Mary Virginia Ellet Cabell"; Biographies of the Presidents General." Manuscripts, Washington, D.C., 1938–40.

"Early History, Daughters of the American Revolution." Washington, D.C.: Board of Management, NSDAR, 1908.

History of New York State Conference Daughters of the American Revolution. New York: New York Daughters of the American Revolution, 1923.

Lockwood, Mary S., and Emily Lee Sherwood. *Story of the Records, D.A.R.* Washington, D.C.: George E. Howard, 1906.

Logan, Mrs. John A. *The Part Taken by Women in American History*. Wilmington, Del.: Perry-Nalle Publishing Co., 1912.

McDuffee, Alice Louise. "History of the National Society of the Daughters of the American Revolution, Our First Decade." Washington, D.C.: NSDAR, 1929

McDuffee, Alice Louise, Elise H. Parcels, ed. "History of the National Society of the Daughters of the American Revolution, Our First Decade." Washington, D.C.: NSDAR, 1964

Minor, Anne Rogers. "The Deeper Meaning of our Daughters of the American Revolution Organization," Washington, D.C.: NSDAR, April 1918.

President General's Subject File. Washington, D.C.: National Society Daughters of the American Revolution.

Proceedings of the Annual Continental Congress.. Washington, D.C., National Society Daughters of the American Revolution, 1909 – 1990.

Report of the Daughters of the American Revolution, 1890 to 1897. et seq. Washington, D.C.: Government Printing Office, 1899.

Somerville, Mollie. *Washington Historic Landmarks: Pillars of Patriotism*. Washington, D.C.: National Society Daughters of the American Revolution, 1985.

St. Paul, John, Jr. and Stuart O. Landry. *The History of the National Society of the Sons of the American Revolution*. New Orleans, Pelican Publishing Company: 1962.

Stevenson, Mrs. Adlai E. *Brief History, Daughters of the American Revolution*. Washington, D.C.: 1913.

Washington, Eugenia. "Our History.," *American Monthly Magazine*, Vol. 6, No. 6. pp.489 – 504.

Washington Landmark. Washington, D.C.: National Society Daughters of the American Revolution, 1976.

Credits: All photographs came from the collection of the *DAR Magazine*, the Office of the President General and the Archives of the National Society Daughters of the American Revolution. The photographers or studios were, where known, the following: Pages iii, 117, Renee Bouchard; page 6, The Historical Society of Washington, D.C.; page 78-79, Matthew Brady; page 104-105, Schutz; page 123, Chase Ltd.; page 133, Judson Smith Studio; page 135, Library of Congress; page 149, Guy Cheek; page 170, David P. Myatt; page 171, National Society Children of the American Revolution; page 190, American Red Cross; page 193, George Starkey; page 197, The Daily Advance; page 202, U.S. Army Signal Corps; page 211, Larry H. Dinsch; page 220, Independence National Historical Park; page 222, Architect of the Capitol.

Index